Essentials of the Essay

Essentials of the Essay

Writing, Reading, and Grammar

Kitty Chen Dean

Nassau Community College

Allyn and Bacon

Boston   London   Toronto   Sydney   Tokyo   Singapore

Vice President: Joseph Opiela
Editorial Assistant: Brenda Conaway
Cover Designer: Suzanne Harbison
Composition Buyer: Linda Cox
Marketing Manager: Lisa Kimball
Editorial-Production Service: P. M. Gordon Associates
Production Administrator: Susan Brown

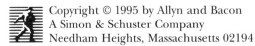
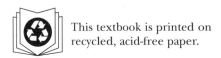 This textbook is printed on
recycled, acid-free paper.

Library of Congress Cataloging-in-Publication Data

Dean, Kitty Chen.
    Essentials of the essay : writing, reading, and grammar / Kitty
Chen Dean.
        p.   cm.
    Includes index.
    ISBN 0-02-322283-2 (pbk.)
    1. English language—Rhetoric.   2. English language—Grammar.
3. Essay—Authorship.   4. College readers.   I. Title.
PE1471.D4 1995
808.042—dc20   94–36094
                                                                    CIP

Printed in the United States of America

10 9 8 7 6 5 4 3 2 1   99 98 97 96 95 94

Credits
Pages 2–3, 146. Excerpts from *The Autobiography of Malcolm X* by Malcolm X, with the
assistance of Alex Haley. Copyright © 1964 by Alex Haley and Malcolm X and copyright
© 1965 by Alex Haley and Betty Shabazz. Reprinted by permission of Random House, Inc.

Credits continue on page 311, which constitutes an extension of the copyright page.

Contents

Preface to the Instructor   xv
Preface to the Student   xvii
Acknowledgments   xix

Chapter 1: Warming Up   1

WRITING AND READING   1
Before Reading "Saved"   1
  Words and Phrases to Look For   1
  Questions to Answer as You Read   1
Malcolm X, "Saved"   2
Before Starting to Write   3
  Exercises in Freewriting, Brainstorming, and Clustering   4
    Exercise 1: Before writing   4
    Exercise 2: Focusing   6
    Exercise 3: Freewrite, brainstorm, and cluster   7
    Exercise 4: Focused freewriting, brainstorming, and clustering   8
Getting Started   8
  Exercises in Narrowing the Topic and Getting Started   9
    Exercise 5: Narrowing the topic   9
    Exercise 6: Getting started   10
    Exercise 7: Narrowing the topic and getting started   11
    Exercise 8: Narrowing the topic and getting started   12
Organizing an Essay   13
  Exercises in Organizing an Essay   14
    Exercise 9: Organizing essays   14
    Exercise 10: Reorganizing an essay   15
    Exercise 11: Reorganizing an essay   16
    Exercise 12: Reorganizing an essay   17
Suggestions for Essay Topics   18

GRAMMAR   19

Learning About Words Often Confused   19

Exercises on Words Often Confused   19

Exercise 13: Words often confused   19

Exercise 14: Fill in the blanks   25

Exercise 15: Fill in the blanks   27

Exercise 16: Writing paragraphs   32

Chapter 2: The Body of the Essay   33

WRITING AND READING   33

Before Reading "Personalize Your Personal Ad"   33

Words and Phrases to Look For   33

Questions to Answer as You Read   33

Advice Column, "Personalize Your Personal Ad"   33

Topic Sentences   34

Exercises in Topic Sentences   35

Exercise 1: Topic sentences   35

Exercise 2: Topic sentences   36

Exercise 3: Topic sentences   37

Exercise 4: Topic sentences   38

Writing Body Paragraphs   39

Exercises in Body Paragraphs and Topic Sentences   40

Exercise 5: Topic sentences and details   40

Exercise 6: Body paragraphs   41

Exercise 7: Body paragraphs   42

Exercise 8: Body paragraphs   43

Suggestions for Essay Topics   44

GRAMMAR   45

Nouns   45

Exercises in Nouns   46

Exercise 9: Finding nouns   46

Exercise 10: Finding nouns   47

Exercise 11: Using concrete and abstract nouns   48

Exercise 12: Using proper and common nouns   49

Pronouns   50

Exercises in Using Pronouns   51

Exercise 13: Finding pronouns   51

Exercise 14: Finding pronouns   52

Exercise 15: Changing nouns to pronouns   53

Exercise 16: Using pronouns   54

Chapter 3: The Beginning and the Ending   57

WRITING AND READING   57

Before Reading "Saving the Elephants"   57

Words and Phrases to Look For   57

Questions to Answer as You Read   57

New York Times, **"Saving the Elephants"**   58

Writing Introductions   58

Exercises on Introductions and Thesis Statements   59

Exercise 1: Introductions and thesis statements   *59*

Exercise 2: Introductions and thesis statements   *61*

Writing Conclusions   **63**

Exercises on Conclusions   64

Exercise 3: Looking at conclusions   *64*

Exercise 4: Looking at conclusions   *65*

Exercises on Writing Introductions and Conclusions   66

Exercise 5: Changing introductions and conclusions   *66*

Exercise 6: Changing introductions and conclusions   *67*

Exercise 7: Changing introductions and conclusions   *68*

Exercise 8: Completing an essay   *69*

Suggestions for Essay Topics   **70**

GRAMMAR   **71**

Verb Tenses I   **71**

Exercises in Verb Tenses I   72

Exercise 9: Regular verbs in present tense   *72*

Exercise 10: Regular verbs   *72*

Exercise 11: Irregular verb tenses   *73*

Exercise 12: Verbs in past tense   *76*

Exercise 13: Verb forms   *77*

Verb Tenses II   **78**

Exercises in Verb Tenses II   79

Exercise 14: Past, present, and future tenses   *79*

Exercise 15: Finding verb tenses   *81*

Exercise 16: Using verb tenses   *82*

Exercise 17: Using verb tenses in writing an essay   *83*

Chapter 4: Describing   85

WRITING AND READING   85

Before Reading "The Story of an Hour"   85

Words and Phrases to Look For   85

Questions to Answer as You Read   86
Kate Chopin, "The Story of an Hour"   86
Writing Descriptions   88
Exercises in Writing Descriptions   90
Exercise 1: Descriptive words and phrases   90
Exercise 2: Descriptive words and phrases   92
Exercise 3: Descriptive words and phrases   93
Exercise 4: Controlling idea   94
Exercise 5: Writing descriptions   96
Using Transitional Expressions   97
Exercises in Transitional Expressions   98
Exercise 6: Finding transitional expressions   98
Exercise 7: Transitions   99
Exercise 8: Writing transitions   100
Exercise 9: Writing transitions   101
Suggestions for Essay Topics   102

GRAMMAR   103
Adjectives and Adverbs   103
Exercises in Adjectives and Adverbs   104
Exercise 10: Finding adjectives and adverbs   104
Exercise 11: Using adjectives and adverbs   105
Exercise 12: Writing descriptions   106
Exercise 13: Paragraphs with descriptions   107
Conjunctions and Prepositions   108
Exercises in Conjunctions and Prepositions   109
Exercise 14: Some common conjunctions   109
Exercise 15: Finding conjunctions   110
Exercise 16: Using conjunctions   111
Exercise 17: Some common prepositions   112
Exercise 18: Using prepositions   113
Exercise 19: Finding conjunctions and prepositions   114

Chapter 5: Voice and Point of View   116

WRITING AND READING   116
Before Reading "Does Language Influence Thought?"   116
Words and Phrases to Look For   116
Questions to Answer as You Read   116
**McConnell and Philipchalk, "Does Language
Influence Thought?" 117**
Using a Consistent Voice   118

Exercises in Voice   118
  Exercise 1: Identifying voice   118
  Exercise 2: Identifying voice   119
  Exercise 3: Identifying purpose   121
  Exercise 4: Using voice   122
Having a Point of View   123
Exercises in Point of View   124
  Exercise 5: Telling point of view   124
  Exercise 6: Third person   125
  Exercise 7: Person and point of view   126
  Exercise 8: Person, voice, and point of view   127
Suggestions for Essay Topics   128

GRAMMAR   129
Sentences (Clauses)   129
Exercises in Clauses   130
  Exercise 9: Writing independent clauses   130
  Exercise 10: Writing dependent clauses   131
  Exercise 11: Writing dependent clauses   132
  Exercise 12: Finding independent and dependent clauses   134
Types of Sentences   135
Exercises on Types of Sentences   136
  Exercise 13: Simple sentences   136
  Exercise 14: Compound sentences   137
  Exercise 15: Complex and compound-complex sentences   138
  Exercise 16: Sentence types   139

Chapter 6: Variety   142

WRITING AND READING   142
Before Reading "Jill Freedman, Photographer"   142
Words and Phrases to Look For   142
Questions to Answer as You Read   142
Studs Terkel, "Jill Freedman, Photographer"   143
Sentence Variety I: Altering Subject-Verb-Object   144
Exercises in Sentence Variety I: Altering
  Subject-Verb-Object   145
  Exercise 1: Before the subject   145
  Exercise 2: Before the subject   146
  Exercise 3: Rewriting paragraphs for variety   147
  Exercise 4: Rewriting an essay   149
Sentence Variety II: Length, Type, It Is/There Is   150

Exercises in Sentence Variety II: Length, Type,
It Is/There Is   151
Exercise 5: Questions and phrases   151
Exercise 6: Questions and phrases   152
Exercise 7: Varying sentence length   154
Exercise 8: It is, there is   154
Exercise 9: Adding variety   155
Suggestions for Essay Topics   156

GRAMMAR   157
Fragments   157
Exercises in Fragments   158
Exercise 10: Correcting fragments   158
Exercise 11: Correcting fragments   159
Exercise 12: Identifying and correcting fragments   160
Exercise 13: Finding and rewriting fragments   161
Run-Together Sentences   161
Exercises in Run-Together Sentences   162
Exercise 14: Finding and fixing run-together sentences   162
Exercise 15: Run-together sentences   163
Exercise 16: Fragments and run-together sentences   164
Exercise 17: Fragments and run-together sentences   165
Parallelism   166
Exercises in Parallelism   167
Exercise 18: Identifying parallel structure   167
Exercise 19: Finding parallel structure   168
Exercise 20: Creating parallel structure   169
Exercise 21: Finding and fixing parallel structure   171

Chapter 7: Getting Down to Details   174

WRITING AND READING   174
Before Reading "Cooking *en Papillote*"   174
Words and Phrases to Look For   174
Questions to Answer as You Read   174
Irma S. Rombauer and Marion Rombauer Becker, "Cooking *en Papillote*"   174
Using Specific Words   175
Exercises in Using Specific Words   176
Exercise 1: Choosing specific nouns   176
Exercise 2: Finding specific nouns   177
Exercise 3: Finding specific nouns   179
Exercise 4: Finding specific verbs   180

Writing Specific Paragraphs 182
　Exercises in Writing Specific Paragraphs 183
　　Exercise 5: Specifics in paragraphs 183
　　Exercise 6: Writing specific paragraphs 184
　　Exercise 7: Specifics 185
　　Exercise 8: Specific paragraphs 185
Suggestions for Essay Topics 186

GRAMMAR 187
Sentence Problems I: Subject-Verb Agreement 187
　Exercises in Subject-Verb Agreement 188
　　Exercise 9: Finding subject-verb agreement 188
　　Exercise 10: Making subjects and verbs agree 189
Sentence Problems II: Pronoun-Antecedent Agreement 191
　Exercises in Pronoun-Antecedent Agreement 192
　　Exercise 11: Finding pronoun-antecedent agreement 192
　　Exercise 12: Using pronoun-antecedent agreement 193
Sentence Problems III: Misplaced and Dangling Modifiers 194
　Exercises in Misplaced and Dangling Modifiers 195
　　Exercise 13: Finding modifiers 195
　　Exercise 14: Finding modifiers 197
Sentence Problems IV: Is when, Is Where, Is Because 198
　Exercises in "Is When," "Is Where," and the Like 199
　　Exercise 15: Finding "is when . . ." 199
　　Exercise 16: Correcting "is when . . ." 200
　Exercises in Sentence Problems 201
　　Exercise 17: Correcting sentence problems 201
　　Exercise 18: Correcting sentence problems 202

Chapter 8: Teaching and Explaining 204

WRITING AND READING 204
Before Reading "Left and Right: The Bias of Language and Custom" 204
　Words and Phrases to Look For 204
　Questions to Answer as You Read 205
Betty Edwards, "Left and Right: The Bias of Language and Custom" 205
Writing to Teach Clearly 206
　Exercises in Teaching Clearly 207
　　Exercise 1: Purpose, audience, and terms 207
　　Exercise 2: Purpose, audience, and language 210

Exercise 3: Purpose, audience, and language *212*
Exercise 4: Writing for an audience *213*
Giving Logical Explanations **214**
Exercises in Giving Logical Explanations 215
Exercise 5: Steps in order *215*
Exercise 6: Step-by-step process *216*
Exercise 7: Writing directions *217*
Exercise 8: Directions in order *218*
Suggestions for Essay Topics **219**

GRAMMAR **220**
Using Commas I: Independent and Dependent Clauses **220**
Exercises in Commas I: Independent and
Dependent Clauses 221
Exercise 9: Identifying commas *221*
Exercise 10: Identifying commas *222*
Exercise 11: Using clauses and commas *223*
Using Commas II: Phrases and Words **224**
Exercises in Commas II: Phrases and Words 225
Exercise 12: Identifying commas *225*
Exercise 13: Identifying commas *226*
Exercise 14: Using commas *228*
**Using Commas III: Series, Titles, Addresses, Dates,
Misunderstandings** **229**
Exercises in Commas III: Series, Titles, Addresses,
Dates, Misunderstandings 230
Exercise 15: Identifying commas *230*
Exercise 16: Identifying commas *230*
Exercise 17: Using commas *232*

Chapter 9: Argumentation 233

WRITING AND READING **233**
Before Reading "The Case Against Bilingualism" **233**
Words and Phrases to Look For 233
Questions to Answer as You Read 234
Trudy J. Sundberg, "The Case Against Bilingualism" **234**
Using Argumentation **235**
Exercises in Argumentation 236
Exercise 1: Analyzing arguments *236*
Exercise 2: Arguments, evidence, and conclusions *237*

Exercise 3: Finding arguments and evidence   238
Exercise 4: Using evidence   240
Avoiding False Arguments   **242**
Exercises in False Arguments   243
Exercise 5: Overgeneralization and distraction   243
Exercise 6: Name-calling and references to character   244
Exercise 7: False authority and the bandwagon   245
Exercise 8: Identifying false arguments   245
Suggestions for Essay Topics   **247**

GRAMMAR   **247**
Using Apostrophes   **247**
Exercises in Apostrophes   248
Exercise 9: Uses of apostrophes   248
Exercise 10: Uses of apostrophes   250
Exercise 11: Using apostrophes   251
Exercise 12: Using apostrophes   253
Using Semicolons and Colons   **254**
Exercises in Semicolons and Colons   255
Exercise 13: Identifying semicolons and colons   255
Exercise 14: Using semicolons   258
Exercise 15: Replacing with semicolons and colons   259
Exercise 16: Using semicolons and colons   260
Using Hyphens   **261**
Exercises in Hyphens   262
Exercise 17: Uses of hyphens   262
Exercise 18: Uses of hyphens   264
Exercise 19: Using hyphens   265
Exercise 20: Using hyphens   266

Chapter 10: Writing to Entertain   268

WRITING AND READING   **268**
Before Reading "The Discovery and Use of the Fake Ink Blot"   **268**
Words and Phrases to Look For   268
Questions to Answer as You Read   269
Woody Allen, "The Discovery and Use of the Fake Ink Blot"   **269**
Writing to Entertain   **270**
Exercises in Writing to Entertain   271
Exercise 1: Analyzing entertaining writing   271
Exercise 2: Analyzing entertaining writing   273
Exercise 3: Adding a thesis, details, descriptions, and exaggerations   274
Exercise 4: Writing to entertain   275

Avoiding Stereotyping, Racism, and Sexism   276

Exercises in Avoiding Stereotyping, Racism, and Sexism   277

Exercise 5: Analyzing paragraphs   277

Exercise 6: Analyzing paragraphs   278

Exercise 7: Finding stereotypes   279

Exercise 8: Identifying stereotypes   280

Suggestions for Essay Topics   282

GRAMMAR   282

Using Quotation Marks and Direct and Indirect Discourse   282

Exercises in Using Quotation Marks and Direct and
Indirect Discourse   283

Exercise 9: Identifying quotation marks and indirect discourse   283

Exercise 10: Identifying quotation marks and indirect discourse   285

Exercise 11: Using quotation marks   286

Exercise 12: Using titles and quotations   287

**Other Punctuation: —, (), . . . , <u>underlining</u>, /, [], *, &, %,
#, @   288**

Exercises in Other Punctuation   290

Exercise 13: Dashes and parentheses   290

Exercise 14: Other punctuation   291

Exercise 15: Other punctuation   293

Exercise 16: Using punctuation   294

Ten Essays for Reading and Analyzing   296

Alice Skelsey, "Eggplant"   296

Joann Faung Jean Lee, "Recently Arrived"   297

Joan Davis, "Young Women, Keep Your Own Names"   298

Nanette Byrnes, "John F. Welch, Jr."   298

**Anthony Brandt, Review of Matt Cartmill's *View to a Death in
the Morning*   299**

S. G. Tyler, "Alice's Snazzy Pajamas"   300

**Otto Ehrenberg, Ph.D., and Miriam Ehrenberg, Ph.D., "Psychotherapy
for Ethnic Minorities"   302**

Andrew A. Rooney, "A Conspiracy Against Silence"   302

Helen Heightsman Gordon, "Improving Reading Efficiency"   304

Surfing Magazine, **"Guns"   305**

Index   307

Preface to the Instructor

Essentials of the Essay: Writing, Reading, and Grammar is sufficiently inclusive to serve as the sole text for a developmental course since it contains readings, instruction in writing, and grammar. Individual chapters, although progressive in organization, may be taught independently of each other or omitted without complication.

Essays of every kind dominate. Each of the ten chapters begins with a professional essay suitable as both a model and an impetus for discussion. Ten additional professional essays at the end serve the same purposes. The instructional essays also serve as models, as well as discussing a particular aspect of writing or grammar. The exercises, as often as possible, are also in essay form and serve as model essays. These latter have been written by the author on the level of a student writer.

The writing instruction progresses from warming up to generation of essay components, sentence writing, and word choice. A set of exercises reinforces each instructional essay.

The exercises always require interaction, progressing from recognition to alteration to generation. Thus, exercise assignments may be tailored to the level of the class or the individual.

Whereas writing instruction goes from the whole essay to the parts of the essay, the grammar instruction progresses from words to complete sentences. The grammar section of each chapter may be taught independently of the writing instruction and follows the same progression from recognition to alteration to generation. Assignments again may be tailored to the class or the individual.

"Suggestions for Essay Topics" range from personal response to discussion of social issues. Again the choice may be tailored to the level of the class or the individual.

The Instructor's Manual contains suggestions for organizing the course, techniques for teaching, methods for encouraging interaction, and answers to the exercises. I believe very strongly that instructors must use their own style, not the dictates of a text. Thus, directions within the text always allow instructors to decide on the approach.

Preface to the Student

This textbook should help you if you want to improve your writing, a skill that becomes more and more necessary in our computer age. Being a good writer helps you not only in your college work but also in your career, whatever it might be.

As you read the assigned essays, no matter for what purpose, notice the general plan of the essay; you will understand the plan of your own essays better. When you do the exercises, note that they also usually turn into essays; notice their plan too. As you write your essays, review what you have learned about essay writing up to that point, and try to apply the methods to your writing.

As you follow the instructions in writing an essay, do not let the requirements hamper you. If you have a method you want to use, then use it. If you don't know what to do, then try one of the suggestions in this book; it will help you find the best method for you.

In playing an instrument or a sport, practice makes perfect. Becoming a good writer also takes practice.

Acknowledgments

A textbook cannot be written without the help of many people, each one with particular expertise and insight. They all deserve my gratitude.

First, I wish to thank my Nassau Community College colleagues Michael Steinman, Elaine Good, and Miriam Cheikin. They read and reread my early proposal and made many valuable comments. I was originally encouraged and greatly assisted by Barbara Heinssen, then by Tim Julet; and finally by Joe Opiela of Allyn and Bacon, who pushed this textbook into its final shape. Along the way I was assisted by Morgan Lance, Brenda Conaway, Karen Stone, and Scott Pass.

I owe thanks to a number of reviewers who made suggestions that transformed the text. They are Cora Agatucci, Louise Baker, Robyn Browder, Roberta Cohen, Jeanne Gunner, Judith Mish, and Carol Wershoven.

My thanks go also to my students over the years who have taught me everything in this book. And finally, I owe much to Richard and to Cecilia.

Chapter 1

Warming Up

WRITING AND READING

Before Reading "Saved"

WORDS AND PHRASES TO LOOK FOR

stock of knowledge: body of knowledge
emulate: to copy behavior with hope of doing as well or better
book-reading motions: looking at words and turning pages but
    not actually reading
riffling: leafing quickly through a book or magazine
painstaking: very careful, diligent
every succeeding page: each next page
inevitable: what cannot be avoided, sure to happen
word-base: stock of words one knows

QUESTIONS TO ANSWER AS YOU READ
1. How do you suppose Malcolm X sounded when he
   talked?
2. What method did he use to learn words and information?
3. What do you think of his method?
4. What other methods could he have used to improve his
   knowledge?
5. Why did he feel free even though he was in prison?

Saved

Many who today hear me somewhere in person, or on television, or those who read something I've said, will think I went to school far beyond the eighth grade. This impression is due entirely to my prison studies.

It had really begun back in the Charlestown Prison, when Bimbi first made me feel envy of his stock of knowledge. Bimbi had always taken charge of any conversation he was in, and I had tried to emulate him. But every book I picked up had few sentences which didn't contain anywhere from one to nearly all of the words that might as well have been in Chinese. When I just skipped those words, of course, I really ended up with little idea of what the book said. So I had come to the Norfolk Prison Colony still going through only book-reading motions. Pretty soon, I would have quit even these motions, unless I had received the motivation that I did.

I saw that the best thing I could do was get hold of a dictionary—to study, to learn some words. I was lucky enough to reason also that I should try to improve my penmanship. It was sad. I couldn't even write in a straight line. It was both ideas together that moved me to request a dictionary along with some tablets and pencils from the Norfolk Prison Colony school.

I spent two days just riffling uncertainly through the dictionary's pages. I'd never realized so many words existed! I didn't know *which* words I needed to learn. Finally, just to start some kind of action, I began copying.

In my slow, painstaking, ragged handwriting, I copied into my tablet everything printed on that first page, down to the punctuation marks.

I believe it took me a day. Then, aloud, I read back, to myself, everything I'd written on the tablet. Over and over, aloud, to myself, I read my own handwriting.

I woke up the next morning, thinking about those words—immensely proud to realize that not only had I written so much at one time, but I'd written words that I never knew were in the world. Moreover, with a little effort, I also could remember what many of these words meant. I reviewed the words whose meanings I didn't remember. Funny thing, from the dictionary first page right now, that "aardvark" springs to my mind. The dictionary had a picture of it, a long-tailed, long-eared, burrowing African mammal, which lives off termites caught by sticking out its tongue as an anteater does for ants.

I was so fascinated that I went on—I copied the dictionary's next page. And the same experience came when I studied that. With every succeeding page, I also learned of people and places and events from history. Actually the dictionary is like a miniature encyclopedia. Finally the dictionary's A section had filled a whole tablet—and I went on into the B's. That was the way I started copying what eventually became the entire dictionary. It went a lot faster after so much practice helped me pick up handwriting speed. Between what I wrote in my tablet, and writing letters, during the rest of my time in prison I would guess I wrote a million words.

I suppose it was inevitable that as my word-base broadened, I could for the first time pick up a book and read and now begin to understand what the book was saying. Anyone who has read a great deal can imagine the new world that opened. Let me tell you something: from then until I left that prison, in every free moment I had, if I was not reading in the library, I was reading on my bunk. You couldn't have gotten me out of books with a wedge. Between Mr. Muhammad's teachings, my correspondence, my visitors . . . and my reading of books, months passed without my even thinking about being imprisoned. In fact, up to then, I never had been so truly free in my life.

Malcolm X,
The Autobiography of Malcolm X

Before Starting to Write

We all have different styles for learning, studying, or getting things done, so of course we have different styles for getting started on a piece of writing. No one way is better or worse than another, but different people find that some work better than others. Some students already have a method for getting started. If you do, you should use it. If not, you need to try out different methods to see which work and which don't. There are many methods, but here are three popular ones.

The first method is **freewriting.** Using scrap paper and paying no attention to grammar or spelling, just keep writing. Even if you can't think of anything to write, you can write that you can't think of anything to write until something comes to mind. If the professor or boss has already assigned a subject, your writing may be limited to that subject.

As you write, particular topics (more specific areas within the subject) might come up that you want to explore further. Then you can continue on these topics. Finally one or two topics will probably emerge that seem worth exploring further. You can then continue this way until you decide that you have an interesting topic.

Brainstorming is another method that works well. If a subject has been assigned (usually the case), just list in one or two words all the ideas that come to mind. After listing around ten items, look over the list to see which items are repeated, which ones might go together, which ones might make good points in an essay, and which ones seem irrelevant. Once you fix the actual topic, you may brainstorm again and again for each part of the essay. This method works well for finding ideas before starting on the actual essay.

The final method, **clustering,** helps you visualize your writing. Draw a circle in which you write the subject of the essay. Then draw lines going out from the circle with words on the subject. These secondary words will result in further lines and words. Eventually one part, or cluster, will be more elaborate and will probably make a good topic for the essay.

If these visual methods don't seem to work, you may try talking into a tape recorder and then transcribing your words onto paper. Or you can talk to another student, who writes down your words. Both of these methods result in a piece of freewriting or brainstorming.

Rather than stare at a blank piece of paper, just start freewriting, brainstorming, or clustering. You will then have some raw material to work with. From there, you can add, change, and delete, but you will have started writing. That is the important thing.

EXERCISES IN FREEWRITING, BRAINSTORMING, AND CLUSTERING

Exercise 1   Before writing

Students were assigned an essay on food, so they had to narrow down the general subject and find a topic.

1. Kim decided to freewrite on food to find a good topic:

> What am I going to say about food. I hate doing this. I eat food every day. So what? We can't live without food every day. Some people probably don't eat every day, but I sure do. I'm really hungry right

now. I wish I had a big bowl of pasta—angel hair pasta—with pesto sauce. That's my favorite sauce, but I like tomato sauce also and also veggies, that's called primavera I think, when the vegs are in a cream sauce mixed with vegetables—broccoli, carrots, peppers, others (?). Pasta goes well with fish or chicken also. And let's not forget spaghetti and meatballs. I love sesame noodles too. I think I have a topic.

What topic should Kim explore?

2. Rosina decided to brainstorm on food to find a good topic:

food	living on potatoes?
fooood	Irish did, could I?
fooooood	starvation
give me food, lots of food	rice
food for thought	beans
junk food	basic foods, mashed potatoes
hamburgers	milk
french fries	boiled potatoes, homefries

What topics might Rosina explore?

3. Larry decided to use clustering on food to find a good topic:

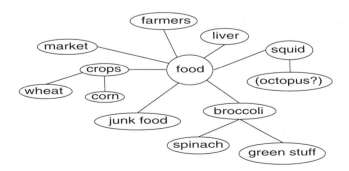

What topic could Larry explore?

Exercise 2   Focusing

1. Kim decided to explore pasta, so she did more freewriting:

> Yeah, pasta! I love angel hair pasta. It is thin and refined. With tomato sauce. Also pesto. Also sesame noodles, also primavera. Japanese restaurants have noodles too. What are they called? Never tried them. So many countries have noodles. American spaghetti and meatballs—not Italian.

What topics could Kim use?

2. Rosina couldn't decide between potatoes and basic foods, so she did some brainstorming on each one:

all kinds of potatoes   rice
Idahoes   black beans
russet   other dried beans
baked   refried beans
french fried   kidney beans
homefries   potatoes
curly fried   brown rice
yams, sweet potatoes   noodles?
mashed
sweet potato pie

Divide Rosina's list into some categories.

3. Larry decided on farming but couldn't find enough to say about it, so he changed to foods he hates. He will discuss liver, squid, octopus, broccoli, spinach, heart, oysters, peas, lobster, and tongue. How can he divide this list into three categories?

   a.

   b.

   c.

Exercise 3   Freewrite, brainstorm, and cluster

Try freewriting, brainstorming, and clustering on one or two of these subjects. Use the methods that appeal to you. If you have another method, use it instead.

1. Music   2. Books   3. Vacation   4. Sports

Exercise 4   Focused freewriting, brainstorming, and clustering

After freewriting, brainstorming, or clustering on one of the above subjects, decide which topic you are interested in and do some focused freewriting, brainstorming, or clustering on it.

Write your topic in sentence form here.

Getting Started

Once you have done some freewriting, brainstorming, or clustering, you are ready to start writing. You should have found a topic within your assignment that is interesting to you. Your professor may have assigned the subject, but you have to make it your own.

Look over your freewriting, brainstorming, or clustering work to see which topic seems most interesting to you. Probably you wandered around at first but then started focusing on one aspect of your subject. That is, you should have **narrowed down** your subject. For example, if you explored the subject of cats, you probably touched on your cat's name, why you have a cat, the funny things your cat does, how your cat looks, other cats you know, what you dislike about cats, where your cat came from. You probably won't find some of them worth exploring further, but one or two of them should be all right. If you have trouble deciding which topic to use, take the one that is most unusual, the one that represents a different point of view; you will have more to write that way.

When you decide which one or two topics are worth continuing, you might want to do more freewriting, brainstorming, or clustering. That will help you narrow down your topic and will help you find some details to discuss. Then right away write the parts that come to mind.

If you want, leave it for a short time. When you come back to it, you will have to start putting the parts in order by topic.

Look at each sentence carefully to see what topic is being discussed. Then try grouping together the sentences that have a similar topic. You may have to write more on some of the topics. You may also find that you have repeated some ideas, so you will have to omit them. The sentences you have grouped together belong in a paragraph.

After you have grouped all the sentences into paragraphs, each with a different topic, you have the major part of your essay. If some sentences are still left over, they probably do not fit your particular subject. Then you must take them out (you have to be brutal with yourself).

Finally, you should read it over and make more changes. You might add parts at the beginning, middle, or end. You might also change parts around or combine parts. This is considered normal editing of your essay.

EXERCISES IN NARROWING THE TOPIC AND GETTING STARTED

Exercise 5　Narrowing the topic

1. Rosina still wants to write about potatoes but can't decide what. List some topics about potatoes.

2. Leslie has done some clustering:

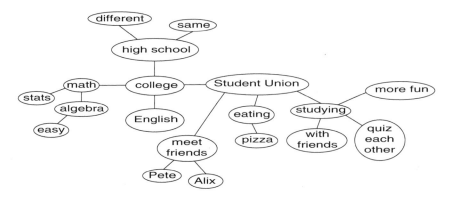

Which topics could she pursue?

Exercise 6   Getting started

1. Kim wanted to discuss noodles from different countries but did not know enough about them. She did not know how to make her favorite pesto sauce, so she decided to tell how to make angel hair pasta with tomato sauce. What steps does she need to discuss?

   Step 1

   Step 2

   Step 3

2. Larry has started this short essay on foods he hates. Find the parts he should group together and number them accordingly.

I like to eat lots of different things. But there are some foods I detest. I am pretty easy to please. Any innards are disgusting to me. Liver is smelly and drippy and has a very strong taste. Take it away. I hate what they call organ meats. Some people actually eat them! I can't stand liver of any kind—chicken, beef, or lamb. Also I don't like most shellfish. Most people like lobsters, but I think they're just a big insect. They are really related to insects. Clams aren't too bad though, and I like breaded shrimp. I'm typical in not liking broccoli, spinach, and other green stuff. Give me corn and carrots any time. I would never eat heart or tongue or brains. Squid and octopus sound really bad. Oysters are slimy and have dark greenish stuff inside—must be their insides.

Exercise 7   Narrowing the topic and getting started

1. Cross out the sentences and parts of sentences that don't fit in this paragraph about the usefulness of a dictionary.

> A dictionary definitely has many uses. When I was small and needed help reaching the dinner table, the large desk dictionary really helped. ~~As a child I liked to climb up on chairs, as well as anything else I could climb—trees, ladders, fences.~~ While in a tree I might collect leaves and blossoms that I could ~~then~~ press in the dictionary. ~~These leaves and blossoms, although flat,~~ ~~really~~ keep their color and fresh look for a long time ~~in the dictionary~~. When my cousins come over, we ~~usually~~ play Scrabble, ~~so~~ the dictionary is very useful then. ~~My cousin Dan always cheats by taking extra letters, but he plays so poorly we don't mind. My mother feels sorry for him.~~

2. Cross out the sentences and parts of sentences that don't fit in this paragraph about riding a bicycle.

> Mara rides her bicycle everywhere. She goes to classes in the morning, ~~so she gets up early to~~ ride twenty minutes to school. At 2:00 she rides ~~about fifteen minut~~es to work. ~~She is a checker in a super-~~

market and stands hours on her feet. She likes the store but wants to be a social worker. In the evening she rides about thirty minutes home. She lives with her father on the edge of town. On weekends when she is not working, she likes to ride in the park and sometimes goes on a picnic in the country with friends—on their bikes, of course.

Exercise 8   Narrowing the topic and getting started

1. Give reasons why your favorite newspaper or magazine is your favorite.

    First reason:

    Second reason:

    Third reason:

2. Give reasons why you like or dislike a course you are now taking in college.

    First reason:

    Second reason:

    Third reason:

Fourth reason:

Fifth reason:

Organizing an Essay

Although people think the standard short essay has five paragraphs (an **introduction,** a three-paragraph **body,** and a **conclusion**), you do not have to follow such a standard exactly. You should know what it is, but let the standard be a guide rather than a rigid framework.

Usually an essay will start with an introduction of several sentences but with a sentence or two that tells the **thesis** (or **theme**) of your essay. This thesis is your main point. Make it one that not everyone will agree with; make it one that you have to prove. For example, rather than saying that you will describe cats you have known (we can't argue with you on that), say that you will tell why cats are unlikable (some people would disagree with that). Then add some sentences before or after the thesis statement that show your knowledge of this subject. You might explain, for example, that you have had four cats in your life and have observed the cats of relatives and friends.

The center of your essay will be the **body.** It may have one or several paragraphs to give your reason or reasons for cats being unlikable. Perhaps you dislike cats because they kill birds, seem unfriendly, and shed fur everywhere. For each of these three reasons you need at least one paragraph and a **topic sentence.** The topic sentence is like the thesis statement, but it serves for the paragraph, not the whole essay. Then give examples and explanations for your topic sentence.

At the end of your essay comes the **conclusion.** Here you summarize your points and say that everyone should agree with you. Don't repeat the same sentences you have already used; write new ones. In a short essay, sometimes you don't even need a conclusion. The final sentence in the last paragraph of the body might be enough.

Finally, put a title at the top of your essay. Make it short, interesting, and relevant to the subject. Do not use the assignment for a title. You should capitalize the first letter of the first word, the first letter of the last word, and the first letter of all important words in the title. For example, Man's Worst Friend, The Abominable Cat, and No Reason for Cats would all be suitable. Something clever—a play on words, a familiar phrase, a line from a song—starts off the essay nicely. The title is not the most important part of the essay, but it is necessary to complete it.

EXERCISES IN ORGANIZING AN ESSAY

Exercise 9   Organizing essays

1. Number each sentence in Kim's essay. Then write the numbers for the sentences that would make an introduction, then a body, and finally a conclusion.

Angel Hair Pasta with Tomato Sauce

Serve this pasta with a simple salad. My favorite dish is angel hair pasta with tomato sauce. I have made this dish many times for myself and for friends and relatives. They all like it very much and so will you.

Start by cleaning and chopping five or six plum tomatoes. Squeeze some of the juice out of them in a colander. Next chop up some garlic. Put some oil in a pan and fry the garlic. After two or three minutes, add the parsley and tomatoes. Season with salt and pepper. Boil a large pot of water and add the angel hair pasta. It cooks in five to eight minutes. The tomato sauce cooks for about fifteen minutes. Drain the pasta and put it in a large bowl. Add the sauce on top.

It makes a great dish for company because everyone likes it.

2. Organize Rosina's essay on potatoes.

Potatoes of Infinite Variety

Potatoes have become a basic food for many people partly because they are very nutritious but mostly because they can be eaten in so many different ways. I wish I had one now. Potatoes can be boiled and can be fried. If they are boiled, many sauces can be put on top. Cheese sauce, tomato sauce, gravy, meat drippings, and butter are just some of the many toppings that go well with boiled potatoes.

They can be cut up and made into french fries, everyone's favorite. Also they can be curled and fried. The easiest is just sliced up and fried, maybe with some onions.

They can be eaten plain, with butter, or with sour cream. The potato just has to be baked an hour or so in the oven. Chopped chives or green onion on top go well also. The most popular and easiest method is baking. Any preparation of potato is just great.

Exercise 10   Reorganizing an essay

1. Organize the sequence of paragraphs.
2. Organize the sentences in the paragraphs.
3. Give the essay an interesting title.

Typing

Don't keep looking at the keyboard. Practice by using a chart of the keyboard placed in front of you. Look at the chart to find where the keys are. Soon you will memorize the different keys.

Use a black pen to write in any corrections or additions after you have finished typing. If you need to erase, use a good eraser that doesn't smudge.

Your thumbs are over the space bar. In order to type different letters, numbers, and punctuation marks, fingers can reach up or down or sideways but the whole hand doesn't have to move much. Place your hands so that the four fingers on the left hand cover a, s, d, and f and the right-hand fingers cover j, k, l, and semicolon.

Have a comfortable chair that is low enough so that your feet reach the floor. You should be able to reach the keyboard with your hands and have your elbows at your sides. The table should be low enough so that you don't reach up.

Even executives have to know how to type because they work at computers at their desks. Learning how to type is an important skill. These days not only do we use typewriters, we also use computers.

Exercise 11   Reorganizing an essay

1. Organize the sequence of paragraphs.
2. Organize the sentences in the paragraphs.
3. Give the essay an interesting title.

My Pet

My pet spider is named Penelope. In the morning as soon as I wake up I see Penelope and wish her good morning. Sometimes she has moved to a different part of her web, but she is still there. She lives in a web at the corner where the wall meets the ceiling just over my bed.

Most people have pets, but they usually have dogs or cats. But my pet is unique: I have a spider. Sometimes they even have rabbits, hamsters, mice, goldfish, or turtles.

Every night I see Penelope as I am getting into bed. I wish her good night after I crawl into bed and just before I turn out the light. I think she notices me because she is very still at that time.

One morning I noticed that Penelope was not in her web. I got rather worried about her. But when I went into the bathroom I saw her in the bathtub. I used a piece of paper to push her into a cup and then put her back in her web. That night she was not in the web, but three days later a spider was there. I'm sure Penelope is back.

Exercise 12   Reorganizing an essay

1. Rearrange the sentences into logical paragraphs.
2. Rearrange the paragraphs into a logical order.
3. Give the essay an interesting title.

Studying

You should review your assignment to make sure you know what it is. Then you need a realistic plan for studying, probably around two hours for a chapter. You may have been studying for many years in school, but you may never have really known how. A few minutes for standing up and stretching or getting a glass of water is all right. Knowing how to study will definitely help you improve your grades and get the most out of your classes. Also you don't need complete silence for studying. You don't need to sit the whole time.

When you review for the test, you will have a good outline to remind you of all the important points.

Concerning the chapter you are actually studying, look for important statements in each section. Before that, if you need to read a chapter in a textbook, you should start by looking at the organization of the whole textbook. The Table of Contents will give you a good idea of the major subjects and topics in it. The chapter title and the subtitles give you a good idea of the general topics.

When you have finished the chapter, go back to your notes and reread what you have written. Try to understand the main points by writing them in your own words. If you did a good job, you outlined the chapter by writing down the most important points. If the chapter has an introductory section or a summary at the end, match your outline with it to see how close you came.

Suggestions for Essay Topics

Use one of the prewriting techniques—freewriting, brainstorming, or clustering—before writing on one of these essay topics.

1. Write a letter to Malcolm X telling him why you liked or disliked his essay. Write specifically about the parts you liked or disliked.
2. Write an essay analyzing Malcolm X's use of language. Find words, phrases, and sentences that help create an impression and explain why they do.
3. Write an essay telling about your experience with reading or writing. What made you become interested in reading and writing? If you think you are not interested in reading or writing, write about why you are not interested.
4. Write an essay telling about the various facts one can learn from the dictionary. Examine a dictionary closely to find out the different areas it covers.
5. Write an essay telling how to do something that you really know and understand. Choose a small task that you can explain in detail.

Once you have written a rough draft of your essay, review "Organizing an Essay" to help revise it.

GRAMMAR

Learning About Words Often Confused

English has many words that are easily confused with each other. Some words sound alike or almost alike but are spelled differently. Other words look somewhat alike but are pronounced differently. Other words are sometimes written as one word and sometimes as two words, depending on the meaning. Yet others seem as if they should be one word or two words but are not. It makes English a confusing language to write.

Some common words that sound alike are *to, too, two,* and *their, there, they're.* Each word has its own meaning and cannot be interchanged with the others. Other common ones are *knew, new; right, write, rite; threw, through;* and *your, you're.* Because these words sound alike, knowing which one to use can be difficult. Using a dictionary and then keeping a list of them will help.

The words that sound nearly alike are a little easier. They just need to be pronounced carefully to see the difference. For example, just saying carefully *advice* and *advise, bought* and *brought, conscience* and *conscious, through* and *thorough* will indicate the differences. But then words like *accept* and *except* may look rather different and yet be pronounced almost exactly alike.

Words that are sometimes one word and sometimes two words can be confusing. We use both *all ready* and *already,* or *every day* and *everyday,* or *may be* and *maybe.* Whether these are one word or two depends on the meaning in the sentence. A few are easy, however. *A lot* and *all right* should always be two words.

The best ways to work with confusing words are to know that they exist, to look them up in the dictionary whenever necessary, and to keep a list.

EXERCISES ON WORDS OFTEN CONFUSED

Exercise 13   Words often confused

Read this list; then (1) put a check next to the words you use often, (2) put a question mark next to words that are confusing to you, and

(3) put a star next to new words. Look up the new words in the dictionary and write the definition next to the word.

a, an

accept, except

adapt, adopt

advice, advise

affect, effect

a head, ahead

a long, along

a lot, allot

already, all ready

all ways, always

amount of, number of

any thing, anything

any way, anyway

are, our

assent, ascent

ate, eight

bare, bear

be, bee

been, being

bought, brought

bread, bred

buy, by

chose, choose

clothes, cloths

coarse, course

complement, compliment

conscious, conscience

counselor, councilor

crowded, crowed

decent, descent

die, dye, dying

difference, deference

do, due, dew

everyday, every day

every one, everyone

farther, further

feel, fell, fill

fewer, less

flour, flower

fryer, friar

guessed, guest

hangar, hanger

have, of

heard, herd

higher, hire

hour, our

idle, idol

its, it's

knew, new, gnu

know, now, no

ladder, latter, later, letter

lay, lie, lye

lead, led

liar, lyre

load, lode

lose, loose

mantel, mantle

may be, maybe

mind, mine

might, mite

moral, morale

morning, mourning

my self, myself

noisy, nosy

not, knot

of, off

one, won

past, passed

patience, patients

pause, paws

peace, piece

peak, peek, pique

peer, pier, pear, pair

personal, personnel

plain, plane

pour, pore

principal, principle

precede, proceed

quiet, quite, quit

rain, reign, rein

raise, rise

recent, resent

right, write, rite, wright

real, reel, rile, rail

road, rode

scene, seen

shore, sure

sight, site, cite

sleigh, slay

so, sow, sew

some one, someone

some times, sometimes

stake, steak

stare, stair

stationary, stationery

straight, strait

than, then

there, their, they're

thought, though

threw, through, thorough

throne, thrown

to, too, two

vain, vein, vane

vale, veil, Vail

want, won't

way, weigh, whey

weak, week

wear, were, where, we're

weather, whether

went, when

whole, hole

who's, whose

whined, wind, wined

yield, yelled

yoke, yolk

your, you're

Exercise 14   Fill in the blanks

Write the correct word in the blank, selecting from the options written under the blank.

Driving

I like _____ drive, but _____
_____to, too, two_____ _____sometimes, some times_____

I'm _____ reckless. I'm _____
____to, too, two____ ____to, too, two____

easily _____ _____ my mood—I
____affected, effected____ ____by, buy____

forget what _____ do, such as paying attention
____to, too, two____

to the _____. _____
____road, rode____ ____Sometimes, Some times____

I _____ _____ sleepy to
____maybe, may be____ ____to, too, two____

drive _____ to the late _____
____do, due____ ____hours, ours____

I keep, but I drive _____. My parents
____anyway, any way____

_____ say _____ me,
____all ways, always____ ____to, too, two____

" _____ _____ bad
____Its, It's____ ____to, too, two____

_____ so _____ _____
your, you're   noisy, nosy   went, when

you come home; can't you be _____ with the car?"
                              quiet, quite, quit

_____ _____, of _____,
There, Their, They're   right, rite, write   coarse, course

but _____ _____ could be
      been, being   quiet, quite, quit

_____ dangerous. I use the car engine just to
quiet, quite, quit

keep _____ awake.
      myself, my self

On campus, _____ I show _____
             were, where, wear   of, off

_____ much, I turn corners _____
to, too, two   to, too, two

fast and take _____ like a _____
                 of, off   plain, plane

on a _____ runway. On _____
      strait, straight   principal, principle

I can't _____ _____
          bare, bear   to, too, two

_____ the last car out of the lot; I'd rather
be, bee

_____ _____ have
die, dye   than, then

_____ _____ out to
to, too, two   lose, loose

_____, so I roar _____
anyone, any one   ahead, a head

of _____.
    everyone, every one

I really like driving in bad _____

weather, whether

_____ conditions are really not _____.

went, when acceptable, exceptable

I like to _____ all alone against the world.

feel, fell

_____ _____ I

Right, Rite, Write, Wright know, now, no

_____ I'm playing with fire, but I _____

know, now, no know, now, no

_____ other way. _____

know, now, no Maybe, May be

_____ I'm older and have _____

went, when been, being

_____ a lot, I won't want to keep moving and

through, threw, though

won't _____ _____ more

mind, mine been, being

_____.

stationary, stationery

Exercise 15   Fill in the blanks

Write in the correct word in the blank, selecting from the options written under the blank.

Cats from Hell

_____ was a time _____ I

Their, There, They're went, when

was convinced _____ _____ a

to, too, two adapt, adopt

cat. I took the _____ of my sister's family,
advice, advise

_____ cats I really liked. _____
who's, whose   *Their, There, They're*

cats _____ friendly, a little _____
wear, were, where   *noisy, nosy*

but _____, and _____ trouble
quiet, quite, quit   *know, now, no*

at all, not fussy about eating _____ cheap cat
plain, plane

food, and wonderful companions. My sister _____
adviced, advised

me to get _____ cats so they would
to, too, two

_____ each other. _____ I
complement, compliment   *Everyday, Every day*

_____ _____ the pound even
went, when   *to, too, two*

_____ it was _____ from my
though, threw, through   *farther, further*

house _____ the pet store because I was
than, then

_____ I would find more grateful cats at the
shore, sure

pound. After about a _____ _____
weak, week   *do, due*

_____ _____ abandoning a
to, too, two   *someone, some one*

litter of _____ kittens, I got _____
ate, eight   *to, too, two*

really cute kittens, _____ black and
one, won

_____ white, _____ but
   one, won   plain, plane

elegant.

The first _____ days they stayed hidden; I
              to, too, two

only saw _____ little _____
              their, there, they're   pause, paws

_____ I peered under the bed. I didn't really
   went, when

_____ because I _____ they
   mind, mine   knew, new

would come out eventually. Little did I _____
                                              know, now, no

that those _____ days would be the only
                 to, too, two

_____ I would have for _____
   peace, piece   along, a long

time.

They would not eat cat food I _____ at the
                                    bought, brought

supermarket _____ they seemed very hungry all
                  though, threw, through

the time. I tried many different brands and finally found one they

liked. It was the most expensive one, but _____
                                                 its, it's

price was not important to me _____. I was just
                                    than, then

happy that they ate. _____ behavior was not
                           Their, There, They're

friendly. They hid _____ I was home, so I never
                          when, went

saw them _____ _____ I
                accept, except   went, when

caught them stealing my _____ in the kitchen.
                                  stake, steak

I couldn't leave _____ on the counter. At night,
                      anything, any thing

they _____ very _____, howl-
          were, where, wear   noisy, nosy

ing at each other and running around. Soon I noticed the rips on

the couch. My _____ white wall became less
                      bare, bear

_____ with _____ scratch
        bare, bear   along, a long

on it.

    One day _____ I came home from work, the
                      went, when

house was a _____ _____
                  scene, seen   of, off

_____ chaos. I _____
  thought, though, thorough   thought, through

_____ had _____ a vase
    someone, some one   throne, thrown

_____ the window. The _____
    threw, through, thought   mantel, mantle

was _____ _____ the statues
          bare, bear   of, off

that usually adorned it. The kitchen floor was completely

covered with _____ I had left out that
flour, flower

_____ for my _____
morning, mourning   weakly, weekly

_____ baking. My fresh pile of dish
bread, bred

_____ had also been _____
clothes, cloths   throne, thrown

around the room. I never _____ that cats
knew, new

liked to climb, but in the _____ closet they
clothes, cloths

had climbed up my _____ and pulled them
clothes, cloths

all _____ the _____.
of, off   hangars, hangers

These events _____ me to call my sister and
lead, led

say, "_____ _____!" She
Their, There, They're   though, through, threw

took them home with her. _____
Its, It's

_____ _____ weeks
been, being   to, too, two

_____ and they've _____
know, now   been, being

perfect. I _____ wrong about myself; I just
guessed, guest

don't get _____ with cats.
along, a long

Exercise 16   Writing paragraphs

Write a paragraph using the following words. Consult the dictionary to make sure of the meanings.

1. a   bought   lie
    an   fewer   moral
    amount   lay   morale

2. peace   raise   site
    piece   rise   want
    proceed   sight   won't

3. through   thorough   thorough
    threw   thought   throne
    there   their   they're

Chapter **2**

The Body of the Essay

WRITING AND READING

Before Reading "Personalize Your Personal Ad"

WORDS AND PHRASES TO LOOK FOR

night shifts: working at a job during night hours
distinctive: unique, different
limitations: limits, what cannot be done
self-sufficient: can take care of oneself
the key to: the answer to
compatible: suitable

QUESTIONS TO ANSWER AS YOU READ

1. Happy Mrs. wrote three ads. How was each one different from the others?
2. According to Happy Mrs., what made her third ad successful?
3. Write some words that describe Happy Mrs.
4. How do you feel about Happy Mrs. thinking that marriage is so important for women? Do you agree with her?
5. What do you think of personal ads? Is it all right to meet people this way?

Personalize Your Personal Ad

Dear Susan:

You support personal ads, but you don't often give tips on writing them. I am happily married to a man who answered my ad, so maybe I can help.

My first ad was written in partnership with an experienced "woman of the world." Since we were both single mothers with jobs, she started our ad with "working women." We received many amusing letters, but met no real boyfriends from the ad.

Then, I decided to go out on my own and write an ad myself. My own judgment couldn't have been worse; I read other women's ads, and they all sounded alike. A man reading them would never have known which one was right for him. Since I was working night shifts then, I included that in my ad; I told what was distinctive about me, and that was very useful. I met some nice "night" people, and I gave my friend the letters I rejected.

But the ad that attracted the man I later married told about my specific situation: "Slightly handicapped, can't dance or run, but like to live and laugh." Then I told what I enjoy doing. I got letters from people worse off than me who became friends. But I met a man with limitations similar to mine, who is self-sufficient, very independent, cheerful, easy-going. We have the same interests and tastes. And he encourages me to do everything I can, just as he does.

So the key to a successful personal ad is to tell about yourself. If you are looking for someone who is compatible with your personality, tastes and lifestyle, write your ad mentioning those details.

Happy Mrs.

Susan Deitz, "Single File,"
Los Angeles Times Syndicate,
New York Newsday,
June 9, 1992.

Topic Sentences

The body paragraphs of your essay give reasons, examples, and details to prove your thesis. Each body paragraph needs a **topic sentence,** which tells the main reason or point in that paragraph. Usually it comes either at the beginning or at the end of the paragraph, but it can also come in the middle. In a way, this topic sentence is like a thesis statement, but it serves only for the paragraph, not the whole essay.

If you know what points you want to make, you can rather easily write down your topic sentences as you need them. But if you are having trouble thinking of a topic sentence, just start writing the rest of the paragraph first. Once you have written it, your point will be clear to you and you will be able to add a topic sentence easily. If the topic sentence does not seem obvious, perhaps you have more than one point in your paragraph.

If you want the paragraph to begin with the topic sentence, think of it as a general statement about the whole paragraph. Then the rest of the paragraph will explain in more detail and give examples of your point. You can see if the detail or example fits by asking yourself if it deals with the topic sentence.

If you want the topic sentence to come at the end of the paragraph, your details and examples will come first and will lead up to that general statement. This way may seem confusing at first, so it needs some practice. But it can be very effective in adding some suspense to your paragraph.

Finally, the topic sentence can either come somewhere in the middle of the paragraph or not even be stated but be obvious by what has been said (an implied topic sentence). Both of these can be difficult if you set out to do them, but sometimes they just fall into place.

Topic sentences are important guideposts that lead a reader through your essay, but you don't need to have them all figured out before you start writing. You might never start writing if you had to do all the work in advance. If you don't know what your major points will be and if you are not sure of the direction of your essay, just start writing and see where it leads. Then you can go back and fill in the topic sentences where they are needed.

EXERCISES IN TOPIC SENTENCES

Exercise 1   Topic sentences

Read this essay, and then do the following:

1. Underline the topic sentences in the middle paragraphs.
2. Give the essay an interesting and personal title.

A Favorite Piece of Clothing

Everybody has a favorite piece of clothing. My particular one is a cotton workshirt that I wear whenever I have the chance. It has served me for many years, and I hope it will serve many more.

The size is extra large, and it fits like a tent. The shoulder line comes to midarm; I have to roll the sleeves way up. The end of the shirt comes almost to my knees. It is so wide that I could get two of me in it.

The shirt is light brown, really a faded medium brown. It goes with anything else I wear, especially my jeans. But I like the color especially because it is almost exactly the color of my eyes, and it makes my hair look really dark.

Most of all I like the shirt's versatility. I can wear it for casual times at home, and sometimes I even sleep in it. I can also wear it to school. Then for work I tuck it in my pants. For a party I wear a fancy belt around it.

I recommend that everyone get a favorite shirt that does everything and goes everywhere. It makes life so much simpler and more pleasant.

Exercise 2   Topic sentences

Read this essay, and then do the following:

1. Underline the topic sentences in the two middle paragraphs.
2. Give the essay a more interesting title.

Baseball

Baseball is the so-called national pastime in the United States. Many people seem to enjoy watching the sport immensely. People go wild during the season and especially during the World Series. But really, baseball takes so long and is such a bore!

First, the batter takes too much time. He swings two bats, then swings one bat, then uses it as a cane and then as a shoe-cleaning device. Then he strolls to the batting position and practices swinging again. Then he takes a break to spit, adjust his helmet, and get dirt on his hands. And then he finally gets ready. The batter takes so much time to get ready, you would think he had never done this before.

The pitcher also has a variety of delaying tactics. He spits, rubs his hands with dirt, and adjusts his helmet and clothing. But he can really delay by having conferences with the catcher, the manager, and anyone else who is around. Then he has to signal mysteriously to the catcher, the manager, and to all the basemen. The pitcher uses even more delaying tactics than the batter.

That is why baseball is a bore. Both the batter and the pitcher take too long to get started. Each bit of action is so short, and then we have to wait and wait again. I find it hard to understand why so many people think baseball is such a fascinating sport. Maybe they know something that I don't know. Or maybe having so much time gives people a chance to buy something to eat, to go to the bathroom, and to chat with their friends.

Exercise 3   Topic sentences

Read this essay and do the following:

1. Add topic sentences to the middle three paragraphs.
2. Give the essay an interesting title.

A Restaurant

I eat out fairly often and used to like going to the Universal Diner. It had some well-prepared dishes that I enjoyed. On my last two visits, however, the Universal Diner had definitely changed for the worse.

The salad was wilted and hardly had any dressing on it. Then the fish I ordered did not seem very fresh. I was afraid to eat it. The dessert tray had such old, dusty pieces of pie and cake that they all looked unappetizing.

wordy!!

Also, the waiter did not bring us water or any rolls until we asked three times. We didn't get any refills on the water either. We had to ask for clean forks. The waiter made a "mistake" on the check and tried to overcharge us by ten dollars.

The table looked dirty, with dead flowers in a vase and crumbs around the silverware. Also, the floor and the front window needed a good scrubbing. The smell from the kitchen almost made me sick one time.

I don't think this restaurant will be around much longer. I am certainly not planning on going there again, and I advise other people to avoid it also.

Exercise 4   Topic sentences

Read this essay and do the following:

1. Add topic sentences to each paragraph.
2. Give the essay an interesting title.

My Room

I moved into my room five years ago when my brother moved out. The room is average size and has two windows on one wall, a closet, and a bathroom. Because it's in the back of the house, nobody has to go through it or even really notice it. So I have decorated it just the way I want it. The walls have posters of some great skiers in the wonderful states of Vermont, Utah, Colorado, and the BEST, California.

The carpet used to be blue but now seems more multicolored. It really doesn't matter because it's so covered with books, clothes, shoes, and sports equipment that nobody can see it.

I have newspapers and magazines that are five or six months old on the desk. Someday I'll get around to reading them. Also, my old high-school notebooks are still there even though I'm in college. On top of that pile, empty cans and bottles, dishes, and glasses encrusted with old food show that I have burned the midnight oil. My bed never gets made except when I change the sheets, about once every month or two. But it stays fairly neat because I don't like to sleep on top of books and clothes. My bookcase has everything but books on it.

Obviously I don't care much for hanging up my clothes, so the closet has some empty hangers and almost empty shelves. The floor, however, has shoes, boots, and boxes piled up on it.

In the bathroom, the tub has a gray film going all around the sides; three or four empty shampoo bottles float around when the water goes on. Layers of underwear cover the floor, but they are useful for soaking up the water when I get out of the shower.

I really should get around to cleaning this mess. I probably will consider doing it for my college graduation. That should be a wonderful gift to myself. Or maybe I'll just move out at graduation like my brother and never clean the room.

Writing Body Paragraphs

The body part of body paragraphs is the meat or flesh that rounds out the topic sentences, the bones. It fills in and completes the paragraphs. You want a complete body, not a skeleton.

If you know your subject but don't really know what you want to say about it, you should do some focused freewriting, brainstorming, or clustering. Then you can think of some points to continue with. Writing on even one point will probably help you think of more.

If you have not written a topic sentence, you can still write the rest of the body paragraph. Write the explanation, example, or details you want. Afterwards you can fill in a topic sentence. You may have to change or take out some of the sentences if they don't fit your topic sentence, but most of the paragraph should be all right.

If you have written a topic sentence, you need to prove that point by explaining it, giving an example, or giving further details. If you are writing about how cats are unlikable and one of your points is that they kill birds, you could explain that cats stalk innocent birds and kill them for no reason. You could explain that such a killer instinct is very unpleasant, cruel, and hateful. If your topic sentence is that cats shed everywhere, you could give examples of where you have found cat hairs: on the couch and bed, in the bathtub, and even in your coffee. If your topic sentence is that cats are unfriendly, give details about their personalities: that they hide, take your favorite chair, hiss at people.

Once you have written the body paragraphs, you should put them in order. All your points should be important ones, but put the least important one first and work up to the most important one, or go from the most obvious one to the most unusual one. If they all seem equal, organize from the shortest one to the longest one. If you can't decide, probably they are all equal and any order will be fine.

Try to have two, three, or four points. Consider whether you have sometimes divided one into two points or if you have included two in the same one. You may not be able to tell until you have done some writing on a point, but after you have finished writing, ask yourself how many points you have raised.

As you can see, body paragraphs are really the most important part of the essay. They give the proof you need; you can't expect readers simply to believe you. After the body paragraphs, the introduction and the conclusion should not be so difficult.

EXERCISES IN BODY PARAGRAPHS AND TOPIC SENTENCES

Exercise 5   Topic sentences and details

Do the following in each paragraph:

a. Underline the topic sentence. It may be at the beginning, middle, or end of the paragraph. Remember, the topic sentence is the main idea of the paragraph.

b. Double underline the details that support the topic sentence in each paragraph.

1.   Start by jogging in place for thirty seconds. Then at the same time swing your arms up and down, side to side, and across your chest for two minutes. Do side swings for another thirty seconds and end by touching your toes ten times. These warm-up exercises should get you ready for a strenuous workout.

2.   There is a hole in the toe of one, and the other has a hole in the heel. The color has turned gray. The top has come unravelled. It is definitely time to throw out this old pair of socks.

3.   Drinking eight glasses of water a day is healthful. It eases the digestion of food. It keeps you from becoming dehydrated. It helps wash out impurities in your system. And it keeps you busy all day long!

4.   Trays and trays full of different frames are beautifully displayed. Who can choose from so many colors and so many styles? Getting new eyeglass frames can be a real problem. The fit must be just right. The earpieces have to be comfortable.

5.   A thesaurus really can be a treasure. It suggests words that are just right. If you forget a word, the thesaurus will have it. And it works perfectly for those words on the tip of your tongue.

Exercise 6   Body paragraphs

Underline the sentences that are examples and details in the following essay.

Talking on the Telephone

Jorge, my cousin, depends on the telephone. His whole life involves talking to people this way. He would not be able to go on living without this mainstay of his life.

Every morning, as soon as he arrives at his office, he receives a pile of memos about telephone calls he has received. He spends from 8:00 to 12:00 calling these people back. Even at lunch in a coffee shop, he brings a portable phone and calls his family or relatives to chat while eating. Just last week, he called me at home to find out about my college classes. He is very proud of me.

He was one of the first people to get a car telephone even though it cost so much money. While he drives to and from work, which only takes half an hour, he sets up appointments and meetings. For exam-ple, he called his dentist for his annual check-up and then invited a business associate for dinner.

At home he might get five or ten calls in the evening from friends and relatives. He advises them, helps them with problems, and catches up on their news. He was the first to know that my other cousin Kim got an A on her English essay.

We all tell him that he should take a vacation at a cottage with no telephone. But we are only kidding because we don't think he could really survive such an ordeal.

Exercise 7   Body paragraphs

Complete this essay by adding body paragraphs; also give the essay an interesting title.

College

Most college students think they should attend class, take notes, do their assignments, read, read, and read. Then they go to the library and read more. After that they write and write. Students should learn the real benefit of going to college: having a good time.

Lounging around in the student union is full of great possibilities for a good time.

The college cafeteria can be more than just a place to grab a bite.

Even the classroom will offer more than just a place to listen to a lecture and take notes.

With so many opportunities, students can practice their skills for having a good time all the time. It's important to make the most of the time because they probably will not be around for long. And once they flunk out they will no longer have all those great places for a good time.

Exercise 8   Body paragraphs

Complete this essay by completing the topic sentences and writing the rest of the body paragraphs; also give the essay an interesting title.

A Happy Event

Taking a trip to _____ was definitely a happy and educational event for me. I went with _____, and we had a wonderful time during our _____ weeks there.

We were really happy because

The trip was also educational because

I have taken other trips before and after this one, but this trip

to _____ really seemed enjoyable. Perhaps some day I will

have the chance to go back to _____ . In the meantime, I

highly recommend it to everyone.

Suggestions for Essay Topics

Using one of the prewriting techniques—freewriting, brainstorming, or clustering—write on one of these topics.

1. Write a letter responding to "Happy Mrs." Tell her what you think of her advice about writing personal ads.
2. Write an essay discussing the specific advice that "Happy Mrs." gives. What is good or bad about her advice?
3. Write an essay that could be your own long personal ad. Tell what good points you have and what is distinctive and special about you.

4. Write an essay about how to meet interesting people. You can discuss how to meet a potential mate or new friends, or how to make business contacts, or how to see famous people.

5. Write an essay about the institution of marriage. Decide if it is no longer possible or if it is a necessity.

When you have written a rough draft, see if you have **topic sentences** in each **body paragraph.** Also see if you have explanations, examples, or details to make up the body paragraphs and if they are all relevant to your topic sentences.

GRAMMAR

Nouns

Nouns make up the basic topics of sentences. Nouns can be **concrete** (we can see, hear, touch, smell, or taste them), such as salad, music, person, book, Susan B. Anthony, Rover, and Seattle. Other nouns are **abstract** (we can't use the senses to know them), such as honesty, idea, love, and horror. We can't always decide whether a noun is concrete or abstract (air, for example), but we should recognize the word as a noun.

Nouns may also be classified as **proper nouns** and **common nouns.** Proper nouns are the names of people, places, titles, and brands; they begin with a capital letter. Proper nouns may be names of people and animals (Kim, José Gomez, Rover), places (Mt. Rushmore, Washington, West Street, Woodrow Wilson High School, Yale University, India), titles (Professor Wang, Dr. Dean, Mr. and Mrs. Parker, King Henry, Lady Montague), and brands (Mustang, General Electric, Jell-O, Sony). Common nouns are all the other nouns that do not take a capital letter unless they appear at the beginning of a sentence. Such words as professor, doctor, king, lady, street, high school, university, and company are common nouns when they do not refer to a particular person or place.

Nouns are used in sentences as **subjects** or **objects. As subjects,** they tell what or who the sentence concerns. For example, in "Maria found the book," if we ask who or what found the book, the answer is "Maria," so "Maria" is the subject. Sometimes the subject is not stated but is understood in commands. "Go to the store," "Please wash the dishes," and "Let's look here" all have "you" understood as the subject. Sometimes the subject has more than one part. In "Maria and Tony found the book," "Maria and Tony" form the subject of the sentence. Also, the subject of the sentence does not have to come at the beginning of the sentence.

Nouns can also be **objects.** In "Maria found the book," "book" is the object because it is what or who was found. In this case, "book" is the object of the verb in the sentence. However, not all verbs need objects. "Maria sleeps," "The cup broke," and "The dog ran away" have no objects. Sometimes a noun can be the object of a preposition as, for example, "window" in "by the window." Thus in the sentence "Maria found the book by the window," "book" is the object of the verb and "window" is the object of the preposition.

These nouns form the topics of sentences and should be chosen carefully so that sentences will be clear and precise.

EXERCISES IN NOUNS

Exercise 9   Finding nouns

In the following essay, underline the nouns. Notice if they are concrete, abstract, or proper nouns. Don't worry if you don't get all of them.

Pizza

Pizza has its roots in Italy, where long ago some cook flattened out some leftover dough, poured some leftover sauce on it, and baked it in the oven. Now, however, pizza has become an American dish with regional differences just as if it had always been an American dish.

New York pizzas have very thin crusts—the thinner the better, according to many New Yorkers. Usually cheese dominates; some people even ask for extra cheese. A white pizza omits the tomato sauce and has three or four kinds of cheese on top. New Yorkers like pizza so much that they can buy just a slice and walk down the street eating it.

"Chicago style" means deep-dish pizza. The crust is thick and rich with lard or other shortening. The ingredients tend to be fillings rather than toppings, but otherwise they are more or less the same as New York pizza, except that rarely would a person have it plain.

California style has more to do with the toppings than the crust, which is of medium thickness. Since Californians are supposed to be health-conscious, their pizzas emphasize vegetables like broccoli, alfalfa sprouts, and avocados. There are a few other local styles (New Haven and Boston) and some unusual ingredients (clams or pineapple, for example), but they haven't hit the big time yet. Maybe a new one is on the horizon, but nobody can make anchovies popular.

Exercise 10   Finding nouns

Underline the nouns in the following essay. Notice if they are concrete, abstract, or proper nouns. Don't worry if you don't get all of them.

Types of Windows

"Home is where you hang your hat." This old saying is not only awkward but also untrue. The truth is that your home is determined by how you open your windows. Different countries in the world have windows that work differently.

In Europe, most windows open inward—the typical "French doors"—and are divided into left and right sides. They usually have a knob in the middle. They allow for rather big windows, and the entire window can be opened for a lot of air. But adjusting them for less openness is hard because they are pushed around by wind.

Asia tends to have sliding windows like the shoji screens of Japan. Usually either side can be slid open, but both sides never can, so one never gets more than half a window open. But they can be easily and precisely adjusted to allow in the air, and they are not blown around by the wind.

The United States likes the "guillotine" window. Only half the window can be opened, but from both the top and bottom. These windows must be small so as not to be too heavy to open. Also they require a sash to keep the open part from crashing down. But they also can be precisely adjusted and don't blow around.

"To each his own" might the motto of the window-makers of the world. But if a clever inventor could design a window that had the best features of each kind, then maybe everyone in the world would have the same window.

Exercise 11   Using concrete and abstract nouns

1. List ten **concrete** nouns. Look around the room, or think of some particular thing.

   Now try to use as many as possible in a paragraph about the room or your particular subject.

2. List five **abstract** nouns. Look around the room, or think of your particular subject.

   Now write a paragraph using all five abstract nouns.

Exercise 12   Using proper and common nouns

List four proper nouns in each category:

People   1.

            2.

            3.

            4.

Places   1.

            2.

            3.

            4.

Titles   1.

            2.

            3.

            4.

Brand names 1.

            2.

            3.

            4.

Which ones could also be common nouns? Use a dictionary if you are not sure.

Write a sentence using four proper nouns, one from each of your four lists.

Write a sentence using a proper noun and the part of it that can also be a common noun.

Pronouns

We could just repeat nouns each time we use them, but our sentences would be repetitive and long-winded. Pronouns replace nouns in sentences and also help give unity and smoothness to an essay.

Some pronouns replace nouns used as **subjects:** *I, you, she, he, it, we, they, who(ever)*. Some pronouns replace nouns used as **objects:** *me, you, her, him, it, us, them, whom(ever)*. For example, we can replace the nouns in "Maria found the book" by "She found it," and "Karl and Pei are looking for Leonard" by "They are looking for him" or "He and she are looking for him."

In informal speech, people often mix subject pronouns and object pronouns. For example, instead of "He and I went to the movies," we hear "Me and him." This is incorrect in writing essays. Even people who say "Me and him went to the movies" would not say "Me went to the movies" or "Him went to the movies." Just testing for each pronoun separately will probably make clear which one to use.

Another group of pronouns is called the **indefinite** pronouns:

anybody, anyone, anything
each, everybody, everyone, everything
either, neither
none, nothing, nobody
some, somebody, someone, something
one, other(s), thing(s), all, few, many

Related to indefinite pronouns are **demonstrative** pronouns: *this, that, these, those*. Another group is the **relative** pronouns: *that, what(ever),* *whichever.* Who(ever) and whom(ever) belong in this group also but were mentioned above with subject and object pronouns.

Some of the indefinite pronouns also serve as adjectives as well as pronouns: *each, either, neither, one, other, some, all, few,* and *many.* And all the relative pronouns also serve as adjectives. For example, the boldface words are pronouns:

Each wants the **other.**	Each person wants the other hat.
A **few** want **many.**	A few people want many hats.
Keep **whichever** you want.	Keep whichever hat you want.
That is my choice.	That green hat is my choice.

In addition, we have the **possessive** pronouns: *mine, yours, his, hers, its, ours, theirs, whose.* Thus we can write: Whose is this; this book is mine; yours is over there; use his instead of ours.

Another group of pronouns is the **reflexive** pronouns: *myself, yourself, himself, herself, itself, ourselves, yourselves, themselves.* We use these pronouns to emphasize that a person has done something herself or himself or to herself or himself: "The boss delivered the mail herself;" "They treat themselves well;" and "You yourself should do the job." Some people have started using "myself" in place of "I" and "me," but this construction is wrong.

These pronouns can be very useful because we don't always want to repeat nouns. Still, it is important to be clear about what the pronoun is replacing. If this is unclear, then it is better to use the noun instead. It is not important to remember the names of the different kinds of pronouns, but it is important to use the correct one.

EXERCISES IN USING PRONOUNS

Exercise 13   Finding pronouns

Circle the pronouns in the following paragraphs. Try to include the subjective pronouns, the objective pronouns, the indefinite pronouns, the demonstrative pronouns, the possessive pronouns, and the reflexive pronouns.

1.   One day a substitute teacher picked me to read aloud from the textbook. When I told her "No, thank you," she came unhinged. She thought I was acting smart, and told me so. I kept calm, and that got her madder and madder. We must have spent 10 minutes trying to

solve the problem, and finally she got so red in the face I thought she'd blow up. She told me she'd see me after class.

2.   One summer my family forced me to go to a camp for children with reading problems. I hated the idea, but the camp turned out pretty good, and I had a good time. I met a lot of kids who couldn't read and somehow that helped. The director of the camp said I had a higher I.Q. than 90 percent of the population. I didn't believe him.

3.   Homework is a real problem. During free periods in school I go into the special ed room and staff members read assignments to me. When I get home my mother reads to me. Sometimes she reads an assignment into a tape recorder, and then I go into my room and listen to it. If we have a novel or something like that to read, she reads it out loud to me. Then I sit down with her and we do the assignment. She'll write, while I talk my answers to her. Lately I've taken to dictating into a tape recorder, and then someone—my father, a private tutor or my mother—types up what I've dictated. Whatever homework I do takes someone else's time, too. That makes me feel bad.

4.   As for what happens after college, I don't know and I'm worried about that. How can I make a living if I can't read? Who will hire me? How will I fill out the application form? The only thing that gives me any courage is the fact that I've learned about well-known people who couldn't read or had other problems and still made it. Like Albert Einstein, who didn't talk until he was 4 and flunked math. Like Leonardo da Vinci, who everyone seems to think had dyslexia. (All four paragraphs from David Raymond, "On Being 17, Bright, and Unable to Read," The New York Times Company, 1976.)

Exercise 14   Finding pronouns

Circle the pronouns in the following essay. Look for objective, subjective, indefinite, demonstrative, possessive, and reflexive pronouns.

My Gal Sally

Little did I know that a two-year-old could be so much trouble. Ever since Sally came along, we have had to change our whole lifestyle. Somebody needs to watch Sally every minute, but no one wants to. All of us are busy, so we decided on some rules: Each of us must keep everything dangerous out of the way, someone always has to be with her, there has to be something for her to play with, and we must leave nothing we value near her.

Sally causes so much trouble. For example, last week, Sally locked herself in the bathroom and got herself all wet in the toilet. Someone called a locksmith, but he couldn't come for an hour, so we ourselves had to pick the lock. She also took somebody's slippers outside. Luckily mine were hidden in the closet, but Doug says his are missing. Then she played with some housekeys. They were not ours, so everybody is worried that someone cannot find his or hers and has not thought to ask us.

We have been asking all the neighbors if they lost any keys; what a chore that is. We also asked a few if they would like to have a cute, but naughty, dog.

Exercise 15   Changing nouns to pronouns

Cross out as many nouns as you can and write in **pronouns.** Be sure the paragraphs still make sense.

1.   Leslie received a letter addressed to Mr. Leslie. Leslie tried to hand the letter back to the mail carrier, but the mail carrier would not take back the letter from Leslie. Leslie said it was not for Leslie because Mr. Leslie was not her name. Leslie said Leslie was female and not male. Also Leslie said that her last name was not Leslie.

2.   The book about dogs belonged to Larry, but Larry did not want the book anymore. Larry decided to give the book to Maria, but Maria did not want the book either. Larry and Maria decided to give the

book to Mr. Sanchez at the public library. Mr. Sanchez was happy to receive the book and thanked Larry and Maria very much for the book.

3.   Kim's party started at eight, but Kim was not ready. Kim had not prepared any snacks or drinks. Maria, Larry, and Rosina arrived on time. Kim knew that Maria, Larry, and Rosina would be hungry and thirsty. Luckily Maria, Larry, and Rosina brought chips and soda along. Kim, Maria, Larry, and Rosina ate and drank all the chips and sodas.

Notice that pronouns are really necessary. Without them these paragraphs do not sound right.

Exercise 16   Using pronouns

Fill in the subject, object, or reflexive pronoun. Also circle the demonstrative, possessive and indefinite pronouns.

My Former and Future Best Friend

Esther and _____ became best friends when
                      I, me, myself

we met in junior high school. She had just come from San Juan, and

_____ from Chicago, so we both felt a little lost.
      I, me, myself

We formed a pair and did everything together. Our friendship

lasted through high school, but then _____ and
                                          her, herself, she

_____ drifted apart for a while.
      I, me, myself

In junior high school, nobody could come between

_____ and _____. Esther
      her, herself, she   I, me, myself

and _____ did our homework together
I, me, myself

either in her house or mine. _____ and
Her, Herself, She

_____ joined the same art club, and
I, me, myself

_____ both became cheerleaders.
ourselves, us, we

In high school, Jason came between _____.
ourselves, us, we

First he dated me and then Esther! _____ and
Her, Herself, She

_____ went steady for about six months. That
he, him, himself

made me so angry I could not talk to _____.
them, themselves, they

But finally they broke up, so _____ and
her, herself, she

_____ became friends again, and
I, me, myself

_____ both could hate Jason!
ourselves, us, we

After graduating, Esther went to college, and I got a job.

Then I met Doug, and _____ and
he, him, I, me

_____ got married last year.
he, him, I, me

_____ and _____
He, Him, I, Me   he, him, I, me

both work, and we decided to go to college also.

Doug and _____ went to register for classes
I, me, myself

and _____ should we meet but Esther, also
who, whom

registering. _____ and _____
Her, She, I, Me   her, she, I, me

had not seen each other for three years. She helped

_____ and _____ register
Doug, I, me   Doug, I, me

and find our way around.

Now that classes have started, _____
Esther, her, I, me

and _____ are pretty busy, but we will see
Esther, her, I, me

each other whenever we can. _____ and
Her, She, I, Me

_____ are going to be best friends again. And
her, she, I, me

both _____ and _____ will
Doug, I, me   Doug, I, me

have someone _____ will help us with our
who, whom

assignments too.

Chapter 3

The Beginning and the Ending

WRITING AND READING

Before Reading "Saving the Elephants"

WORDS AND PHRASES TO LOOK FOR

elusive: hard to find
emit: send out
ultrahigh-frequency signals: extremely fast radio waves
pitfalls: hidden dangers
deflect: to turn aside
Cameroon: a country in western Africa
Zaire: a country in central Africa
dense vegetation: crowded-together plants
savannah-dwelling: living on a flat, open plain
curator of mammology: person in charge of the study of
    mammals, usually in a museum or institute

QUESTIONS TO ANSWER AS YOU READ

1. Why are wildlife biologists tracking the African elephants?
2. How are the biologists tracking the elephants?
3. Name some difficulties involved in tracking the elephants.
4. Where are these elephants located? What sort of land do they live in?
5. Should we be spending money on this project? Why or why not?

Saving the Elephants

Wildlife biologists are using new technology to track the elusive African forest elephant in the hope of finding the best way to insure the animal's survival.

Wildlife Conservation International, a division of the New York Zoological Society, put collars that emit ultrahigh-frequency signals on two African elephants this summer; the signals are picked up by weather satellites, and the information is relayed to the Bronx Zoo.

About a third of the 700,000 African elephants are thought to live in the rain forests and may be endangered, but information on them is sketchy. Dense forests make it difficult to track the elephants with standard technology, collars that emit very high-frequency radio signals.

But just switching to satellite technology does not eliminate all the pitfalls of forest tracking. The ultrahigh-frequency signals can still be absorbed or deflected by the 8,000-pound animal's bulk, dense vegetation, or weather conditions. In a trial run of the technology, the researchers have collared a forest elephant in the area of Korup National Park, Cameroon, and a savannah-dwelling elephant in Garamba National Park, Zaire.

Since mid-June, nearly all of the signals from the savannah elephant have been picked up, but the satellite is detecting only a third of the signals from the forest elephant. The project's director, Dr. Fred W. Koontz, curator of mammology at the zoo, said that transmission should improve when the rainy season ends in late fall. The scientists also plan to test a new transmitter design.

"Science Watch," *New York Times,*
Tuesday, September 8, 1992.

Writing Introductions

Starting to write an essay, even after freewriting, brainstorming, or clustering, can be quite difficult. You must find a thesis statement and then find a way to make it sound interesting and worth reading. Several ways can work well.

The **thesis statement** should be a complete sentence that states a point of view, an idea, or an argument. For example, instead of stating that your essay will be about camping, make a clear point: "Camping is the cheapest form of vacationing"; "Camping provides fun for an entire family"; "Camping means nothing but cold, hunger, and mosquito bites"; "Camping can be dangerous." Write down different thesis statements to decide which one to use, even if all the statements could work.

The thesis statement usually comes at the end of the introduction, but it may also be the first sentence. Then you can mention the points that will be discussed in the body of the essay. For example, if the cheapness of camping is the thesis, state that costs for hotels, eating out, amusement park fees, and airline fares can be saved. But this method is somewhat mechanical and predictable. You should consider starting another way.

Starting with a short **anecdote,** a little story, can engage the reader immediately. It can be your own or someone else's experience, or it can be made up, but remember that writing fiction is hard. The anecdote should lead into the thesis statement, which can be the last sentence of the introduction.

Or ask a **question** that can be answered by your essay. then state the thesis and add another sentence or two. Rather than "Why do people go camping?" which is too general to answer, ask "Why do people risk being eaten alive by hordes of mosquitoes?"

Setting the scene can also create interest for the readers. Describe each person's activities to illustrate that camping can be fun for the whole family, for example. However, describing people killed by bears for a dangers-of-camping thesis may overstate your case if you will discuss mostly topics more familiar to you, such as mosquitoes and collapsing tents.

Using a **quotation** is also a possible beginning. You can find one in a book of quotations or think of a common saying. "Misery loves company," for example, will work for the pitfalls of camping. But don't quote the definition of "camping" from a dictionary; that's too obvious. Quoting a **statistic,** such as the number of campers in the United States, is also a possibility.

No one method is best. Try different beginnings and choose the one that will make people want to read your essay.

EXERCISES ON INTRODUCTIONS AND THESIS STATEMENTS

Exercise 1   Introductions and thesis statements

For these **introductions** for an essay called "Umbrellas," do the following:

a. Underline the **thesis statement.**

b. Number the type of introduction (1) anecdote, (2) question, (3) setting the scene, (4) quotation, or (5) statistic.

c. Write one or two sentences stating what the rest of the essay should be about.

1. "An umbrella for every occasion, an occasion for every umbrella." That is my motto for my unusual collection of twenty umbrellas. I have made a point of collecting umbrellas for different uses, not just for rain.

2. I was in my expensive new linen outfit chatting with elegant guests in the rose garden. A summer shower started suddenly and forcefully. Everyone opened up little umbrellas—except me. I had to run for cover and miss the party. I made a vow that I would never be caught empty-handed again.

3. Why would anyone need twenty umbrellas? Yes, I have that many, and I use every one of them, sometimes more than one at a time. But mostly I have that many because I collect useful but unusual umbrellas.

4. The street is shiny with rain. One man runs by with a sturdy cane-handled classic black umbrella. Another man fights with a flimsy red folding one that flips inside out. A woman struggles to keep a large blue plaid one over herself and another woman. Three people huddle

under an enormous striped golf umbrella. I love the scene because I love umbrellas.

5.   I did not understand the old saying, "when it rains, it pours" until I moved here. Now I am prepared for the elements because I have a collection of twenty umbrellas. I need all twenty of them to continue living here.

If you did not like any of these introductions, write your own:

Exercise 2   Introductions and thesis statements

For these five **introductions** for an essay called "Watching Television," do the following:

a. Underline the **thesis statement.**
b. Number the type of introduction (1) anecdote, (2) question, (3) setting the scene, (4) quotation, or (5) statistic.
c. Write one or two sentences stating what the rest of the essay should be about.

1.   She curls up in the overstuffed armchair placed just ten feet from the enormous screen. The lights have been dimmed; the remote is in hand; the TV guide is nestled at her side. She is about to indulge in her one and only "activity": watching hour upon hour of television.

2.   "There's a sucker born every minute." Television is the greatest huckster of them all, beating out P. T. Barnum by a long shot. People who succumb to television are being duped every minute they watch, but especially during the commercials.

3.   America has gone way beyond the standard television that sits on a TV stand in the middle of the living room. Now there are TVs for the bedroom, the recreation room, and the kitchen. We even have TVs for cars. Televisions are really everywhere.

4.   The average eighteen-year-old person in the United States has watched the equivalent of almost two years (710 days) of television. This great waste of time and energy should be channeled into reading. We would be a nation of intellectuals if it were not for television.

5.   Why do I watch the Academy Awards every year? The show is too long, too slow, and too boring. Yet, when the time comes, I settle down on the couch and watch the whole thing. Why?

Write your own introduction if you prefer.

Writing Conclusions

An essay needs to be completed with an interesting conclusion that gives the sense that you have done a thorough job. Indicate that the essay is finished with one of the following techniques.

A **quotation** can work well, but only if you have the right one. Use one you know or from a book of quotations rather than from the dictionary, and choose one that sums up your thesis concisely. If you started your essay with a quotation, perhaps you can relate or contrast the two quotations.

Consider asking a **question** whose answer will be obvious because of your discussion in the essay: "With all these benefits, don't you think everyone should go camping?" or "Don't you feel like grabbing your backpack and hiking boots right now?" If you asked a question in the introduction, then answer it in the conclusion.

Another method is to make a **prediction** or a **recommendation.** Be sure that the prediction or recommendation follows naturally from your points in the essay. You don't want to sound as if you are launching into a whole new subject. This type of conclusion can be tricky but it's wonderful when it works well. Try different predictions or recommendations to see if one of them works. For example, you might predict "More and more people certainly will be going camping considering the low cost and the state of our economy." Or recommend that people try camping to have a good time *and* save money.

A **summary** of your points is the most obvious method, but it works better for long essays. For short ones, summarizing will seem repetitive. Still, you can combine one or two sentences of summary with a question, quotation, prediction, or recommendation.

Sometimes the conclusion need not be a separate paragraph at the end, especially in a short essay. It might be included in the final point. Or perhaps just one more sentence at the end of the paragraph will be enough for a satisfactory conclusion.

EXERCISES ON CONCLUSIONS

Exercise 3   Looking at conclusions

Read the following essay; then decide which conclusion you like. If you don't like any of them, write your own.

Movie Etiquette

The lights are off; my popcorn is making a steady path to my mouth; I'm enjoying a great movie. Then in front of me a dark figure blocks my entire view—a latecomer. From two rows back, shouts drown out the dialogue. Next to me a couple talks instead of watching. They should learn some movie etiquette.

People should arrive on time for movies and take their seats before the lights go off. They should buy their popcorn beforehand, so they don't disturb everyone by going back and forth. People should not exclaim or talk during the movie. Laughing and gasping are expected, but only at appropriate times.

Pick one of the following **conclusions,** or write your own. Then see if your choice was a quotation, question, prediction, recommendation, or summary.

1. Why go to the trouble and expense of going to the movies if not to enjoy the film? People should stay home and do what they like instead of disturbing others at the movies.

2. Matters are getting worse. Soon people will do whatever they want at the movies. They'll come at any time, leap up and down to buy drinks and food, shout to each other, yell obscenities at the screen, and talk about their intimate lives.

3. Movie theaters should post a sign in the lobby about proper etiquette and show the sign on the screen before every movie. Ushers should be stationed in the theater to warn people or ask them to leave. These simple steps would make going to the movies much more enjoyable.

4. "The times, they are a-changing." Maybe I should accept the fact that people no longer behave as they used to. They are enjoying the movie in a different way. If I can't join them, then I'll have to get a VCR and watch movies at home.

5. Movie etiquette is nonexistent. People come late and disturb others. They shout at the screen, and they talk to each other during a movie. They probably don't know any better.

Write your own conclusion if you wish.

Exercise 4   Looking at conclusions

Read the following essay; then decide which conclusion you like. If you don't like any of them, write your own.

Eating with Chopsticks

"Slow and easy wins the race." Learning to use chopsticks slowly one at a time will keep you from starving in a Chinese or Japanese restaurant. The food tastes better too.

Hold one chopstick between your thumb and forefinger, letting it rest mostly at the base of the thumb. Rest it on your bent ring finger near the tip. Then hold the other chopstick with the tips of your thumb, forefinger, and third finger. You should be able to move the top chopstick up and down, meeting the end of the lower chopstick. Tap the ends of the chopsticks on the table to make them even.

Pick one of the following **conclusions,** or write your own. Then see if your choice was a quotation, question, prediction, recommendation, or summary.

1. Follow these simple instructions and you will enjoy great food, impress your friends with your sophistication, and gain the admiration of the waiters.

2. Just follow these instructions step by step, one chopstick at a time. Start with the first one, carefully; then do the second one. With a little practice, you will master chopsticks.

3. Why not just grab a fork? You could; lots of people do and have lived to tell about it. But wouldn't you rather fit into the scene? Don't you want some new experiences?

4. Once you have mastered chopsticks you should go on to learn other aspects of Asian dining: how to order a well-balanced meal, how to eat Asian foods properly, and how to behave at the table.

5. Some day you will be thankful for this skill. You could be stranded on a deserted island. Will you have a fork handy? Probably not. But you will be able to grab a couple of twigs and eat anything you want.

Write your own conclusion if you wish.

EXERCISES ON WRITING INTRODUCTIONS AND CONCLUSIONS

Exercise 5   Changing introductions and conclusions

Change the introduction and the conclusion so they will be more interesting. Try one or more of these introductions: **anecdote, question, setting the scene, quotation, statistic.** Try one or more of these conclusions: **quotation, question, prediction, recommendation, summary.**

Warming Up Before Exercising

Here is how to warm up before you start exercising.

Start by bending your neck first to one shoulder and then to the other three or four times. Then raise and lower your shoulders ten times. Next swing both your arms to the same side ten times. Then with hands on your waist, twist your upper body to the right and then to the left ten times.

Next you should do some stretching. Bend forward at the waist while reaching forward with your arms. Lower your arms and touch the floor while your legs are slightly apart and straight. Hang there for ten seconds and then slowly straighten up. Then bend forward again and do the same thing, but instead of straightening up, put both hands on one ankle and try to touch your head to your knee. Hold for ten seconds. Do this again with the other ankle and knee. Then slowly straighten up. Finally jog in place for one minute.

Now you are warmed up and ready for an exercise routine.

Exercise 6   Changing introductions and conclusions

Change the introduction and the conclusion so they will be more interesting. Try one or more of these introductions: **anecdote, question, setting the scene, quotation, statistic.** Try one or more of these conclusions: **quotation, question, prediction, recommendation, summary.**

My Bedroom

When I was assigned this topic, I really didn't know what to write because I don't have a bedroom.

I sleep on the couch in the living room, so maybe the living room can be called my bedroom. We only have one bedroom in our apartment. My mother and father sleep there and share the room also with my baby sister and eight-year-old brother. Maybe I'm lucky because I'm the only one with my own room at night.

However, the living room is not only a living room and my bedroom, it is also the dining room. The whole family eats meals at the table next to the kitchen. In the evening after dinner, I do my homework at the dinner table. My father plays checkers with my brother at the table too. My mother sometimes uses the table for her sewing machine. My two-year-old sister usually plays on the floor. The living room is pretty crowded with all of us. We also watch television in this room and everybody sits on the couch, my bed.

Sometimes I wish I had my own room.

Exercise 7   Changing introductions and conclusions

Change the introduction and the conclusion so they will be more interesting. Try one or more of these introductions: **anecdote, question, setting the scene, quotation, statistic.** Try one or more of these conclusions: **quotation, question, prediction, recommendation, summary.**

If I Had a Dog

I want a dog.

We could go for walks in the streets. I wouldn't mind pausing for the dog to do its business because I like to look around at the people. I also have errands that seem tedious, like buying the newspaper or mailing letters, but having a dog to take with me might make the errands seem more fun.

The dog would also be good protection at home. It would bark if someone came to the door or window and probably scare the person away. My friends would know that I had a dog, so they wouldn't be afraid, but everyone else would.

I could get some exercise by running with the dog. We could go to a park on weekends and really have a workout. Or we could just run around the block in the neighborhood. I feel foolish running around the block alone.

That is why I want a dog.

Exercise 8   Completing an essay

Complete this essay:

1. Complete the **introduction** and add a **thesis statement.**
2. Write the **topic sentence** and **body paragraphs.**
3. Complete the **conclusion.**
4. Change the **title** to an interesting one.

Movie

Recently I attended a showing of "_____."

Although I _____, the movie was really

_____.

The plot

The actors

This movie has _____. I think

people should _____. They will be

_____.

Suggestions for Essay Topics

Do some freewriting, brainstorming, or clustering on one of these topics before you start writing your essay.

1. Write a letter to Dr. Fred W. Koontz, Curator of Mammology, expressing your approval or disapproval of his work in trying to save the African elephants.

2. Write an essay that tells why tracking the savannah elephant is easier than tracking the forest elephant.

3. Write an essay telling what you have done or should do to help save animals or to help save the environment.

4. Write an essay about conservation methods for other animals besides elephants. What have we been doing in our country about saving whales, dolphins, tigers, bald eagles, or others?

5. Write an essay about why we should be concerned or not concerned with saving elephants and other animals that might be endangered.

When you have completed a rough draft of your essay, try out different **introductions** and **conclusions.** Then make sure you have a **thesis statement** in your introduction. See that you have **topic sentences** in each body paragraph and that each **body paragraph** deals with the subject of the topic sentence.

GRAMMAR

Verb Tenses I

The verb in a sentence tells what happens. Without the verb, the subjects would be there, but they would have nothing to do. Verbs, and only verbs, may change time (tense): past, present, and future.

Verbs change their spelling depending on the subject the verb goes with and depending on the tense. Some verbs follow a pattern and are called *regular verbs;* other verbs change in different ways and are called *irregular verbs.*

First, we change the form of the verb for third person singular (he, she, it) verbs by adding *-s* or *-es.* This rule about third-person singular does not just apply to pronouns and people. It also applies to all kinds of nouns. So we write "The chair breaks," "The house looks nice," "Love conquers all." Obviously, we use third-person singular very often. First-person singular and plural (I and we) verbs, second-person singular and plural (you for both) verbs, and third-person plural (they) verbs all keep the same form of the verb with regular verbs. For example, we write *I break, we break, you break, they break,* but *he breaks, she breaks,* and *it breaks.*

To form the past of regular verbs, we add *-ed:* The cat scratched, the cat has scratched, the cat has been scratched.

Turning to irregular verbs, we see that many of our most common verbs take different forms in the past tense and the past participle (the part that goes with *has* or *have*). For example, we write "The chair broke" for the past tense. For the past participle, we write "The chair has broken" and "The chair has been broken." You already know most of the common irregular verbs, but you should also check in the dictionary to make sure you are right.

All this may seem complicated, but actually the *-ing* forms (for example, *breaking, looking*) are almost all regular. Also, the future tense is regular.

Different dialects in the United States use different forms of verbs in speaking. For writing in college and at work, however, only certain forms may be used even though there are some variations. All students need to study and learn these forms.

EXERCISES IN VERB TENSES I

Exercise 9   Regular verbs in present tense

After reading this chart, answer these questions:

1. Which verbs change form?
2. Which person is the most complicated?
3. Which person is the simplest?

	First person	*Second person*	*Third person*
Singular	I walk	you walk	she or he walks it walks the boy walks
Plural	we walk	you walk	they walk the boys walk

Exercise 10   Regular verbs

Read this chart and then do the following:

1. Tell why *need* is included as an example.
2. Add five more regular verbs to the list. If you are not sure of one, look up the present tense in the dictionary.

3. Write the rule for changing present tense to other tenses.

Present	Past	Past participle	Present participle
need(s)	needed	needed	needing
walk(s)	walked	walked	walking

Exercise 11   Irregular verb tenses

Read this chart and answer the questions at the end.

	Present	Past	Past Participle	Present Participle
Type 1	burst(s)	burst	burst	bursting
	knit(s)	knit	knit	knitting
	set(s)	set	set	setting
Type 2	come(s)	came	come	coming
	run(s)	ran	run	running
Type 3	bring(s)	brought	brought	bringing
	catch(es)	caught	caught	catching
	dig(s)	dug	dug	digging
	dive(s)	dived (dove)	dived	diving
	drag(s)	dragged	dragged	dragging
	fight(s)	fought	fought	fighting
	hang(s) (person)	hanged	hanged	hanging
	hang(s) (thing)	hung	hung	hanging
	lay(s)	laid	laid	laying
	lead(s)	led	led	leading
	lie(s) (untrue)	lied	lied	lying
	lose(s)	lost	lost	losing
	raise(s)	raised	raised	raising
	read(s)	read (say *red*)	read (say *red*)	reading
	sit(s)	sat	sat	sitting
Type 4	begin(s)	began	begun	beginning
	drink(s)	drank	drunk	drinking
	ring(s)	rang	rung	ringing
	shrink(s)	shrank	shrunk	shrinking
	sing(s)	sang	sung	singing
	sink(s)	sank	sunk	sinking
	spring(s)	sprang	sprung	springing
	swim(s)	swam	swum	swimming

	Present	*Past*	*Past Participle*	*Present Participle*
Type 5	blow(s)	blew	blown	blowing
	do(es)	did	done	doing
	draw(s)	drew	drawn	drawing
	fly (flies)	flew	flown	flying
	grow(s)	grew	grown	growing
	know(s)	knew	known	knowing
	lie(s) (recline)	lay	lain	lying
	swear(s)	swore	sworn	swearing
	tear(s)	tore	torn	tearing
	wear(s)	wore	worn	wearing
Type 6	arise(s)	arose	arisen	arising
	bite(s)	bit	bitten	biting
	break(s)	broke	broken	breaking
	choose(s)	chose	chosen	choosing
	drive(s)	drove	driven	driving
	eat(s)	ate	eaten	eating
	fall(s)	fell	fallen	falling
	forget(s)	forgot	forgotten	forgetting
	freeze(s)	froze	frozen	freezing
	get(s)	got	gotten	getting
	give(s)	gave	given	giving
	hide(s)	hid	hidden	hiding
	ride(s)	rode	ridden	riding
	shake(s)	shook	shaken	shaking
	speak(s)	spoke	spoken	speaking
	steal(s)	stole	stolen	stealing
	take(s)	took	taken	taking
	write(s)	wrote	written	writing
Type 7	am (is, are)	was (were)	been	being
	go(es)	went	gone	going

1. What do Type 4 verbs have in common with each other?

2. Why is hang(s)(person) on the Type 3 list?

3. How are Type 3 verbs the same as regular verbs? How are they different?

4. List the present participle forms that are irregular.

5. Explain the two forms of *lie.*

6. Why is *lie* (untrue) not a regular verb?

7. Why do people confuse *lie* (recline) and *lay?*

8. What is the past tense if you hang up your coat?

9. Figure out the different forms of *become.*

10. Which verb is our most commonly used verb? Can you think of reasons why such a common verb is so irregular?

Exercise 12   Verbs in past tense

Change the verbs in this essay to the **past tense.** That is, make the events occur in the past rather than in the present.

Working in a Clothing Store

People tell me working in a clothing store is fun, but I think it is really inconvenient, often boring, and expensive. I am not at all happy with my job and am looking for other work.

First, I have to dress nicely for the job. That means wearing my fashionable but not very comfortable shoes and standing up all day. Also I wear neat and well-coordinated clothes and keep them nice looking and clean all the time. I do the laundry often and iron many shirts. Going to the dry cleaner also takes time.

Usually I am bored and the time passes very slowly. Sometimes we have customers, so I try to help them find the right styles. When the customers are nice, I enjoy going back and forth from the fitting room for them. But usually there are no customers and I have nothing to do. I stare at the clothes on the racks, I look out the window, or I stroll up and down the aisles.

The biggest problem is that I find the expense a big surprise. I like new clothes—that is why I have this job—and I get to see the latest fashions as soon as they come into the store. Lots of them are simply irresistible to me. I spend a large part of my salary on clothes right from the store. Of course, I get a 25 percent discount on everything, but the expense still adds up.

So I am looking for a new job where I can't use the merchandise and where there is lots of action. Or maybe I can just feel lucky that I don't work in a liquor store, or a pet shop, or a candy store.

Exercise 13   Verb forms

Add the correct form of the verb in the blank space after the present tense form. If you are unsure of the form, look up the present tense form in the dictionary.

Smoking

Many people (give up) _____ smoking in recent times,

and I (be) _____ one of them. I (smoke) _____

for almost ten years, and I (fight) _____ for my right to

continue. But about a year ago some events finally (shake)

_____ some sense into me.

I (cough) _____ every morning right after I (wake)

_____ up. My throat (feel) _____ irritated and

scratchy and (keep) _____ feeling sore for long periods of

time. I (catch) _____ colds very easily. Every winter I

(think) _____ I (get) _____ more colds.

Then I (read) _____ a lot about lung cancer and

other diseases caused by smoking. When I (hear) _____

that nonsmokers (breathe) _____ "passive smoke," I (start)

_____ to worry about my children. I (try) _____

smoking outside or in my room when they (be) _____ not

there. Smoking (become) _____ a lonely activity for me; I

(hide) _____ my habit so that it (become) _____

a vice.

   I (choose) _____ to go "cold turkey." I (finish)

_____ the last cigarette from my last pack when I (say)

_____, "I (buy) _____ my last pack." After I (eat)

_____ dinner that night, I really (crave) _____ a

cigarette. But I (understand) _____ the feeling. I (know)

_____ I (do) _____ the right thing when my son

(cling) _____ to me and (keep) _____ me there. I

(break) _____ into tears and (stay) _____.

═══

Verb Tenses II

   The simple past, present, and future tenses of verbs seem like all we need for expressing time, but we actually use many subcategories of past, present, and future tenses. Memorizing them is not necessary, but knowing they exist is important.

   The past tense tells us about completed conditions or actions. Sometimes the condition or action happened once: Kim *lived* in Texas. Or the condition or action happened over a period of time: Kim *was living* in Texas during the recession. Or the condition or action continued over time in the past but has ended: Kim *had been living* in Texas until last year.

   The present tense tells us about conditions or actions now and also conditions or actions that continue over time. "Kim *lives* in Kansas" tells the present action, but "Kim *is* living in Kansas" makes the present action more continuous. "Kim *has lived* in Kansas" shows action in the past to the present. "Kim *has been living* in Kansas" shows continuous action from the past to the present. The present tense can also indicate the future if other words in the sentence tell us so: Next week, Kim *leaves* for Florida. We see that the present tense is not so simple.

The future tense uses *will, shall,* and *going to* to indicate actions or conditions in the future. "Kim *will live* in Florida" and "Kim *is going to* live in Florida" both state a future action. "Kim *will be living* in Florida when Larry visits there" shows continued future action. "Kim *will have been living* in Florida a year when Larry arrives" shows continued action to a certain time in the future. "Kim *will have left* Florida when Rosina goes there" shows completed action in the future. We see that the future can be complicated.

We need to use the right verb tense in order to be clear and precise in our sentences. Sometimes we need to change tense to express past, present, or future actions, but sometimes we don't really need to shift tenses. Writers must be careful about choosing the right verb tense and not changing tenses unless necessary.

EXERCISES IN VERB TENSES II

Exercise 14   Past, present, and future tenses

Past tense *(completed condition or action)*

Happened in past:	He *walked* in the park.
Happened over period of time:	He *was walking* in the park.
Happened over time but ended:	He *had been walking* in the park.

1. Write sentences with these three forms of the past tense using a different regular verb.

2. Write sentences with these three forms of the past tense using an irregular verb.

Present tense *(conditions or actions now)*

Happening often:	He *walks* in the park.
Happening continuously:	He *is walking* in the park.
Happens from past to present:	He *has walked* in the park.
Happens continuously from past to present:	He *has been walking* in the park.
Future:	He *walks* in the park tomorrow.

1. Should the fifth present tense (future) be listed under future tenses instead of present tenses? Why or why not?

2. Write sentences with these five present tense forms using a different verb.

Future tense *(conditions and actions later)*

Happening in future:	He *will walk* in the park.
	He *is going to* walk in the park.
Continuing in future:	He *will be walking* in the park.

Continuing in future to a certain time:	He *will have been walking* in the park for two hours.
Completed in future:	He *will have walked* in the park for two hours.

1. Try to explain the difference between the third and fourth future tenses (continuing in future to a certain time and completed in future).

2. Write sentences with these four future tenses using a different verb.

Exercise 15 Finding verb tenses

1. Underline the complete verbs in the following essay.

2. Match up the verbs to the charts on previous pages.

3. Give this essay an introduction. It needs it.

4. Decide if this essay needs a conclusion.

I Need a Nap

When I was working the morning shift at a fast food restaurant, I always went home at two in the afternoon. I got in the habit of napping until four. Even on my days off I got sleepy at two and took a nap. After I had been working about a year at this job, I decided that I needed a change.

Now I work at a regular restaurant and have been working here for about two weeks. Since I have worked before in restaurants I thought I could adjust easily. Unfortunately, I start at noon and at two

I get sleepy. Next week I will quit. I will have worked only three weeks, but I will have been used to napping at two o'clock for over a year.

Exercise 16   Using verb tenses

1. Try writing a paragraph using these verbs. Use any order, and add *not* if you want.

   have gone   have been going   will have been going   went

2. Try writing a paragraph with these verbs. Use any order, and add *not* if you want.

had been swimming   will have swum   is going to swim   swam

3. Try writing a paragraph with these verbs. Use any order, and add *not* if you want.

will have ridden   rode   is riding   has ridden

Exercise 17   Using verb tenses in writing an essay

Fill in the following outline with an essay about this person, his past, and his plans for the future. Change him to a female if you want.

What will the Future Bring?

As _____ sits in his English class trying to improve his

writing, he thinks about his past, his hopes, and his plans for the fu-

ture. If he continues working as hard as he is doing, his dreams will

come true.

If only he had _____, he would have

But he did not know what he wanted and did not

In the future, he will

So he sits writing his essay, thinking about the past, and dream-ing about the future. Someday, he will look back at his college days and know that they helped him fulfill his dreams.

==

Chapter 4

Describing

WRITING AND READING

Before Reading "The Story of an Hour"

WORDS AND PHRASES TO LOOK FOR

afflicted: hurt, diseased, suffering
veiled hints: hidden, not openly expressed, suggestions
to forestall: to head off, to delay or prevent
aquiver: shaking, trembling
eaves: the roof part that hangs over the side of a building
bespoke: told of, revealed
repression: keeping unconscious thoughts (impulses, ideas)
    from reaching consciousness
reflection: thought
suspension: stopping temporarily
subtle: hard to understand, hard to detect
elusive: puzzling, hard to grasp, hard to keep
tumultuously: greatly disturbed, agitated, riotous
coursing blood: fast-flowing blood
elixir: medicine for eternal life
importunities: repeated disturbances
unwittingly: unknowingly, unintentionally
composedly: calmly
gripsack: small suitcase

1. How did Brently Mallard die, according to Josephine and Richards?
2. How did Mrs. Mallard react at first to the news?
3. How did Mrs. Mallard feel later about her husband's death?
4. What happens at the end and why?
5. Describe Mrs. Mallard.

The Story of an Hour

Knowing that Mrs. Mallard was afflicted with heart trouble, great care was taken to break to her as gently as possible the news of her husband's death.

It was her sister Josephine who told her, in broken sentences; veiled hints that revealed in half concealing. Her husband's friend Richards was there, too, near her. It was he who had been in the newspaper office when intelligence of the railroad disaster was received, with Brently Mallard's name leading the list of "killed." He had only taken the time to assure himself of its truth by a second telegram, and had hastened to forestall any less careful, less tender friend in bearing the sad message.

She did not hear the story as many women have heard the same, with a paralyzed inability to accept its significance. She wept at once, with sudden, wild abandonment, in her sister's arms. When the storm of grief had spent itself she went away to her room alone. She would have no one follow her.

There stood, facing the open window, a comfortable, roomy armchair. Into this she sank, pressed down by a physical exhaustion that haunted her body and seemed to reach into her soul.

She could see in the open square before her house the tops of trees that were all aquiver with the new spring life. The delicious breath of rain was in the air. In the street below a peddler was crying his wares. The notes of a distant song which some one was singing reached her faintly, and countless sparrows were twittering in the eaves.

There were patches of blue sky showing here and there through the clouds that had met and piled one above the other in the west facing her window.

She sat with her head thrown back upon the cushion of the chair, quite motionless, except when a sob came up into her throat and shook her, as a child who has cried itself to sleep continues to sob in its dreams.

She was young, with a fair, calm face, whose lines bespoke repression and even a certain strength. But now there was a dull stare in her eyes, whose gaze was fixed away off yonder on one of those patches of blue sky. It was not a glance of reflection, but rather indicated a suspension of intelligent thought.

There was something coming to her and she was waiting for it, fearfully. What was it? She did not know; it was too subtle and elusive to name. But she felt it, creeping out of the sky, reaching toward her through the sounds, the scents, the color that filled the air.

Now her bosom rose and fell tumultuously. She was beginning to recognize this thing that was approaching to possess her, and she was striving to beat it back with her will—as powerless as her two white slender hands would have been.

When she abandoned herself a little whispered word escaped her slightly parted lips. She said it over and over under her breath: "free, free, free!" The vacant stare and the look of terror that had followed it went from her eyes. They stayed keen and bright. Her pulses beat fast, and the coursing blood warmed and relaxed every inch of her body.

She did not stop to ask if it were or were not a monstrous joy that held her. A clear and exalted perception enabled her to dismiss the suggestion as trivial.

She knew that she would weep again when she saw the kind, tender hands folded in death; the face that had never looked save with love upon her, fixed and gray and dead. But she saw beyond that bitter moment a long procession of years to come that would belong to her absolutely. And she opened and spread her arms out to them to welcome.

There would be no one to live for her during those coming years; she would live for herself. There would be no powerful will bending hers to that blind persistence with which men and women believe they have a right to impose a private will upon a fellow creature. A kind intention or a cruel intention made the act seem no less a crime as she looked upon it in that brief moment of illumination.

And yet she had loved him—sometimes. Often she had not. What did it matter? What could love, the unsolved mystery, count for in face of this possession of self-assertion which she suddenly recognized as the strongest impulse of her being!

"Free! Body and soul free!" she kept whispering.

Josephine was kneeling before the closed door with her lips to the keyhole, imploring for admission. "Louise, open the door! I beg; open the door—you will make yourself ill. What are you doing, Louise? For heaven's sake open the door."

"Go away, I am not making myself ill." No; she was drinking in a very elixir of life through that open window.

Her fancy was running riot along those days ahead of her. Spring days, and summer days, and all sorts of days that would be her own. She breathed a quick prayer that life might be long. It was only yesterday she had thought with a shudder that life might be long.

She arose at length and opened the door to her sister's importunities. There was a feverish triumph in her eyes, and she carried herself unwittingly like a goddess of Victory. She clasped her sister's waist, and together they descended the stairs. Richards stood waiting for them at the bottom.

Someone was opening the front door with a latchkey. It was Brently Mallard who entered, a little travel-stained, composedly carrying his gripsack and umbrella. He had been far from the scene of the accident, and did not even know there had been one. He stood amazed at Josephine's piercing cry; at Richards' quick motion to screen him from the view of his wife.

But Richards was too late.

When the doctors came they said she had died of heart disease—of joy that kills.

Kate Chopin (1851–1904)

Writing Descriptions

Entire essays may be devoted to describing a person, a place, or a feeling. But even when an essay has a different purpose, it probably also contains some descriptions within it. Thus, writing good descriptions will always be useful.

For your description, you should start by deciding what you want to prove; this is called the **controlling idea.** What kind of person, for example, do you want to show? A slob? A fashion plate? Then think of the descriptive words that advance your controlling idea; ignore any that don't fit. For example, if you want to describe a rich woman, mention her fancy dress, her gold shoes, her jewelry. But omit her height and her weight. On the other hand, height and perhaps weight would be important for describing a basketball player. If you want to describe a place, decide also on the controlling idea. A tranquil garden? A messy room? Then choose the descriptive words that give that picture. The same follows for describing feelings—that is, thoughts, wishes, or emotions. Seething jealousy? Raging anger? Use the descriptive words that suit those feelings.

Once the controlling idea and the descriptive words have been established, you should organize the description. In describing people or places you may use almost any direction, but use a consistent one: left to right, right to left, top to bottom, near to far, far to near, clockwise or counterclockwise. In describing the rich woman, you might start with her hair, then her dress, jewelry, and shoes. For the tranquil garden, you could start with the path in the foreground that leads into the flower beds and on into the background. For feelings, start with the first instance and go step by step. For example, if you want to describe someone's anger at his boss, concentrate on this anger and keep descriptions of his job, his appearance, and his surroundings to a minimum.

Many times, however, going in a logical direction may seem mechanical and less effective for your point. Perhaps starting with the minor parts and leading to the major part will be more effective. Or start with a dominant aspect and then show how other aspects support the dominant one. For the rich woman, perhaps her quantity of elaborate jewelry dominates the whole picture. For the tranquil garden, perhaps a marble birdbath in the center makes the rest of the garden seem tranquil. For feelings of anger, perhaps blaming the employee for a heavy snowfall will epitomize the boss's unjust accusations.

When writing the actual description, use words (usually **adjectives** and **adverbs**) to describe the nouns and verbs. Use a **picturesque noun** when possible instead of attaching descriptions ("coward" rather than "frightened person," "mansion" rather than "large house"). Use **descriptive verbs** also: "the train *thundered*," "the lake *glistened*," "his anger *exploded*." Also use **comparisons:** "He danced like a stampeding elephant"; "Her room was a junk yard." Comparisons are especially good for describing emotions. For example, compare his anger to a dam breaking or to a spreading forest fire. In this way an unseen emotion becomes something we can see.

But don't feel that every noun and verb must be preceded or followed by two or three descriptive words, and don't get carried away with too many vivid comparisons. Also don't fall into clichés, such as "neat as a pin," "in a month of Sundays," "out of the blue." If the expression leaps to mind, it is probably a cliché. Try for fresh, original descriptive words and comparisons.

EXERCISES IN WRITING DESCRIPTIONS

Exercise 1   Descriptive words and phrases

Underline the descriptive words and phrases in the following para-graphs. Then ~~number them in the margin as follows:~~

1. Description (adjective or adverb) of noun or verb.
2. Picturesque noun.
3. Descriptive verb.
4. Comparison.

vivd
viv. descr

a.   Norman, on the other hand, had always had "difficult" hair, coarse, bristly and now iron-grey, which in his younger days had re-fused to lie down flat at the crown and round the parting. Now he did not have to part it and had adopted a medieval or pudding-basin style, rather like the American crew-cut of the forties and fifties. (Barbara Pym, *Quartet in Autumn*)

b.   An old man sits on Ralph's bench, white hair as fine as spun glass poking out under his green feed cap, his grizzled chin on his skinny chest, snoozing, the afternoon sun now reaching under the faded brown canvas awning up to his belt. He is not Ralph. Ralph is the thin man in the white apron who has stepped out the back door of the store, away from the meat counter, to get a breath of fresh, meatless air. He stands on a rickety porch that looks across the lake, a stone's throw away. The beach there is stony; the sand beach is two blocks to the north. (Garrison Keillor, *Lake Wobegon Days*)

c.   Niagara Falls beckoned. The sweet white rush of the water was as luscious as I had hoped. When I pushed on to another local wonder, a deserted knoll a short drive away, I was not surprised to smell the faint tang of something like benzene. Just one indication of the name of the place was painted on a varnished sign of the type used to mark trailheads for hikers. I had arrived at Love Canal. (Mark D. Uehling, "Beauty and the Bleak," *New York Times*)

d.   Before you buy a bicycle, think about what you are going to use it for. If you are going to ride over plowed fields, or on sand flats at low tide, or if you plan to take only short rides to the corner store, get a sturdy coaster-brake model, a balloon-tire bomber. If you plan leisurely shopping jaunts, weekend excursions up to 30 miles, or commuting for short distances, all on reasonably even terrain, get a 3 speed. If you like a comfortable ride and maneuverability, you might try one of the newly introduced small-wheeled bikes. If you plan to cover long distances over varied terrain, and if you are willing to accommodate yourself to a specialized riding position for the sake of vast improvement in cycling speed and responsiveness, get a 10 speed. (Tom Cuthbertson, *Anybody's Bike Book*)

e.   This sort of sublime forgiveness was not natural to my father. I had thought that he would be angry, say hard things, and strike his forehead. But he was so wonderfully peaceful, and I believe this was due to my clean confession. A clean confession, combined with a promise never to commit the sin again, when offered before one who has the right to receive it, is the purest type of repentance. I know that my confession made my father feel absolutely safe about me, and increased his affection for me beyond measure. (Mahatma Gandhi, *An Autobiography*)

f.   Life is a copiously branching bush, continually pruned by the grim reaper of extinction, not a ladder of predictable progress. Most people may know this as a phrase to be uttered, but not as a concept brought into the deep interior of understanding. Hence we continually make errors inspired by unconscious allegiance to the ladder of progress, even when we explicitly deny such a superannuated view of life. (Stephen Jay Gould, *Wonderful Life: The Burgess Shale and the Nature of History*)

g.   Some transformations are overt and heroic; others are quiet and uneventful in their unfolding, but no less significant in their outcome. Karl Marx, in a famous statement, compared his social revolution to an old mole burrowing busily beneath the ground, invisible for long periods, but undermining traditional order so thoroughly that a later emergence into light precipitates a sudden overturn. But intellectual transformations often remain under the surface. They ooze and diffuse into scientific consciousness, and people may slowly move from one pole to another, having never heard the call to arms. (Stephen J. Gould, *Wonderful Life: The Burgess Shale and the Nature of History*)

Exercise 2   Descriptive words and phrases

Underline the descriptive words and phrases in the following essay. Then number them in the margin as follows:

1. Description (adjective or adverb) of noun or verb.
2. Picturesque noun.
3. Descriptive verb.
4. Comparison.

James Cagney

James Cagney's genius lay in movement. When he was tripping the light fantastic or shooting up the town, this former vaudeville dancer had split-second control. Whether in the pink of youth or sporting a sizable middle-age paunch, he would strut and gyrate as if he were a marionette pulling his own strings—a punk Pinocchio with kapow. Imagine a wire running from his rump through his neck, giving his torso and head a swivelling motion and letting his feet tap and hands dangle, and you've got the basic Cagney posture for both dance and destruction. He made that posture infinitely flexible. In his 1942 George M. Cohan biopic, "Yankee Doodle Dandy," it allowed him to tap like a percussion team and to fly like Peter Pan—all over the stage, and even up the proscenium walls.

He won his only Academy Award for his characterization of Cohan. He stuffed the part with exuberance, freshness, and cock-of-the-walk wit—and funnelled all that into his phenomenally visceral and graceful dancing. He created a Horatio Alger hero with chutz-pah—a wisecracker and flag-waver rolled into one. In some ways, Cohan was the fulfillment of the rough-and-ready, likable go-getter Cagney had already fleshed out (in films like "G-Men" and the aptly titled "Great Guy") as a change of pace from his hardened crimi-nals. What puts across Cagney's inspired showboating as Cohan is the glee he takes in performing. His acting here is a form of con-trolled euphoria; fifty years after "Yankee Doodle Dandy" premiered, Cagney still blows audiences sky-high. (Michael Sragow, *The New Yorker*)

Exercise 3 Descriptive words and phrases

Underline the descriptive words and phrases in the following essay. Then number them in the margin as follows:

1. Description (adjective and adverb) of noun or verb.

2. Picturesque noun.

3. Descriptive verb.

4. Comparison.

Nunan's Lobster Hut (Cape Porpoise, ME)

The best thing about Nunan's Lobster Hut, other than the lob-ster, is the plumbing. In particular, the sinks. Should you desire to wash your hands before, during or after eating, the sinks are right there, out in the open dining room, ready for immediate action. They are serious, proletarian sinks, like you'd want to have next to your workbench in the basement. For drying hands, Nunan's supplies rolls of paper towels.

In some restaurants, this arrangement might not be so appealing, but at Nunan's Lobster Hut—which really is a hut—the sanitary accommodations are exactly right because this place is designed for serious lobster eating. Tables have easy-wipe surfaces with ribs around the edge to keep the inevitable mess from falling to the floor. The floor is painted battleship gray, which makes it easy to swab at the end of the day. Overhead lights are unadorned tubes. A touch of romance is provided in the form of a utility candle stuck in a thick cork on every table.

Lobsters are brought to tables on pizza pans, accompanied by bags of potato chips and store-bought rolls. Coffee is served in mugs. Water comes in paper cups. Bring your own wine or beer.

No frills at Nunan's will distract you from the perfection of the lobster (except maybe the view, when the panels on the sides of the dining room are raised and reveal a pleasant vista of Cape Porpoise marshlands). Each lobster is steamed to order in several inches of salty water for exactly twenty minutes, emerging with silky tender claw meat, its knuckles and tail succulent and chewy. The only secrets to her lobsters' deliciousness, Bertha Nunan told Mel Allen of *Yankee* magazine, are that the water must be **fresh** for each batch, and the lobster must be cooked immediately before serving.

The Nunan family has been lobstering for three generations, so by now they have the process of enjoying their catch down to its essence. After you've polished off the lobster, there are homemade brownies or a slice of one of Bertha Nunan's pies, the recipes for which have been perfected over the last thirty years. Blueberry and apple are memorable, their subtly sweetened fruits encased in sugar-dusted crusts. (Jane and Michael Stern, *Roadfood*)

Exercise 4   Controlling idea

Read the following descriptive essay and then:

1. Underline the controlling idea. *same as if thesis*
2. Cross out words and phrases that do not suit the controlling idea.

My Beautiful Cat

I have no doubt that my sleek black cat, Katzie, is the most beautiful cat in the world. Her whole body is perfectly proportioned and always graceful, no matter what she is doing. I've had her for many years and have been through a lot with her. Only last week I had to take her to the cat dentist again.

She holds up her perfectly shaped round head regally one moment, comfortably nestled on a cushion the next. She likes to be with people so she stays alert and seems to listen to conversation, but soon she nods off and starts sleeping. Either way, she has perfectly symmetrical pointy, mite-infested ears covered with smooth black fur. And her green eyes sparkle like emeralds and change shape depending on her mood, one moment wide-eyed and alert, the next half-closed, and then shut tight for a nap on the book I happen to be reading, of course. Either way, she could be a painting.

The rest of her small body is well proportioned even though she eats a lot. She gets a medium-size can a day plus a continuous supply of dry cat food. Her straight legs and paws stretch out elegantly or curl up luxuriously. And her whole body undulates rhythmically as she walks. Then her long, tapered tail sways as gracefully as a dancer or flicks as ominously as a time clock. Sometimes she leaps effortlessly in the air in a perfect arch to catch a fly with her two front paws. Then she crunches noisily on the fly—a perfect predinner snack!

Katzie is at her most beautiful when sitting upright. Her head is alert; her back curves in a smooth line. She daintily tucks up her front paws so they are exactly aligned with her back paws, all four in a row. Her tail curves snugly around half her body so that the tip rests softly across her front paws. She often chooses the edge of a bookcase, table, or chair to sit on, so she looks just perfect. I wish I had photos of her in this elegantly simple pose.

Some people keep cats for catching mice and for companionship, but I keep Katzie for her pure aesthetic value. Naturally, she is good at catching mice and showering me with affection too.

don't have to do

Exercise 5   Writing descriptions

Write descriptive paragraphs about the following topics using descriptions (adjectives and adverbs) of nouns and verbs, picturesque nouns, descriptive verbs, and comparisons. You do not have to use all types in each paragraph, but try to use more than one kind.

1. a very cute baby

2. the room you are in (choose a controlling idea)

3. how you feel when you first wake up in the morning (choose a controlling idea)

4. the feelings of a person who has eaten too much (choose a controlling idea)

Using Transitional Expressions

An essay, like a road, needs signs that tell where you are going next and what to expect. Signs are useful in every essay to keep the reader following the direction of your thought. In essays, such signs are called **transitional expressions.**

There are many transitional expressions, some simply a word, others phrases. Here are some common ones listed in categories according to their meaning:

Addition	also, in addition, too, and, besides, furthermore, next, then, finally
Contrast	but, yet, however, nevertheless, in contrast, on the contrary, still, at the same time, on the other hand
Comparison	in comparison, similarly, likewise, in the same way, in the same manner
Result	consequently, so, therefore, thus, due to this, as a result, hence, in conclusion, on the whole, finally
Example	for example, for instance, namely, specifically
Time	first, second, third, next, then, finally, soon, later, afterwards, during, before, meanwhile, eventually, currently, immediately, in the past, in the future
Place	in back, in front, at the side, nearby, next to, in the distance, here, there, between

Aside from these transitional expressions, you may also make transitions in other ways. One way is by using pronouns for clearly indicated nouns in previous sentences. Another way is through repeating a word

or words from a previous sentence in the next or a later sentence. These
approaches help make your essay run smoothly and logically.

You don't need to use transitions in every sentence or even every
paragraph, but probably you need them now and then in your essay. Use
them at the beginning or near the beginning of sentences within a
paragraph and usually near the beginning of paragraphs after the introduction.

EXERCISES IN TRANSITIONAL EXPRESSIONS

Exercise 6   Finding transitional expressions

Underline the transitional expressions in the following essay. You
may consult the list on the previous page.

Untied Shoelaces

To the Editor:

Data that I have recently collected at schoolyards and on com-
muter trains indicate that there is likely to be an epidemic this year of
untied shoelaces. Although I originally hypothesized that this problem
was limited to teenagers, I must now report that my $8\frac{1}{2}$-year-old son
and many of his classmates have succumbed.

Some of the public health consequences of this disease are obvious, such as an increased incidence of falls. However, investigations
should begin immediately into the problems of clenched toe, a common strategy to keep untied sneakers on the feet, and bowlegged
walking, a strategy to avoid tripping over one's laces.

Meanwhile, health professionals should consider a number of
options, including legislation and education. First of all, a bill should
be enacted by state legislatures to prohibit untied shoelaces. A
stronger solution might be the banning of tie shoes for persons under
21 years of age. This would have the additional benefit of relieving
parents of the burden of teaching their children the skill of tying laces.

A second strategy is to use the talents of health educators. Perhaps advertising campaigns featuring television and recording stars

demonstrating the satisfaction one gets from tying one's laces and untying them at the appropriate time would do the trick.

Finally, more research is needed. Foundations must come forth and fund projects on shoestrings. Not to act vigorously is to take the risk of allowing an entire generation to flip-flop in their own footsteps.

Seth B. Goldsmith, Sc.D.
University of Massachusetts

Shirley Blotnick Moskow, ed.
Hunan Hand and Other Ailments

Exercise 7   Transitions

Underline the transitional expressions, pronouns, and other transitions in the following essay. Don't worry if you don't find all of them.

Big City Versus the Suburbs

Many people think moving to the suburbs is the ultimate dream of most families. No doubt this is true for many, but many other people want to remain in the big city and prefer it even if they can afford to move to the suburbs.

First, employment opportunities are easier to find in big cities. And one can change jobs more easily without having to move. In the suburbs, people need to keep the same job because they are afraid they won't make enough money to support their suburban lifestyle.

Second, one can save a lot of money by living in the big city. One does not need to own a car or buy gas and insurance for it. Moreover, one will not need to pay for maintenance and antitheft devices. Maintaining an apartment is much cheaper than maintaining a house whether one rents or owns.

After saving money on a car, one can spend it on entertainment, which is more diverse in the big city. Of course, the suburbs have malls and multiplex cinemas, but they don't have the big sporting events, theaters, nightclubs, and museums that one finds in the big city.

In addition, one has more time to enjoy life in the big city. In the suburbs, the house, the lawn, the trees all need care. The whole weekend can be taken up by such chores. Our former neighbors, the Levines, tell us that they are busy all the time with the house. They may not want to move back, but in the city, someone else takes care of the leaking roof, the snow-covered sidewalk, and the falling leaves.

In conclusion, people should revise the great American dream of moving to the suburbs. I know I have. Eventually, however, maybe I will change my mind.

Exercise 8   Writing transitions

Write a paragraph about how to avoid studying. Use some or all of the following transitional expressions: **first, second, then, next, also, while, but, finally.**

Write a paragraph about the place where you study. Use some or all of the following transitional expressions: **in front, in back, next to, nearby, here, also, in addition.**

Write a paragraph to convince someone to buy a frog. Use some of the following transitional expressions: **also, in addition, furthermore, yet, however, meanwhile, thus, in the same way, as a result, afterwards.**

Exercise 9   Writing transitions

Write a paragraph telling how to get from your home to your school. Use some of the following transitional expressions: **first, next, then, immediately, here, there, after, eventually, nearby, and, also.**

Write a paragraph persuading a friend to go to college. Use some of the following transitional expressions: **in addition, too, besides, furthermore, for example, so, however, eventually, in the future, as a result, on the whole.**

Write a paragraph telling how to write an essay. Use some of the following transitional expressions: **at first, then, next, afterwards, but, nevertheless, still, at the same time, in the same way, specifically, thus.**

Suggestions for Essay Topics

Using one of the following techniques—freewriting, brainstorming, or clustering—write on one of these topics.

1. Write a biography of Mr. and Mrs. Mallard's lives. You might include where they went to school, how they met, where they live, what work he does, and how they get along with each other.
2. Write an essay that explains Mrs. Mallard's feelings about her husband and her married life.
3. Write an essay defending Mr. Mallard. That is, describe his attitudes and his side in their relationship.
4. Write an essay about discrimination against women. Use examples from your friends', your relatives', or your own life.
5. Write an essay about some solutions to discrimination against women. Cite examples of solutions and then propose further solutions.

Once you have written a rough draft of your essay, see if the **body paragraphs** have **topic sentences** and **descriptions**. See if the **introduction** has a **thesis statement** and if you have used one of the techniques for writing introductions. See if you have used one of the techniques for writing **conclusions.**

GRAMMAR

Adjectives and Adverbs

Adjectives and adverbs describe (modify) other words. They are not absolutely necessary, as nouns and verbs are in sentences, but our essays would be much less interesting without them. They would be vague and unspecific without adjectives and adverbs.

Adjectives describe nouns and pronouns by telling us more, such as their color, size, number, or material. Adjectives also help give the writer's opinion on a subject. One might use the adjectives large, shiny, and red to describe a car. To add an opinion, one might use the adjectives beautiful, favorite, or best to describe how one feels about the car. Also we tell quantity (one car, two cars, many cars), ownership (my car, her car, their car), and other aspects.

Adverbs describe verbs, adjectives, or other adverbs and work the same way as adjectives. If we just write "The red car moves," we have not made a precise statement. But if we write "The red car moves quietly" or "The red car moves smoothly," we can be quite precise about how the car moves. When adverbs modify adjectives and other adverbs, we can be even more precise and detailed. To "The red car moves quietly" we can add an adverb to make "The bright red car moves quietly" or "The red car moves extremely smoothly." *Bright* modifies red; that is, *bright* tells us more about the redness of the car. In the same way, *extremely* tells us more about the smoothness of the car's movement.

Adjectives and adverbs often come just before the word they will modify, as in the examples in the previous paragraph. But they do not always have to be there. Adjectives may come later in a sentence: "The car was red." And adverbs may also be elsewhere in a sentence: "Quietly and smoothly, the car moves through the streets." These changes help add variety to sentences and make them seem more interesting.

Adjectives and adverbs that are used over and over again can become tiresome, so you need to pick precise and less common ones instead of the more common ones. Instead of describing the car as bright red, you might choose, for example, scarlet, maroon, candy apple red, fire engine red, or blood red. Each word will give a different picture.

Choosing just the right adjectives and adverbs takes some practice, but they can make all the difference in changing an average essay into a good one. In the same way that we choose nouns and verbs carefully, we should choose adjectives and adverbs carefully.

EXERCISES IN ADJECTIVES AND ADVERBS

Exercise 10   Finding adjectives and adverbs

In the following essay:

1. Circle the adjectives and adverbs. Don't worry if you don't get all of them.
2. Underline the thesis statement.
3. Underline the topic sentences.

The Perfect Room

If I had my own bedroom, I would decorate it very beautifully. People would want to visit just to see this stunningly decorated room, which would be the most interesting room they had ever seen.

The high white ceiling would have a huge crystal chandelier that gave off twinkling light. The four walls would be elegantly covered with shiny soft pink brocade that perfectly matched the intricately draped curtains around the floor-to-ceiling French doors. The wall-to-wall black carpet would be thick and deep. The general atmosphere of the room would be elegant.

I would have a round water bed with a custom-made black satin bedspread. Lots of fluffy round and square pillows would be propped up luxuriously at the head. Over the bed would be a large black canopy with flowing scarlet drapes hanging loosely around. This fabulous bed would be the center of attention.

If I had this wonderful bedroom, I would be the happiest person in the whole wide world. I would spend my sleeping and waking hours there.

Exercise 11   Using adjectives and adverbs

Fill in the blanks with appropriate adjectives or adverbs.

A _____ Person on the Street

One day while I was on my way to school, I saw a _____

dressed man on the corner. I stopped to look at him because his

outfit attracted my attention. Lots of other people were staring

_____ at him too.

The first thing I noticed was his _____ hat. It was

_____ and _____. In the middle, swaying

_____, was a _____ feather. It was unlike anything

I had ever seen.

His _____ suit caught my eye next. The cut seemed

_____ for his _____ shape and must have been

specially made. The lapels were _____ and _____.

Under the _____ jacket I could see a _____ vest.

The pants were _____ and _____. I especially no-

ticed his _____ belt because the buckle was _____.

His shoes were as _____ as the rest of the outfit. They

were _____, _____, and _____. I wonder

how he got them so _____ because his socks were also

_____.

Since seeing this _____ person on the street that time

I have seen him _____ times. I always stop and stare

_____ at him.

Exercise 12   Writing descriptions

Find and write down adjectives and adverbs for the following:

1. *The room you are in*
   Size:
   Color(s):
   Atmosphere:
   Other:

2. *Your bathroom*
   The floor:
   The tub and shower:
   The washbasin:
   Other:

3. *Your face*
   Your eyes:
   Your nose:
   Your mouth:
   Your skin:
   Other:

4. *Your best friend*
   Personality:
   Attitude:
   Other:

Exercise 13 Paragraphs with descriptions

Don't have to do (handwritten in left margin)

Using the adjectives and adverbs you listed before, write a paragraph about each of the subjects. You may add more adjectives and adverbs if you want. Also add topic sentences to each paragraph at the beginning, middle, or end.

1. *The room you are in*

2. *Your bathroom*

3. *Your face*

4. *Your best friend*

Conjunctions and Prepositions

Both conjunctions and prepositions are connecting words. We need them to join words and to add parts of sentences to other parts of sentences.

Common conjunctions are **and, or,** and **but.** They can join words together (the dog *and* cat). They also join parts of sentences together (after dinner *or* before the party). And they can also join complete sentences together (That book is quite long, *but* students will enjoy it.). In addition to **and, or,** and **but,** other common conjunctions that can join complete sentences together are **for, nor, yet,** and **so.** They can be remembered because the first letters of the seven words spell "fanboys."

Some other common conjunctions are **after, although (even though, though), because, before, if, since, until, when,** and **while.** These conjunctions join two sentences together also, but one part of the sentence will not be able to stand alone. In the sentence "If we study hard, we will pass the test," we can easily figure out which part will not stand alone as a sentence. Aside from these mostly one-word conjunctions are two-part conjunctions: **both . . . and, either . . . or, neither . . . nor,** and **not only . . . but also.** It is not useful or possible to remember all the conjunctions because there are so many, but becoming familiar with the common ones is helpful.

Prepositions are also connectors, most often in **prepositional phrases.** Some common prepositions are **after, at, before, by, for, from, in, of, on, to, until,** and **with.** There are many more, but these prepositions are the common ones. Most often these prepositions join with other words to make **prepositional phrases: after** the party, **at** the school,

before the test, **by** the street, **for** the dog, **from** the store. As you can see, prepositional phrases are very common and useful in sentences.

It is fairly easy to see the difference between conjunctions and prepositions, but distinguishing them from each other is sometimes difficult, especially since they can also be confused with one kind of adverb, the conjunctive adverb. Also some words can be both a conjunction and a preposition (notice **for,** for example). Realizing that these parts of speech exist and that they are common as parts of sentences is sufficient for now.

EXERCISES IN CONJUNCTIONS AND PREPOSITIONS

Exercise 14   Some common conjunctions

Here are some common conjunctions:

after	nor
although	or
and	provided
because	since
before	so
both . . . and	though
but	unless
either . . . or	until
even though	when
for	where
if	whereas
neither . . . nor	while
not only . . . but also	yet

1. Make sentences by continuing the following conjunctions.

   After she

   Before we

   Since he

   Until I

   When you

   While the game

2. Use these two-part conjunctions in sentences.

either . . . or

not only . . . but also

Exercise 15   Finding conjunctions

Underline the **conjunctions** in this short essay. Don't worry if you don't get all of them. Add some **topic sentences** where they seem necessary.

My Brother and I

My brother and I are very much alike. We look alike, have the same interests, and go to college. We only have one difference.

Both my brother and I have black hair, although his is a little lighter than mine. Our faces are so much alike that people sometimes think we are twins, but my face is rounder. Neither his build nor mine is outstanding since we are both of average weight and height, even though I am a little heavier and taller.

Not only do we both watch basketball and tennis, but also we both play these sports. If we play against each other, we compete seriously and fiercely. We also listen to the same music. When he turns on the radio and starts humming and dancing, I do the same.

My brother started college before I did. After he had attended for a year, I decided to register also. I did not consider college until he told me about it, but he said he would not continue unless I attended also.

Our one big difference is that he is studying English and I am studying accounting. Believe me, we have some big arguments about the future.

Exercise 16   Using conjunctions

don't do

Write a paragraph about one of your former teachers using most or all of these conjunctions: **and, although, but, since, because, after, or, when, before, while.**

Write a paragraph about your future plans using most or all of these conjunctions: **either . . . or, until, after, if, yet, both . . . and, so, when, while, even though.**

Write a paragraph about your daily schedule using most or all of these conjunctions: **not only . . . but also, though, before, after, neither . . . nor, but, while, until.**

Exercise 17   Prepositions

Here are some common prepositions. Some illustrative phrases are included because prepositions are most often used in such phrases. Read the list while doing the following:

Just
#1

1. Complete all the prepositions by adding appropriate words.

2. Check the prepositions that are also conjunctions.

3. Circle prepositions you have never used before.

about two hours	**behind**
above	**below**
according to	**beneath**
across	**beside**
after	**between**
against	**beyond**
along	**by**
along with	**despite**
among	**down**
around	**during**
as	**except** Kim
as for	**except for**
at	**for**
because of	**from**
before breakfast	**in**

in addition to	throughout
in front of	**till** the end of time
in place of	to
in regard to	toward
inside	under
in spite of	underneath
instead of studying	until
into	up
like	upon
near	with
of	within
off	without
on	
on account of the weather	
out	
out of	
outside	
over	
past	
since	
through	

Exercise 18 Using prepositions

1. Write a paragraph about your ears using all or most of these prepositions: **above, across, at, below, beside, between, by, near, over, to.**

2. Write a paragraph about the front of your home using all or most of these prepositions: **about, after, against, around, behind, beyond, down, from, in, through.**

3. Write a paragraph about your shoes using all or most of these prepositions: **along, for, inside, near, on, throughout, toward, under, with, within.**

Exercise 19   Finding conjunctions and prepositions

Circle the conjunctions and prepositions in the following essay. Don't worry if you do not find all of them.

Different Kinds of Libraries

Finding materials in a library can be complicated and time-consuming, especially if one does not know that there are different kinds of libraries. In order to use one effectively, we must know which kind of library we want or which kind we happen to be using. Otherwise, the experience will be frustrating, and we will not find the materials we need.

First, there are small specialized libraries. They usually deal with materials on a particular subject and are found in an academic department. For example, if one wants materials on women's issues, the Women's Studies Department or a Women's Center might have a small library holding only books, pamphlets, and an article file dealing with women's issues. Larger libraries may have some of the same materials, but sometimes they are easier to find when they are all in one place.

Then there are the public libraries and high-school libraries. We can group them together because they both use the Dewey Decimal system for cataloging the holdings. The books are divided into categories by subject matter; the categories are numbered. This system is easy to use.

Finally there are college libraries. They tend to be large, and all of them use the Library of Congress system for cataloging. Although this system seems more complex, it is not much different from the Dewey Decimal system. It just has longer call numbers involving letters and numbers so that more material may be categorized. The Library of Congress system is also based on cataloging the holdings by subject matter and then assigning groups of letters and numbers to them.

A library may seem daunting for a first-time user, but it is not really difficult to use. In addition, there are always friendly librarians willing to help find something or just explain the system. Also, every library probably has a pamphlet or instructions on the wall about how to use it.

Chapter 5

Voice and Point of View

WRITING AND READING

Before Reading "Does Language Influence Thought?"

perceive: understand, grasp mentally, become aware of
linguistic, linguistics: of language, study of language
relativity: comparison, in relation to
hypothesis: theory, educated guess
finer distinctions: smaller and smaller differences
implications: resulting effects
syntax: the arrangement of words to make a sentence
dialect: speech peculiar to a region or group
perception: understanding, awareness of

QUESTIONS TO ANSWER AS YOU READ

1. What is the *linguistic relativity hypothesis?*
2. Why does Benjamin Whorf think Eskimos see snow differently from other people?
3. Do English-speaking people have a great concern for time?
4. Do we always think in words?
5. Do we limit people's thinking when we use terms such as *businessman* and *paper boy* or *he* to refer to males and females?

Does Language Influence Thought?

Obviously we use language to influence and persuade other people. They in turn influence our thinking by what they say. But does our own language influence what we think and even what we perceive? The ancient Hebrews, for example, had a word for God which could not be pronounced, because they did not want to limit their concept of God. If we used different words, or spoke a different language, would we experience the world differently?

This idea, known as the *linguistic relativity hypothesis,* is most clearly associated with Benjamin Whorf. Whorf claimed that the language we speak affects the way we think and even the way we experience the world. For example, if a language possesses words for certain concepts, the speakers of that language are much more likely to think in terms of those concepts than are speakers of a language without names for the concepts. Whorf observed that Eskimos have several different words for different kinds of snow. He suggested that this caused them to see snow differently—with finer distinctions than someone from the tropics (Whorf, 1956). Critics point out that even someone from the tropics can learn to discriminate between different kinds of snow, if, for example, they became interested in cross-country skiing.

The linguistic relativity hypothesis has some interesting implications for the relationship between different groups. For example, some native North American languages do not make clear distinctions between past, present, and future (Solso, 1988). Speakers of these languages may find it difficult to understand the English-speaking person's concern with time. Benjamin Lahey has pointed out that many American blacks speak a version of English with its own sound, words, and syntax (Lahey, 1973). Does this distinct dialect lead to a different pattern of thought or perception of the world? Some research says "yes" (Bernstein, 1970). Other research says "no" (Labov, 1970).

It seems safe to conclude that language influences thought to some degree. The extent of the influence remains an exciting topic for further research (Bourne et al., 1986).

James V. McConnell and Ronald P. Philipchalk,
Understanding Human Behavior

Using a Consistent Voice

Most students don't think they have a voice in their essays, but they usually do. The voice in an essay deals with the style, whether you are being formal or informal, humorous or serious, lighthearted or concerned, terse or chatty. Also voice has to do with intentions: What is the purpose of your essay? Do you want to share an experience, teach a skill, explain an action, argue for or against a proposal, or describe something? (Don't confuse this voice with the grammatical active and passive voices.)

When writing an essay, you should decide on the voice you will use. Sometimes the voice will fall into place naturally. If you give instructions in how to do something, you will surely use an instructional voice, but it still can be lighthearted or serious depending on the topic. How to eat pizza should have a very different voice from how to perform CPR.

If you can't decide on a voice or if you can't tell what voice you are using, think about the topic you have chosen. Decide what you want to do with that topic. Are you sharing, teaching, explaining, arguing, or describing? Is the topic light or serious? (Don't assume that serious topics are necessarily better.) Then start writing about the topic.

Having a clear idea of the purpose of your essay helps you decide how you will write it. Your voice will come through, and your essay will really be yours. Then after you have written a rough draft, you can see if you succeeded in sharing, teaching, explaining, arguing, or describing. Then you can change, add, or delete.

EXERCISES IN VOICE

Exercise 1   Identifying voice

Decide if the following paragraphs are formal or informal, humorous or serious, lighthearted or concerned, terse or chatty. You may circle more than one word. If none seems to fit, use your own word.

1.   Golf is so weird. Only old geezers and tough old ladies get out on the course. They walk and walk and walk and then swing and swing and swing. Sometimes they don't even bother with that. They ride and ride and ride and then miss and miss and miss. Is this a sport?

formal/informal   humorous/serious
lighthearted/concerned   terse/chatty

2. Golf requires concentration both mental and physical. First one must choose the ball and club with great care. Then one must do a number of practice swings before taking a careful stance, addressing the ball, and lining up the club. One must be aware of each movement of the arms, wrists, torso, and legs in order to swing and follow through perfectly.

    formal/informal   humorous/serious
    lighthearted/concerned   terse/chatty

3. People should give it a try to see if they like it. Golf doesn't require much besides a bag of clubs and some comfortable shoes. Then it's just a matter of finding a public or private course and going at it.

    formal/informal   humorous/serious
    lighthearted/concerned   terse/chatty

4. Golf is a sport recommended for people of all ages. For the young, the exercise of carrying heavy clubs, swinging the whole body, and walking many miles will put them in good condition for their active lives. For older people, the fresh air and the club swinging will benefit the heart. If carrying the clubs and walking prove too strenuous, caddies and golf carts may be used.

    formal/informal   humorous/serious
    lighthearted/concerned   terse/chatty

5. Golf is recommended for everyone. Youths find beneficial exercise through carrying clubs, swinging, and walking. The elderly benefit from the air and swinging. Caddies and golf carts may be used.

    formal/informal   humorous/serious
    lighthearted/concerned   terse/chatty

Exercise 2   Identifying voice

Decide if the following paragraphs are formal or informal, humorous or serious, lighthearted or concerned, terse or chatty. You may circle more than one word. If none seems to fit, use your own word.

1. I couldn't believe my eyes! There she was—my own mother on television. Can you believe such a thing? The reporter wanted to speak with someone about the street fair and looked around and chose my mother out of the blue. She didn't have much to say, but

she sure made the most of it. The reporter could hardly get a word in edgewise after he got her started. Oh, Mom!

formal/informal   humorous/serious
lighthearted/concerned   terse/chatty

2.   Corresponding with acquaintances and relations hardly comprises the most difficult of accomplishments, yet so many of us neglect this crucial endeavor. Spending the requisite time with writing instrument and stationery in this epistolary effort will realize enormous benefits.

formal/informal   humorous/serious
lighthearted/concerned   terse/chatty

3.   Eating meat means killing animals. Every steak or chop in a person's mouth means a cow, a lamb, or a pig killed. People say that the animals were raised in order to supply us with food, but who says we have the right to kill what we have raised? We don't have the right to kill a child after we give birth to it.

formal/informal   humorous/serious
lighthearted/concerned   terse/chatty

4.   Fingernails are hardly a woman's greatest asset, but they have become so important that entire shops are devoted to them. No more do we get nails done at a hair salon; now we go to "Nails-R-Us" for a complete job. Do fingernails deserve such attention and such expense?

formal/informal   humorous/serious
lighthearted/concerned   terse/chatty

5.   Use high-quality, heavyweight white $8\frac{1}{2}$" × 11" paper for your essays. Leave one-inch margins all around, number in the upper right-hand corner, and double space entirely. Type on an electric or electronic typewriter or computer. Handwritten essays should be clear and follow the same format.

formal/informal   humorous/serious
lighthearted/concerned   terse/chatty

Exercise 3   Identifying purpose

Decide what each paragraph wants to do, and then in the margin write one of the following letters:

S   (Share an experience)
T   (Teach or explain a skill)
A   (Argue or persuade people)
D   (Describe something)

1.   I think of my grandmother as bubbly. Her shape reminds me of a bubble—round and small. Her personality also bubbles; she's always talking and has a high, squeaky voice. She seems to bounce around like a bubble too, saying a few words to each of us and then moving on.

2.   This digital watch not only tells you the time to the split second but also the date. It can also be programmed to be an alarm and a timer. Besides that, it will beep on the hour and the half hour if it is set that way. And for entertainment, it will play "Happy Birthday."

3.   Changing a lightbulb is easy but dangerous. First, be sure the light switch is off. Using a towel, unscrew the old bulb carefully; it might be hot. Screw the new bulb in slowly and regularly; tighten it well. Try not to drop a bulb, but if you do, cover your eyes and get out of the way. They explode.

4.   Desserts have healthful benefits that we often neglect. Ice cream is made of milk or cream and fruit; we need the vitamin B and D in milk and the vitamin C in fruit. Any fruit pie also has the vitamin C of the fruit as well as the carbohydrates in the crust. We should all pay more attention to nutritious desserts.

5.   My recent birthday party turned out to be very pleasurable. My best friend gave a surprise party with my family, relatives, and friends. We ate cake and ice cream, and I got many gifts. I especially liked getting a new shirt, a book of poems, and a gift certificate at a sports store. I was very touched.

6.   Aerobic exercise should be a part of everyone's life because everyone needs a healthy heart. People of all ages can run or jog, fast or slow, for long or short periods of time, depending on their condition. Jumping, jogging in place, or aerobic dancing

also benefits people of all ages and, in addition, can be done indoors.

7.   Wear shorts or sweat pants with an adjustable elastic waistband and a T-shirt. If the weather is chilly, add a sweatshirt that you may remove later. Wear smooth fitting cotton socks and, most important, comfortable running shoes that are broken in but not worn out.

Exercise 4   Using voice

1. Write an argument paragraph persuading people to eat or not eat broccoli. You may choose to be formal or informal, humorous or serious, lighthearted or concerned, terse or chatty.

2. Write a paragraph explaining how to sit in a classroom. You may be formal or informal, humorous or serious, lighthearted or concerned, terse or chatty.

3. Write a paragraph describing your hair. You may be formal or informal, humorous or serious, lighthearted or concerned, terse or chatty.

Having a Point of View

In writing essays, **point of view** deals with both having an *opinion* or attitude and expressing it through *first, second,* or *third person.* Both these aspects of writing are called point of view, and both need to be planned for a good essay.

In everyday life, we have points of view that we express to others. For example, now that you have attended classes, you probably have very definite opinions about each of your courses. You have probably described them to your family and friends as great, boring, hard, or fun. Or perhaps you have differing opinions about the professor, who is nice and friendly, and the subject, which is boring and hard. Perhaps you will alter your opinion as the term continues. In any case, you have expressed your point of view.

When you are writing an essay, you need also to have a point of view. You need to argue for or against some proposed action, such as capital punishment or gun control. Or you may explain that a particular method is best, for example, to stop smoking or to go camping. If you are describing a room, you still must decide on a point of view. You can't just name the pieces of furniture: You need a controlling idea, a point of view, about the room.

Choosing the right *person* can make your essay effective or not. In *first person* (I, we), you give a personal opinion. Using first person is good for sharing an experience because it is informal but can be lighthearted or serious. Using *second person* (you) is good for teaching a skill since it naturally has an instructional tone. Using *third person* (he, she, it, they, one) is good for arguing and persuading since it takes the topic outside the personal and into the world. Still, these are not hard-and-fast rules. Using first person sometimes while mainly using either second or third person can add an informal or personal observation. Using third person while mainly using first person can add a persuasive touch. But you should not shift needlessly from one person to another.

Being aware of these aspects will help make your essay effective and interesting. Think about the purpose of your essay. Try out different voices in rough drafts. Don't be afraid to change, add, or delete parts. Read your rough draft aloud to see what voice it has.

EXERCISES IN POINT OF VIEW

Exercise 5   Telling point of view

Write a sentence telling your point of view; that is, give your opinion on the topic, not just that you have heard of it or know something about it.

1. Living in the suburbs

2. Grand opera

3. Wearing fur

4. Mandatory physical education in college

5. Raising the drinking age

6. Mandatory seat-belt laws

7. No smoking in indoor public places

8. Year-round public school

9. Mandatory retirement age

10. Higher salaries for teachers

Exercise 6   Third person

Change the following essay from second person (you) to third person, using *everyone, everybody, they, people.* You will have to change some other words also to make the essay sound right.

Get a Dog

You should have a dog. Dogs can give you something to do every day. They also can be good companions when you are lonely. Dogs also can help you make new friends. You should not live without a dog in your life.

You have to take care of a dog every day. Dogs need to be fed every day, so you have to go shopping often to get dog food. Also you have to walk a dog, usually three times a day and sometimes more. You get some exercise and a nice outing each time you take Rover out.

You get a wonderful companion not only on walks but also at home. You can tell Rover all your problems and hopes, and you will feel the comfort of having a sympathetic ear, and Rover probably has a big one. Rover will also sit near you while you eat or watch television. He won't make you change the channel either.

Finally, you won't be alone for long with Rover. You will make friends on the street, in the park, and in the neighborhood. You will seem like a nice person because you love dogs, so people will make friends with you. You will get to meet many other dogs too.

Exercise 7   Person and point of view

Change parts of the following essay:

1. Where the person shifts. Consider the use of first, second, and third person.

2. Where the point of view shifts. Do you want the essay to share, teach, explain, argue, or describe?

My Garden

My dream is to have a big flower garden with tulips, roses, and chrysanthemums. You should choose these three because they each bloom at a different time of year, so you will have flowers most of the year.

These flowers are all so beautiful. Tulips have that modern, streamlined, stripped-down look and muted, understated colors. I especially like the striped red and white ones. Roses, of course, are my favorites. In contrast to tulips, roses can be almost garish in their bright showiness. Roses also are multifaceted. The delicate, silky petals remind you of a baby's skin, but the rough leaves and the rougher thorns remind me of life's hard side. Then chrysanthemums bring the end of summer and a sad reminder of impending winter. The many little petals and the convoluted leaves tell us of life's complications.

Tulips, as well as daffodils and crocuses, come up in the spring, but you must plant the tulip bulbs the previous autumn. I want lots of them together, so you would plant dozens of bulbs at once. Roses need their own rose garden because you get them in bushes rather than individually. You should set aside a large sunny section for them and plant in the early spring. They usually plant rosebushes about six feet apart. They should also give chrysanthemums lots of room; plant them where there is not too much sun. You don't want them to burn.

I live in an apartment where you don't have any sun, so you can't even grow anything in a pot. But some day you will see me in a house with a garden.

Exercise 8   Person, voice, and point of view

Change these parts of the following essay:

1. Where the person shifts. Consider first, second, and third person.

2. Where the voice shifts from lighthearted to serious.

3. Where the point of view shifts. Decide if the essay should share, teach, explain, argue, or describe.

Why Go to College?

There are many reasons why you should go to college. You can learn a skill and get a better job. I can also meet different people and have some high-class friends (for a change?). But the main reason most people go to college is so they can improve their minds.

I can learn how to use computers and maybe get a high-paying job in a nice company that also gives you benefits. If you have a skill that people want, you can ask for and get more money. Also the company will value me and want to keep me, so they will "invest" in you with nice medical plans, sick leave, and pensions. I am sick and tired of working for peanuts and being afraid that I will be fired.

Lots of people on campus have improved their social lives. You can meet new classmates all the time and go out with them after class. They can also join clubs on campus and meet people who have the same interests as you. I like to sit in the student union or the cafeteria and strike up conversations with students around me. You should pick someone who looks a little lonely. I have made several new friends and often meet them for lunch in the cafeteria.

"A mind is a terrible thing to waste." I can believe that, but do I still have one (ha, ha). You can learn philosophy, psychology, history, biology, and literature, just to name a few. All these subjects will help you think better and will also give you something to think about. I mention ideas I have learned in class to my friends all the time. They must think I'm a real snob! So maybe you'll lose those old friends, but you'll gain all those new ones you met in college.

College definitely has benefits for everyone. You won't lose anything except your money, time, and friends. Only kidding. You will gain enough to change your whole life.

Suggestions for Essay Topics

Using one of the getting-started techniques—freewriting, brainstorming, or clustering—write on one of these topics.

1. Write a story about a person who goes from one country to another and has to learn new words for things she or he has never known.
2. Write an essay explaining the implications of the linguistic relativity hypothesis.
3. Write an essay showing how English speakers are limited by the words we know (consider, for example, food or clothing).
4. Write an essay about a subject in which English speakers make fine distinctions (for example, cars, sports, colors, or time).
5. Write an essay about how to evaluate the two sides of an issue. What are the steps necessary for a full analysis?

Once you have written a rough draft of your essay, see if it has an **introduction, body paragraphs** with **topic sentences,** and a **conclusion.** Does it have **descriptive words** to make it interesting? Also see if you have been consistent with **voice** and **point of view.** Revise it carefully by changing, adding, or deleting parts.

GRAMMAR

Sentences (Clauses)

Technically, if a group of words has at least a subject and a verb, it is called a **clause.** If this clause can stand alone, it is called an **independent clause.** If this clause cannot stand alone, it is called a **dependent clause.** A **sentence** is really just an informal way of saying independent clause. Having an understanding of clauses will be helpful to writers.

An independent clause can be short or long but must be able to stand alone as a sentence. For example, "The dog barked" is an independent clause. It has a subject (dog), a verb (barked), and can stand alone as a complete sentence. A much longer clause, for example, "The huge dog named Rover barked loudly at all the cats and cars passing in the street" still has the same subject (dog) and the same verb (barked). It also has other modifiers in it, but it is still an independent clause.

A dependent clause also can be short or long but cannot stand alone as a sentence. For example, "When the dog barked" is a dependent clause. It has a subject (dog) and a verb (barked), so it is a clause. But it cannot stand alone because of the word "when." Even if we make the clause much longer, for example, "When the huge dog named Rover barked loudly at all the cats and cars passing in the street," it still is a dependent clause.

Since a dependent clause cannot stand alone, it must be changed. One obvious way is to remove the word that makes the clause dependent, in this case "when." However, since "when" probably served some purpose, taking it out probably will not be helpful. Another way is by adding an independent clause to the end or to the beginning. For example, the clause could become "When the dog barked, the neighbors complained." In this sentence, "When the dog barked" is a dependent clause and "the neighbors complained" is an independent clause. Or we could write it the opposite way: "The neighbors complained when the dog barked." We could do the same thing with a longer dependent clause.

Understanding clauses simply helps writers know what they are doing. When writing an essay, one should not, however, start thinking about when or where to write an independent or a dependent clause. Nobody could write that way!

EXERCISES IN CLAUSES

Exercise 9   Writing independent clauses

Here are some dependent clauses that need to be attached to independent clauses. Add the independent clause in the space provided. Remember a dependent clause cannot stand alone; an independent clause can stand alone.

1. While the city sleeps, _____.

2. If you study hard, _____.

3. Since my watch broke, _____.

4. Because Kim works, _____.

5. When the clock strikes three, _____.

6. After Joe eats dinner, _____.

7. Although it's late, _____.

8. Once you try it, _____.

9. _____ if Ming will go.

10. _____ because she studies hard.

11. _____ while they wait for you.

12. _____ once we get started.

13. _____ so that she is pleased.

14. _____ as soon as they can tell.

15. _____ even if the train is late.

16. _____ unless it is cancelled.

17. _____ that you recommended

_____ .

18. _____ who lives in Ohio

_____ .

19. _____ , which starts today,

_____ .

20. _____ that we all like

_____ .

Exercise 10   Writing dependent clauses

Write in a dependent clause to go with the independent clause in these sentences. Choose from these words to start the dependent clause:

after	although	as soon as	because	before
even if	if	in order that	since	so that
though	unless	until	when	while

1. _____ , he still wanted to party.

2. _____ , it looked comfortable.

3. _____ , they should be wrapped well.

4. _____ , he wore his best suit.

5. _____ , she wouldn't take no for

an answer.

6. _____ , it will be too rough.

7. _____ , the bread will be baking.

8. _____, life will go on.

9. _____, we will not have enough time.

10. _____, Jaime likes the plan.

11. That Chihuahua barks a lot _____.

12. The college looks small _____.

13. The garbage can smelled awful _____.

14. My cup will crack _____.

15. Don't break your promise _____.

16. We cleaned the room _____.

17. Kim likes junk food _____.

18. Joe exercises often _____.

19. Japan is not a big country _____.

20. Walking has many health benefits _____.

Exercise 11   Writing dependent clauses

Write in a dependent clause to go with the independent clause in these sentences. Choose from these words to start the dependent clause:

after	although	as soon as	because	before
even if	if	in order that	since	so that
that	unless	until	when	while

1. Kim wants to buy a graduation present for Joe

_____. She went to Johnson's Gift Shop

_____. She looked at the silver trays and

bowls _____. _____

she looked at tablecloths and napkins. She finally decided on a

set of mugs with a wall rack _____.

2. The College Union always has many students in it

_____. Students sometimes study there

_____. _____

others come for just a moment; they probably do it

_____. Most of them stay about an hour

_____.

3. _____ people like to go camping. They

often go to the mountains _____. They

can hike _____ and swim in a lake

_____. _____,

they can also go boating.

4. My English professor likes seeing plays

_____. He goes to the theater

_____. _____, he

goes alone. _____, he prefers it that way

_____.

5. I have worn glasses _____. They have

gotten thicker over the years _____.

_____, I will continue getting thicker and thicker

glasses. Everyone calls me "four eyes" _____

and _____.

Exercise 12   Finding independent and dependent clauses

Underline the dependent clauses and double underline the independent clauses. Remember that independent clauses can stand alone, and dependent clauses cannot stand alone.

How to Cook Perfect Broccoli

Nothing is better than a big bowl of broccoli with a little garlic sauce on it. Broccoli is really not difficult to cook, but it needs some care.

When you choose broccoli, pick stalks that are light green with tight dark green flowerets on top. If the flowerets have turned yellow or brown, don't take that stalk.

Put about two inches of water to boil in the bottom of a steamer. If you don't have a steamer, use a metal strainer in a pot. Wash the broccoli and scrape the top layer of each stalk while the water comes to a boil. Cut up the broccoli into bite-size pieces, but try to keep small whole flowerets, which will make the dish look better. When the water has come to a boil, put in the broccoli and cover the pot. Steam it for about ten minutes. Take out an average-size piece after ten minutes are up, and taste it. If it suits you, then turn off the heat; otherwise, cook it longer and taste it again.

While the broccoli is cooking, heat about a quarter-cup of oil. Add two or three minced cloves of garlic to the oil. Before the garlic turns brown, take it off the heat. Let the oil cool a minute or so, and then add a quarter-cup of soy sauce to it. Mix these together, and pour this sauce on the broccoli, which has been placed in a serving bowl.

Other sauces that may be used are oil and vinegar, diluted hot chili sauce, or butter and garlic. The broccoli will be good no matter what you use. Or you can eat the broccoli just plain with no sauce at all.

Types of Sentences

Considering the infinite number of sentences we can make in English, it is remarkable that all these sentences can be divided into just four types: **simple sentences, compound sentences, complex sentences, and compound-complex sentences.** The final one really just combines the second and third types.

A simple sentence has just one independent clause. "The dog barked" is a simple sentence; "The huge dog named Rover barked loudly at all the cats and cars passing in the street" is also a simple sentence. A simple sentence is not as simple as it may seem at first because it may have more than one subject and more than one verb. For example, "The huge dog named Rover and the tiny Chihuahua barked and growled at all the cats and cars passing in the street" is still a simple sentence. It has two subjects (dog, Chihuahua) and two verbs (barked, growled) and several modifiers, but it cannot be divided into two sentences, because it has just one independent clause.

A compound sentence has two or more independent clauses that have been joined together. For example, "The huge dog barked, but the tiny Chihuahua growled" is a compound sentence because the two parts ("The huge dog barked" and "but the tiny Chihuahua growled") could be separated into two simple sentences without changing any of the words. The only changes would be a period instead of a comma and a capital letter.

The two or more parts of a compound sentence may be joined by a comma and a coordinating conjunction (for, and, nor, but, or, yet, so): "The huge dog barked, *but* the tiny Chihuahua growled." Or the parts may be joined by a semicolon: "The huge dog barked; the tiny Chihuahua growled." When using the semicolon, do not use a coordinating conjunction.

The third kind is the complex sentence, which has one independent clause and one or more dependent clauses. For example, "The huge dog barked when the tiny Chihuahua growled" combines an independent clause ("The huge dog barked") with a dependent clause ("when the tiny Chihuahua growled"). The dependent clause may come at the beginning, the middle, or the end of the independent clause. Complex sentences can be complicated!

The final kind, the compound-complex sentence, just combines these two so that it has two or more independent clauses and one or more dependent clauses. For example. "When cats and cars passed in the street, the huge dog barked and the tiny Chihuahua growled" combines a dependent clause ("When cats and cars passed in the street") with two independent clauses ("the huge dog barked," "and the tiny Chihuahua growled"). Once again, the dependent and independent clauses may appear at various places in the sentence.

Figuring out sentence types is not always easy, but knowing about sentence structure is important. Still, essay writers should not concentrate on writing particular types of sentences. It is more important to express one's ideas. After that, the other aspects can be examined and changed, if necessary, so that the essay is interesting as well as grammatically correct.

EXERCISES ON TYPES OF SENTENCES

Exercise 13   Simple sentences

Underline the simple sentences in this essay; don't bother with the other types. Remember that a simple sentence has just one independent clause that cannot be divided.

I Love the Beach

My favorite relaxation is going to the beach. I love the sun, the sand, and the water. I love to look at the other people there. I love to wear very little clothing. I feel so free and happy when I spend a day, or even part of a day, at the beach.

All the talk of skin cancer has changed my sunbathing habits a little. I wear more sunblock, and I put it on more frequently. I sit in the shade more. I can still enjoy the sand and the water. I like to cover myself with sand, and I like to build sand castles. But I only build sand castles when kids are with me. The water always feels great. I like to dive in and fight the waves.

Other people always seem to have a good time at the beach too. Whole families gather there for the day. I like to see them eating, swimming, running around, and playing in the water. Also I like to watch the volleyball games. I don't play myself, but someday maybe I will. At some beaches I have seen surfers, water skiiers, and wind surfers. Also I like seeing the graceful sailboats and the elegant motorboats.

Maybe I'm a nudist at heart! I like to wear as little clothing as possible and feel the air on my body. Most of the time I have to wear lots of clothes. At the beach I can get away with just one small item. I don't have the courage yet to try nudism, but maybe it's the right thing for me. I just love the freedom of so little clothing. And not wearing shoes is great.

I want to spend more time at the beach. Unfortunately, I have school and work and lots of other responsibilities. I don't really have the money for a long beach vacation, so I take the bus out to the beach on my free days.

Exercise 14   Compound sentences

Underline all the compound sentences in this essay. Remember that compound sentences have two parts that could stand alone. Try dividing the sentence into its two parts and reading each part to see if it forms a complete sentence. Don't worry if you're not sure about some of the sentences.

Wearing Glasses

So many people wear glasses. Do they all really need to, or has it just become fashionable?

Some people really need glasses. They may be nearsighted or farsighted, or they may have some other eye problem. Elderly people almost all need glasses for something. Changes in the eyes must come naturally with old age. In the old days people probably just could not do some things because of their eyes.

These days some people have nothing wrong with their eyes, but they still might wear glasses. Lots of people wear dark glasses. Sometimes the sun is not very bright, but people walk around with "shades." They must feel stylish. Sometimes people wear dark glasses indoors in dark rooms. The glasses are not helping them see well, and, in fact, the glasses probably prevent them from seeing well.

On television, especially in commercials, people wear glasses for effect. The "doctor" recommending some medicine wears glasses, and other "authorities," such an lawyers and professors, also impress us with their knowledge by wearing glasses. These people must have done lots of reading, so we are supposed to trust their information. Actually no one has proven that reading weakens the eyes.

All the fancy frames and name-brand sunglasses on the market probably will keep us wanting to wear glasses. Movie stars, doctors, lawyers, and other famous or intelligent people keep wanting to put on glasses; so do I!

Exercise 15   Complex and compound-complex sentences

Underline the complex sentences and the compound-complex sentences in this essay. Remember that these types of sentences have dependent clauses and independent clauses in them.

My Study Habits

Since I have been in college, I have changed my study habits. I have decided to put all my effort into studying so that my grades will be good. I have to do this if I want to succeed in college.

When I was in high school, I did not study very much because other activities seemed more interesting. While I was in class, I did not pay attention, and I didn't remember anything after I left the room. I rarely did any homework because I did not know the assignments.

After I worked for a year and saved some money, I decided to get an education. Although I still work, I try to spend three hours studying every night. Weekends are hard because I want to enjoy myself, but I still study three hours a day. When I started this habit two months ago, I thought I would hate it. Now I am beginning to enjoy the subjects that I am studying. Well, I am beginning to enjoy *some* of the subjects.

Exercise 16   Sentence types

Figure out each type of sentence in the following essay. Then underline the simple sentences, double underline the compound sentences, and triple underline the complex and compound-complex ones.

Using the Library

When students have to use the library, they get nervous. The library always looks so big and so complicated. They feel foolish asking someone, so they just suffer in silence. These students should learn how to use the library.

To find books, students should use either the card catalog or the computerized catalog. Card catalogs are divided by author, title, and subject. They should look alphabetically under one of those, but they should be sure to look at the correct one. Most libraries now have a computerized system for finding books; such a system is a great help. Usually booklets next to the computer tell how to use it, but asking the librarian is no shame. The computerized system is also divided by author, title, and subject. So again, it is important to look at the correct one.

To find an article from a journal or magazine, students must use the reference room. This room will have lots of big volumes on different subjects. One useful reference is the *Reader's Guide to Periodical Literature,* which helps students find articles about particular subjects in popular journals and magazines. It can be a big help. If students want more specialized articles in a particular field, they can ask a reference librarian for help in locating those indexes. Finding information in these big indexes is not always easy. Each has a particular format and organization, so each one takes some work to figure out. It may seem tedious at first, but the next time around the work will be much easier.

When some articles have been found, their titles and authors should be written down carefully. Then students should look at the file that tells whether the library has that particular journal or magazine. Often the library just does not have any of the journals; that can be very frustrating. A librarian might be able to help, but probably students will just have to find other articles or go to another library.

Finding newspaper articles can be easier. Most libraries have a newspaper index, which lists articles by subject. This index might be mechanical, or it might be computerized. When students have located particular articles, they usually go to the microfilm room. In this room, they can find the right date on the box of microfilm, so they can read the microfilm by putting it in the microfilm machine. Using this machine takes a little practice, but directions are always written on or next to the machine. Some microfilm machines even make copies, so students don't have to stay there to do all the reading.

Using the library takes practice, but the rewards are great. Every student should learn early how to find books and articles there; then reading up on a subject can be easy.

Chapter **6**

Variety

WRITING AND READING

Before Reading "Jill Freedman, Photographer"

WORDS AND PHRASES TO LOOK FOR

Greenwich Village: area of New York City formerly inhabited by
   artists, writers, and musicians
darkroom: room for developing photographs
state of disorder: messy condition
higgledy-piggledy: scattered messily
singular care: unusual care
ego trip: making yourself feel important, self-aggrandizing
Weegee: (real name Arthur Fellig) New York photographer in
   1940s and 1950s
My Lai: town in Vietnam where Americans killed Vietnamese
   civilians

QUESTIONS TO ANSWER AS YOU READ

1. What does Freedman mean by "I was taking pictures long
   before I had a camera?"
2. What does Freedman mean by "cheap pictures?"
3. Why did the photographer in My Lai continue taking pictures?
4. Is Freedman really sorry that she did not take pictures of kids
   being beaten at the stock car race?
5. Do you agree with Freedman that photographers should stop
   events from happening?

Jill Freedman, Photographer

(We're in a studio in Greenwich Village, a steep flight of stairs above a small theater. It's in a state of some disorder; things are higgledy-piggledy—all save one. Singular care is evident in the matter of photographs, camera equipment, and the darkroom.)

I took my first picture five years ago. I was taking pictures long before I had a camera. I always wanted to sit back and watch things. There are times where if I'd used the hidden camera I'd've had things that I don't have. But I'd never use it. I hate sneaky photographers. There's no respect.

Sometimes it's hard to get started, 'cause I'm always aware of invading privacy. If there's someone who doesn't want me to take their picture, I don't. When should you shoot and when shouldn't you? I've gotten pictures of cops beating people. Now they didn't want their pictures taken. (Laughs.) That's a different thing.

I hate cheap pictures. I hate pictures that make people look like they're not worth much, just to prove a photographer's point. I hate when they take a picture of someone pickin' their nose or yawning. It's so cheap. A lot of it is a big ego trip. You use people as props instead of as people. To have people say of the guy, "Oh, isn't he great?"—that's easy.

Weegee took a picture of that woman and daughter crying. The sister had just been burned in a fire. It's one of the most touching pictures in the world. Yet I know I could never have taken that picture. Especially shooting off the flash in their face at the time. And yet I'm glad that he took that picture. But the guy in My Lai—I couldn't have done it.

When I think of that guy taking those pictures. He was part of the army, too. He took a picture of those two children gunned down. He took a picture right before they were massacred, instead of running up to those kids. He just stood there and took the pictures. How could he? I don't think he had any moral problems at all. Just from what he said and those pictures. How is it possible to shoot two children being shot down without doing something?

There was a time when I was at this stock car race. With a bunch of motorcycle guys there. They were drinkin' and they were doin' that whole phony, masculine, tough guy s—t. There were these two kids came by in a Corvair. They took these kids and stomped that car and they beat 'em up so bad. People were standing around lookin'. I was there with my camera. I had been shooting these motorcycle guys up till then. It was cool. But when they were beating up these guys, I found myself running up to the biggest guy, who was doing the punching. I grabbed his arm—one of the kids who was being beaten up had a little camera and it was smashed to the ground. I grabbed his arm and I was hollerin', "Stop it! stop it!" That's what I was doing. I was up all night mad at myself that I didn't take that picture. Because that's where it's at; a picture of people beating up on other people.

I was so mad. Why didn't I take the picture and *then* grab the guy's arm? Because that picture is one of the reasons I take pictures. To show: Look at this. (Sighs.) But I didn't. I would like to if it happens again. (A pause.) I don't know what I'd do. I hope I can take it.

Studs Terkel, *Working*

Sentence Variety I: Altering Subject-Verb-Object

The basic English sentence follows the order of subject first, then verb, then object. For example, in "Maria pulled out an apple," the subject (Maria) is followed by the verb (pulled out) and the object (apple). Although this order should be used often, if it is used all the time, the essay will sound boring and monotonous. Thus, it is important to alter this basic sentence pattern sometimes to add variety to one's sentences.

One of the most common variations consists simply of starting the sentence with a dependent clause instead of the independent clause. When writing a sentence this way, however, consider that you want the more important part of the sentence to come at the end. Formulate your sentence so it comes out that way. Instead of writing "Maria threw an apple after she pulled it out," change the order to "After Maria pulled out an apple, she threw it to Joe," since "she threw it to Joe" is probably more important in the sentence.

Starting the sentence with a prepositional phrase makes an interesting variation. For example, instead of "Maria pulled out an apple from her backpack," try putting the prepositional phrase first: "From her backpack, Maria pulled out an apple." This method adds some variety and also puts the more important part of the sentence at the end.

Starting with a verbal or a verbal phrase is possibly the most common method for sentence variation. For example, instead of writing "Joe was startled by the apple, so he knocked it to the floor" consider writing "Startled, Joe knocked the apple to the floor," which uses the verbal, "startled." Or consider using a verbal phrase: "Startled by the apple, Joe knocked it to the floor." In addition to -ed verbals and verbal phrases, you may also use -ing verbals or verbal phrases: "Laughing, Maria pulled out an apple," or "Laughing softly, Maria pulled out an apple." In addition, you could also change part of the sentence to a verbal phrase: "Pulling out an apple, Maria threw it to Joe." The final type of verbal or verbal phrase is the *to:* "To pull out an apple, Maria opened her backpack."

One of the easiest variations is to use an adverb or adjective or an adjective phrase at the beginning of the sentence. "Suddenly, Maria pulled out an apple" and "Fearful, Joe knocked it to the floor" use an adverb or an adjective at the beginning. Adding more words to the adjective will make an adjective phrase: "Already very fearful, Joe knocked it to the floor."

Varying your sentences will make your essay more interesting, but don't think that every sentence has to be different. Use each method in moderation.

**EXERCISES IN SENTENCE VARIETY I:
ALTERING SUBJECT-VERB-OBJECT**

Exercise 1   Before the subject

Underline the dependent clause, phrase, or word that comes before the subject in the following essay. Give the essay a more interesting title.

My Adventure

When I was visiting my cousins last year, we went for a picnic by the lake. After eating, I wanted to go for a walk in the woods behind the lake. Although I asked both my cousins to go with me, they were too lazy, so I went alone. Sadly, I have learned that I should not go for a walk alone in the woods.

To get to the woods, I crossed a small bridge and walked along a dirt path. In the woods I saw a nice opening in the trees. I headed for it and sat under a tree. Before I knew it, the sky became dark; I must have fallen asleep under the tree. I decided to return, but I did not know which way to go. I could no longer look at the sun's position to help me. Feeling rather scared, I walked quickly in the growing darkness. Deeper and deeper I went into the woods.

Knowing they couldn't hear me, at first I did not yell for my cousins. Then desperately I started calling their names. Worried and annoyed at me, my cousins had come to the woods looking for me. I was so happy to hear their voices. Now I know that I should not wander alone into the woods.

Exercise 2   Before the subject

Underline dependent clauses, phrases, and words that come before the subject in the following paragraphs.

1.   Whenever you set up a new friendship, you have begun an inter-action group. That is, you have given up some part of your own personal *independence* to create a *state of interdependence* between you and the other person. Whenever you join or create a group, you lose the privilege of "just being yourself" and of ignoring the other group members. But you may gain many things that compensate for this loss (Newcomb, 1981). (McConnell and Philipchalk, *Understanding Human Behavior*)

2.   When I had progressed to really serious reading, every night at about ten P.M. I would be outraged with the "lights out." It always seemed to catch me right in the middle of something engrossing. Fortunately, right outside my door was a corridor light that cast a glow into my room. The glow was enough to read by, once my eyes had adjusted to it. So when "lights out" came, I would sit on the floor where I could continue reading in that glow. (Malcolm X, *The Autobiography of Malcolm X*)

3.   Yawning typically occurs when you get tired and your breathing slows down, or else when you're in a crowded room and the air gets stale. Since most people keep roughly the same hours and thus get tired around the same time, we may theorize that toward the end of the evening everybody is on the verge of yawning anyway, and that the power of suggestion from seeing one person do it is enough to push everybody else over the edge. Similarly, when you're in a room full of stale air, everybody else there is in the same boat; so you all tend to yawn together. (Cecil Adams, *More of the Straight Dope*)

4.   I do not know whence I got the notion that good handwriting was not a necessary part of education, but I retained it until I went to England. When later, especially in South Africa, I saw the beautiful handwriting of lawyers and young men born and educated in South Africa, I was ashamed of myself and repented of my neglect. I saw that bad handwriting should be regarded as a sign of my imperfect education. I tried later to improve mine, but it was too late. (Mahatma Gandhi, *An Autobiography*)

5.   Better than hide-and-seek, I like the game called Sardines. In Sardines the person who is It goes and hides, and everybody goes looking for him. When you find him, you get in with him and hide there with him. Pretty soon everybody is hiding together, all stacked in a small space like puppies in a pile. And pretty soon somebody giggles and somebody laughs and everybody gets found. (Robert Fulghum, *All I Really Need to Know I Learned in Kindergarten*)

Exercise 3   Rewriting paragraphs for variety

Rewrite these paragraphs so that some of the sentences start with a dependent clause, a prepositional phrase, a verbal or a verbal phrase, or an adverb or adjective or adjective phrase.

1.   Joe gets postcards of cows from his best friend. He likes cows and hopes to work in a dairy. He is always happy and pleased to receive the cards. He looks at them for a long time.

2.   Kim was happy. She was excited. She went to the party at 8:00. She was annoyed by 8:30. Nobody else came until 10:00. All her friends came. She was still angry at them and did not enjoy the party.

3.   I was walking down the street. A homeless man asked me for some money. He said he wanted to buy some food, and he did not seem drunk or on drugs. I offered to buy him some food. A fruit stand was on the corner. I bought him a dollar's worth of bananas. I hope I did the right thing.

4.   Tony went home from work. The door to his apartment was unlocked and open. He was frightened and did not want to go

inside. He called the police. A police officer came in a few minutes. She looked around the apartment. Tony was relieved that nothing had happened. He thanked the police officer.

5. Five o'clock is my time to relax at home. I kick off my shoes. I settle into my armchair. I do the crossword puzzle. I feel refreshed after finishing the puzzle. I tackle the evening's chores.

Exercise 4 Rewriting an essay

Rewrite this essay so that some of the sentences start with a dependent clause, a prepositional phrase, a verbal or a verbal phrase, an adverb or adjective, or adjective phrase. Don't worry if you can't use all these variations.

Train Ride

My five-year-old brother Lou had never been on a train. He really wanted to take his first ride. We went on the train to Union Station in Washington, D.C. Lou liked many parts of the trip, but not the parts I would have predicted.

He really liked looking at the huge board that had all the trains listed with their times and tracks at the station. He couldn't read most of it, but he wanted to watch the letters and numbers changing. He would have done that for the rest of the day if I had let him.

He wanted to climb on the luggage rack over our seats on the train. I had to pull him off a couple of times. He said he wasn't any heavier than the suitcases up there and that he wanted to ride there the whole time. I couldn't get him to look out the window or enjoy sitting in our seats. He got very bored during the trip.

Lou really liked Union Station and did not want to leave it. He found the stores and the displays absolutely fascinating. And of course there was that huge board again. He could not take his eyes off it and would have stayed there forever.

Lou says he really enjoyed his "train ride," but next time we can just visit the station. That won't cost anything and will keep Lou happy.

Sentence Variety II: Length, Type, It Is/There Is

Aside from starting a sentence with a dependent clause, a phrase, or a describing word, there are also several other ways to give variety to your sentences. You don't need to use all of them all of the time, but a good writer knows them and uses them.

First, an easy technique is to vary the *length* of your sentences. In every paragraph try to have long, medium, and short sentences in any order that works for the sentences. You may combine to make long compound sentences or divide long ones into two short ones. After you have written a paragraph, look at the sentences to see if they could benefit from some variation in length.

Other techniques consist of *questions, exclamations,* and *commands* to vary the standard subject-verb-object order of most sentences. Adding a question that can be answered in the next sentences (What happened next?) or one that has an obvious answer (What could she do?) makes an interesting break in a paragraph. Mild exclamations, such as "What a day" or "Enough said," make the paragraph lively. A mild command, such as "Consider this fact" or "Be careful of such people," adds a personal note that makes an essay interesting sometimes. But be careful not to use questions, exclamations, and commands often; once or twice for each one in a whole essay will be enough.

Yet another technique is to write a *series* of adjective phrases or verb phrases, making rather long but interesting sentences. For example, write "Kim was thrilled to be invited, excited about the train ride, and fearful about the weather." This sentence combines three adjective phrases instead of dividing it into three sentences. In the same way, you can write verb phrases: "Kim answered the invitation, bought her ticket, and prayed for sunshine." This combines three verb phrases into one sentence. Don't overdo this technique, however; use it at most two or three times in a whole essay.

Next are some phrases to avoid. New writers sometimes rely too much on "it is" and "it was." Try to have "it" refer to a specific thing. For example, if you write, "I enjoyed the play; it was a comedy," the "it" refers to "play" and works all right. If the "it" does not refer to anything, for example, in "It was good seeing Kim," try changing the sentence around: "I liked seeing Kim" or "Seeing Kim was good." Although you need "it is" and "it was" sometimes, you can often rewrite the sentence to avoid it.

As with "it is/was," "there is/was/are/were" can also be used too often. Nothing deadens an essay more than using "there is" and "there are" too many times. But changing them means rewriting the whole sentence and takes some work. For example, instead of writing "There was a huge desk in the room," you might write "A huge desk dominated the room" or "The room contained a huge desk."

When you are writing your essay, keep some of these ideas in mind, but don't let them stop you from writing. After you finish a rough draft, go back and make changes. See if you have varied the length of your sentences; see if a question, exclamation, or command is appropriate; see if some sentences can be combined into a series of phrases; see if "it is/was" and "there is/are/was/were" can be eliminated. Try out different ways of writing the sentence to see which way you like.

EXERCISES IN SENTENCE VARIETY II:
LENGTH, TYPE, IT IS/THERE IS

Exercise 5   Questions and phrases

Underline the sentences in this essay that are questions, exclamations, or commands, and that use a series of adjective phrases or verb phrases.

A Terrible Day

I work as a waitress, and I am almost always rushed. Take yesterday. For the dinner crowd, I set up the tables, made coffee, got a fresh order pad, and put on my uniform. I did all this starting at 5:00. Did I have a minute to catch my breath? A party of four came in at 5:30. A couple came in two minutes later. Another couple came in a minute later! Then four more people. Menus. Water. Rolls and butter. Change a chair. Extra butter. Where's the men's room? What does rollatini mean? Can you fry fish without oil? Do you have broccoli? Give me another spoon. Help.

The other waitress arrived at 6:00. Plenty of time. But she could hardly get her coat off. In fact, before changing to her uniform, she took two orders, led three people to a table, and got some water. She still had her purse over her shoulder. Did she deserve this?

What a night. I never stopped taking orders, answering questions, serving dinners, cleaning tables, and writing bills. I made out great in tips, and I'm glad we get so many customers. But give me a break!

Exercise 6   Questions and phrases

In the following paragraphs, underline sentences that are questions, exclamations, or commands and that are a series of verb phrases or adjective phrases.

1.   In my lifetime I've resolved to do a thousand things I have not done. I have been determined, on countless occasions, to stop doing the things I do badly. I've promised myself to think things through more carefully, not to be so careless with money, not to eat so much, not to make so many cutting remarks either in writing or in conversation, and to finish every project I start. These are my weaknesses, and I must add to those my inability to correct them by resolv-

ing to do so. (Andy Rooney, "Resolutions Don't Work," *Not That You Asked*)

2.   The medical experts tell you to exercise but you're always reading of some jogger keeling over. Why chance it? You certainly wouldn't get me out on a golf course with the number of people hit by lightning. Eighty-five people struck dead last year. If we want to last forever, we should stay home, eat whole grains and vegetables, breathe through a mask, boil the water, avoid making close friends. Have a complete medical checkup often. See your dentist twice a year; avoid eye strain and loud noises. (Andy Rooney, "Living Longer but Less," *Not That You Asked*)

3.   Yesterday afternoon we had a torrential downpour. Where did the chipmunks go? I've never seen a chipmunk out in the rain. I'm kind of surprised animals don't like getting wet. Even the robins disappear when it rains. Where do all the robins go that are usually picking worms out of our front lawn? I can't believe the robins all go to nests. I see an awful lot more robins than robins' nests around here. (Andy Rooney, "Bless the Beasts," *Not That You Asked*)

4.   Anything in a supermarket that doesn't go away doesn't come back. This is especially true at a store like Sunshine, where each item has to be stocked, get sold, and be reordered regularly to make it worth having around. In grocery language, this process of coming and going is called a turn. (Susan Orlean, "All Mixed Up," *The New Yorker*)

5.   Let every young man and woman be warned by my example, and understand that good handwriting is a necessary part of education. I am now of the opinion that children should first be taught the art of drawing before learning how to write. Let the child learn his letters by observation as he does different objects, such as flowers, birds, etc., and let him learn handwriting only after he has learnt to draw objects. He will then write a beautifully formed hand. (Mahatma Gandhi, *An Autobiography*)

Exercise 7   Varying sentence length

Notice that all the sentences in this essay are about the same length. Vary the lengths by combining some sentences and shortening some sentences. If you want, make some into questions, exclamations, or commands.

Lateness

The one trait that I find the most annoying is lateness. In our busy lives, everyone should be aware of time. Everyone who has appointments should keep strictly to time schedules. If they can't be on time, they should not make appointments. But that is impossible, so they need to be precise.

When people have jobs, they know they should arrive on time. Some companies have time clocks for employees to punch. That must show the importance of punctuality to them. Employees also have to punch the time clock when they leave. Their pay is probably based partly at least on their being on time.

In their personal lives people should also be punctual. It is rude to make a friend wait on a street corner. Or this friend could be in front of the movie theater. These situations are the worst for being late. But being at home and expecting someone is also difficult. If a friend shows up an hour late, you have been waiting anxiously.

Going to college probably helps some people to be punctual. If a student is an hour late, the class is over. If that happens a few times, the student will be hopelessly behind. Having a strict schedule in this way probably helps many people. Punctuality might be the most important thing students learn.

Exercise 8   It is, there is

This essay uses "it is/was" and "there is/are/was/were" too often. Change as many as you can so that the sentences seem more lively. Also give the essay an interesting title.

Noses

There are several kinds of noses in the world. It is a way that some people judge others, but really all noses are equal. No group of people have better noses than any other group.

First, there are the small noses. Probably there are more people in the world with small noses than any other. They are asked often, however, why they have such small noses. Scientists guess that perhaps it was due to cold weather. It is the scientists who don't have small noses who think of this.

Then there are the big noses. People make all kinds of jokes about big noses, calling them elephants or ski jumps. It is quite insulting to be compared this way, as if it were a kind of defect to have such a nose.

Next, there are the wide noses. Scientists study the causes for the development of these noses as if it is not normal to have a wide nose. It was something in the environment that made these noses develop this way, they say. However, there are no studies about why narrow noses are narrow. So it is implied that wide noses are not normal.

It is important that there is no discrimination about noses. We should all accept each other as we are and not make these kinds of comparisons, as if one kind of nose is normal and all others are defective.

Exercise 9   Adding variety

Make this essay more interesting by doing the following:

1. Vary the lengths of the sentences.
2. Add or change some sentences into questions, exclamations, or commands.
3. Change some sentences into series of adjective phrases or verb phrases.
4. Eliminate "it is/was" and "there is/are/was/were."

The Unsurprise Party

It was soon to be my birthday, and there was going to be some kind of celebration. It was just in the air, and I felt it coming before it actually came. The party itself, however, was a real anticlimax although I appreciated the effort of my friends.

I first realized something strange was going on when Leslie wanted me to go to her house on a particular night. It was two weeks before that night, and there was no reason to make the date in advance. I agreed as if it was not unusual to do that, but she thought I was being strange. She said that she wanted me to meet her cousin from out of town at first. I asked her if that was the cousin I had met before, and she got confused. So she said she really wanted me to come for a long talk about her problems.

It was a few days later when I saw my friend Joe coming out of a poster store that we both go to often. He got very embarrassed and said that he was just browsing. Then he said that the rolled-up poster he was carrying was for himself, not for anybody else. There was no reason for him to say that; it was none of my business if he bought a poster.

I got all dressed up in my best clothes on the night of the party and went to Leslie's apartment. I was ready to act surprised, but actually only Leslie was there when I arrived. All the guests came about an hour later, so they couldn't yell surprise because I was already there. I liked the poster Joe gave me, and I am grateful that my friends wanted to have this surprise party for me.

Suggestions for Essay Topics

Using one of the prewriting techniques—freewriting, brainstorming, or clustering—write on one of these topics.

1. Write a biography for Jill Freedman. Think of where and how she might have been raised, what made her interested in photography,

how she makes a living, what kind of person she is. Use clues from her essay to help you.

2. Write an essay explaining Freedman's views about invasion of privacy by photographers.

3. Write an essay about Freedman's choice of words. Does she sound formal or informal, humorous or serious, lighthearted or concerned, terse or chatty? Give examples.

4. Write an essay explaining the duties of the news media (television, radio, newspapers, news magazines) towards the public. Does the public have the right to know everything? Do the news media have the right to find out everything?

5. Write an essay giving your view on public responsibility. Is it the public's duty to help others even if their lives are in danger?

Once you have written a rough draft of your essay, see if it has an **introduction, body paragraphs** with **topic sentences,** and a **conclusion.** Do you have **descriptions?** Also see if you have a consistent **voice** and **point of view.** Consider also **sentence variety;** have you tried to write varied and lively sentences?

GRAMMAR

Fragments

A fragment is a part of a sentence that has been punctuated as a sentence. Sometimes a fragment just needs to be connected with what comes before it or after it. Sometimes it needs to be rewritten.

Many fragments are dependent clauses that simply need to be connected to an independent clause, at either the beginning or the end. Here is an independent clause followed by a dependent clause fragment: "Kim is entering a talent contest. Although she has no talent." "Although she has no talent" may be attached either at the beginning or end of the independent clause "Kim is entering a talent contest." It is possible to remove "Although," but the meaning of the sentence would be changed too much.

Another frequent fragment is simply having the -ing part of the verb and thus not having a complete verb. There is an -ing fragment in this example: "Kim is entering a talent contest. She playing the violin." Changing "She playing the violin" to "She *is* playing the violin" will solve this fragment problem.

Some fragments are phrases that need a subject and a complete verb to make them into independent clauses, or they need to be attached to an independent clause. For example, "Kim is entering a talent contest. Having no talent at all." Adding a subject and complete verb would make the second part "She has no talent at all." Or this fragment could be attached to the independent clause: "Kim is entering a talent contest, having no talent at all."

Some of these fragments may sound all right because we often do see fragments in writing, especially in advertisements, and we often speak in fragments. But we should avoid them in essays to be sure not to cause misunderstandings.

To test for fragments, read each sentence separately, but from the end of the essay to the beginning. This will isolate each sentence for analysis. If the sentence does not sound as if it could stand alone, it probably needs to be attached or changed. Being aware of fragments and testing for them will probably solve most fragment problems.

EXERCISES IN FRAGMENTS

Exercise 10   Correcting fragments

The following paragraphs are made up mostly of fragments. Get rid of the fragments using these methods:

a. Attach dependent clauses to independent clauses.

b. Complete the verb.

c. Attach the phrase to an independent clause.

d. Remove a word to make a dependent clause into an independent clause.

1.   What a treat. Sleeping late in the morning. Because I usually have to work on Saturday mornings, only on Sunday morning. Staying in bed until 10:00, even 11:00, and listening to the radio. Then getting up and having something to eat in the kitchen without having to get dressed and rush out the door. If only I could sleep late every morning. That would be living.

2.   Summer being over and since I started college and have to work and take care of a family. No time to myself. I am so busy. Which really is not easy and makes me tired all the time. Having so many assignments in school. My job as a cashier bringing in so little money and

taking so much time. Also taking the bus back and forth every day. And having to take care of my four-year-old as well as my cousin's child to make a little extra money.

Exercise 11   Correcting fragments

Underline the fragments in the following paragraphs. Then correct the fragments using one of these methods:

a. Add it to the beginning or end of the sentence.

b. Add a complete verb.

c. Add a subject and complete verb.

d. Remove a word.

Don't rewrite the whole paragraph to avoid the fragments.

1. Halloween. Kids love it. Dressing up in costumes. Getting all those treats. Rubbing soap on windows. Tipping over garbage cans. Running around late at night. For many kids it is the best holiday of them all.

2. I hate this story. No plot. Characters so weird. Can't follow what's going on. Although I know I can't relate to it at all. And even worse. I have to read it over again.

3. Most of us have a set routine every morning. Such as brushing our teeth and taking a shower. Then having breakfast in a hurry and rushing out the door. Weekends, however, mean something else. A change of pace.

4. Leslie, taking charge of the whole class and leading us through the exercises, with no one to help out at all. Doing a fine job of making us understand what we had to do and when we had to do it. She was better than the teacher.

5. Many people would rather watch television than read a book. Needing no practice to watch. Reading takes more time and concentration. According to them, "A picture (on the TV set) is worth a thousand words."

6.   Being entirely too smart to be doing nothing at all with his life except sitting at home or wandering the streets. He decided to get his GED, which led to his wanting to learn about computers. He signed up for a course in adult education. Then he wanted more courses in computers and other subjects as well. Now he is a full-time college student. My brother.

7.   The students started to hate fragments. Because they had so many of them to correct. Which made them examine their own essays very carefully. Being very thorough and knowing a lot about fragments, they were rarely mistaken and managed to correct almost all the fragments.

Exercise 12   Identifying and correcting fragments

Underline the fragments in the following essay. Then correct the fragments by making a dependent clause into an independent clause, by attaching the fragment to an independent clause, by changing the verb to a complete verb, or by adding a subject and complete verb.

Nontraditional Students

Colleges often call minority, older, handicapped, and even women students *nontraditional*. This term gives the wrong message. Even though it may have these students' best interest in mind.

Calling someone a nontraditional student immediately implies that there is a traditional student. Who somehow has more ability and more right to be in college just by historical precedent. These "traditional" students, the white, 18-year-old, male, usually Anglo-Saxon ones, with middle-class or wealthy families behind them.

Instead of having this separate term, students should just be students. No matter what their race, color, age, physical ability, or gender. If colleges would just accept students because of their desire to learn. That would be a step in the right direction.

Exercise 13   Finding and rewriting fragments

In the following essay, find and correct the fragments. This essay is rather dull; try making it a little more interesting using some techniques you have learned.

Recycling

My community has been recycling metal cans, plastic bottles, and newspapers for some time. I think it is a good idea because we will benefit. And the environment as well. At home it is my job to prepare all the recycled materials.

On Friday nights I have to bundle up all the newspapers. I tie them in packets that I can carry. I include magazines and cardboard boxes. If we have any. I have to flatten the boxes by cutting them up.

Then every day washing any cans and bottles we had that day. I usually let them drain after washing them and then put them in a cardboard box where I keep them. Then I put that container out to be collected. Which is done on Tuesday mornings.

I'm glad that I can do these things to help the recycling effort. I know I am helping to improve the environment.

Run-Together Sentences

A **run-together sentence** happens when two sentences have been put together as one sentence. The run-together sentence has either no punctuation or the wrong punctuation between the two sentences. It must be corrected by putting in the right punctuation. (Run-together sentences may also be called *run-on sentences* and divided between fused sentences and comma splices. Many people wrongly think that a run-on sentence simply means a long sentence.)

Most people write run-together sentences because the two independent clauses sound as if they belong together without a pause between them. For example, "The bookcase looks nice it suits the room" can be spoken as if it were all one sentence. But looking at it in writing, one can see that it is made up of two independent clauses: "The bookcase looks nice" and "it suits the room." These two parts can each stand alone.

Correcting this run-together sentence is easy. One may simply separate the two parts with a period and add a capital letter, making two simple sentences: "The bookcase looks nice. It suits the room." Or else one may use a semicolon (;) between the two independent clauses, making a compound sentence: "The bookcase looks nice; it suits the room." Or one may add a word: "The bookcase looks nice, and it suits the room." Or one may recast the sentence: "The nice-looking bookcase suits the room." The best choice depends on the context of the essay.

Sometimes the run-together sentence is more a problem of wrong punctuation than anything else. Students often do hear or see the two parts so they simply add a comma between the two parts. This comma actually reveals a good sense of sentence structure. But a comma alone is not strong enough.

Run-together sentences can be found by reading each sentence slowly in an essay. Then one should try dividing up sentences to see if the parts can form separate sentences. If they can, then they need to be punctuated differently.

EXERCISES IN RUN-TOGETHER SENTENCES

Exercise 14   Finding and fixing run-together sentences

Underline the run-together sentences in these paragraphs. Then correct the run-together sentences in one of these ways:

a. Separate into two sentences.
b. Add a semicolon.
c. Add a comma and conjunction, making a compound sentence.
d. Recast the sentence.

1.   I wish I could learn how to surf it would be so much fun. I would go to the beach every day and surf all day long. I would not want to leave I would enjoy it so much.

2.   Many people enjoy photography as a hobby they find it very rewarding. They take their cameras everywhere with them, and they can take pictures of scenery, people, and buildings. Most people have the film developed in a lab some people do their own developing.

3. My cousin started smoking cigarettes recently, but I told her that smoking was very bad for her. She still wants to continue smoking it makes her feel grown up and sophisticated. But these days smoking is a sign of unsophisticated youth or else of people who have a terrible addiction.

4. Joe's uncle sends him postcards from all over the world. He always has a message in the language of the country that he is visiting. Joe gets then translated at school he really enjoys receiving them.
and

5. Working in a nursery school is very rewarding it can be a lot of fun too. Small children like to learn from adults, and they are so open to new ideas. When they misbehave, they usually have a reason. I try to find out the reason and help them solve the problem.

6. My little brother did not know how to eat an ice cream cone he licked it so hard it fell on the ground he was so mad. I bought him another one.

7. Leslie has become very interested in geology since she took a science course last semester. She wants to take a specialized course about geological formations in this area she says that all areas can be studied geologically.
recast

8. The library has many uses I like to sleep there on the third floor after my morning class. I also can do my homework it is peaceful and quiet there. Sometimes I read magazines too they have *Sports Illustrated, Time,* and *National Geographic.*

Exercise 15   Run-together sentences

In the following essay,

1. underline the run-together sentences

2. correct the sentences by separating them into two sentences, by adding a semicolon, by adding a comma and conjunction, or by recasting the sentence

3. give the essay an interesting title.

My Job

My job is to answer the telephone and take messages I also sort the mail and put it in the right mailboxes I sign for packages and deliver them right to the person also I sharpen pencils and make coffee and send out the mail I am in charge of the copier and the fax they keep me busy most of the day. Now I enjoy being an office worker before I wasn't so sure.

At first I did not know how to work in an office. I came every day and waited until someone told me what needed doing. My boss usually did that but sometimes she had a meeting I did not see her until much later. I felt bored so I read magazines I also called my friends sometimes just to have someone to talk to.

My boss has been very nice to me she really helped me learn how to work in an office it was difficult at first now I understand better about performing duties without being ordered to I feel more capable and reliable, and I enjoy working more.

Exercise 16   Fragments and run-together sentences

Underline the fragments and run-together sentences in this essay. Then correct the sentences by separating them into two sentences, by adding a semicolon, by adding a comma and conjunction, or by recasting the sentence.

Finger Food

Eating with my fingers. That is the way I like to eat. I don't like using any utensils at all. I enjoy food more when I have direct contact with it.

Pizza can be eaten with the fingers, I like it that way. Picking up a whole slice with one hand and not using a fork and knife. For the same reason, I also like hamburgers, hot dogs, and barbecued ribs. Lunch is easy, I always have a sandwich.

For vegetables I can eat french fries, pickles, carrot sticks, radishes, and celery with my fingers peas can be a problem, however. I prefer these vegetables raw (except the french fries) they are easier to pick up that way. I especially like fruit apples, tangerines, and bananas are my favorites they naturally belong in the hand.

I don't miss out on dessert. Which is my favorite part of the meal. Cookies, cookies, and more cookies will do just fine. And I like fruit for dessert also. But cake, pie, custard, and ice cream can be real problems as finger food.

Exercise 17   Fragments and run-together sentences

Underline fragments and run-together sentences. Then correct them using the methods you have learned. Also give the essay an interesting title.

My Favorite Book

The Grapes of Wrath. This novel by John Steinbeck tells about the Joad family moving from Oklahoma to California during the 1930s. The Great Depression in the United States. People did not have jobs they had nothing to eat.

The entire family of about ten people all ride a really old car. Which is about to fall apart at any minute. They have many difficulties along the way. Partly from trying to find food. Partly from getting in trouble with the law. Partly from being cheated by hustlers. And partly from birth and death along the way.

We have to feel sorry for these people who are victims of the bad times. Which they did not cause. But this novel does not just tell about one family's troubles it is about humanity struggling to survive. Steinbeck shows a ray of hope through people pulling together for the good of all rather than individuals fighting each other.

Parallelism

Sometimes also called *parallel construction,* **parallelism** means that words in a series of two or more parts should have the same construction—that is, the same grammatical structure. The sentence then will flow more smoothly and read more clearly. Faulty parallelism makes sentences seem rough, unclear, and disorganized. Parallelism occurs in clauses, phrases, and words.

In both independent clauses and dependent clauses, if a series has been set up, the clauses must be parallel. For example, in this compound sentence, notice that the three parts all have the subject-verb-object order: Kim wanted ice cream; Joe wanted pizza; Ming wanted papaya juice. Dependent clause parallelism is a little harder. If you wrote "Since Kim wanted ice cream and pizza being Joe's desire, they went out to eat," the dependent parts are not parallel. The sentence should read "Since Kim wanted ice cream and Joe wanted pizza, they went out to eat." In this case "Kim wanted ice cream" and "Joe wanted pizza" both are dependent clauses with "since." In the same way, if the dependent clause comes later it must also be parallel: "Ming knew that Kim wanted ice cream, that Joe wanted pizza, and that she herself wanted papaya juice."

If you use a series of phrases—prepositional phrases, verbal phrases, adjective phrases, verb phrases—they must also be parallel. Notice the parallelism in these phrases:

Kim studies *at* home, *in* the store, and *on* the telephone.
Tired of studying and *disgusted* with English, Kim left.
Kim went out *feeling* bored and *looking* for some fun.
She *visited* Ming, *went* to a movie, and *ate* ice cream.

If you use a series of words, also keep them parallel by using the same part of speech. Only nouns, verbs, adjectives, and adverbs apply with parallel words. Note the parallelism in the following words:

Kim, Joe, and *Ming* enjoyed their snack. (nouns)
Joe *ate, paid,* and *left.* (verbs)
The pizza was *hot, delicious,* and *filling.* (adjectives)
Quietly and *quickly,* Joe ate his pizza. (adverbs)

You never need to use parallelism, but if you have started to write a series of clauses, phrases, or words, you need to make them parallel. Use parallelism three or four times in your essay; it adds grace and force to your writing.

EXERCISES IN PARALLELISM

Exercise 18   Identifying parallel structure

Underline the parallelism in the following paragraphs:

1.   Welcome to the wonderful world of pigs. Pictures, cartoons, statuary, piggy banks, and memorabilia in this downtown Detroit sandwich shop on Cadillac Square are all of the porcine persuasion (there is even a small toy pig in a bird cage); and in case you didn't guess, the specialty of the house is pig meat—ham in particular, in every cut, shape, and size a chef can imagine. (Jane and Michael Stern, "Ham Heaven," *Roadfood*)

2.   Going down the long dirt road, headed for the country road, I passed a row of maple trees. Several of the smaller trees had been overrun by wild grape, an eastern version of kudzu, the scourge of the South. Wild grape wraps itself around tree trunks, climbs the tree, and pulls down its branches in a vicious stranglehold. (Andy Rooney, "Nature Seems So Unnatural," *Not That You Asked*)

3.   In the industrial world, capitalists and socialists alike know that you get ahead in the world by adding more dollars or rubles or yen to your bank balance than you subtract. Another thing that people in currency-using economies agree upon is that bank balances, coins, paper money, and electronic transactions are symbols for other kinds of wealth—arms, food, heavy machinery, works of art. (Harold Rheingold, *They Have a Word for It*)

4.   In 1986, a group of computer enthusiasts—a notoriously skeptical group—were addressed by former psychedelic guru Timothy Leary, whose slogan "Turn on, tune in, drop out" was one of the hallmarks of the American youth revolution of the 1960s. "I have a new slogan," Leary told the assembly: "Think for yourself; question authority." He had barely finished his sentence when a voice rang out from the back of the room: "I question that!" (Harold Rheingold, *They Have a Word for It*)

5.   Noted for the height, range, and drama of their twirls, members of the Ventura Baton Twirling Troupe surprised even themselves on one occasion in the late 1960s. During an Independence Day march, one of their batons hit a power cable, blacked out the area, started a grass fire, and put the local radio station off the air. "They were in form," the mayor said. (Stephen Pile, *Cannibals in the Cafeteria and Other Fabulous Failures*)

Exercise 19   Finding parallel structure

Underline the parallelism in this essay.

Going on a Trip

Going on a trip even for a week takes a lot of planning. We had to plan when to go, how much to spend, how to get there, and what to see. In our case, we were invited by friends to visit in Washington. D.C., so we had a place to stay. The whole trip was a lot of trouble but worth it.

Before leaving, we had to stop the mail, find a place for our cat, and take our plants to my mother's house. Then we consulted schedules, bought train tickets, and asked my brother to drive us to the station. We had to shop for a house gift, to pack for a week, and to read our guidebook. I had to be prepared for walking around town, for swimming in a pool, for visiting museums, and for entertaining our friends in a restaurant. Packing was not easy.

We did not have much money, so we had to budget carefully for the gift, the tickets, the restaurant. and other expenses. We did not want to buy the guidebook at first, but it suggested ways to cut costs. After returning, we decided that we had had a good time, that the expense was worth it, and that we would do it again.

Exercise 20　Creating parallel structure

Underline the one sentence in each paragraph that needs parallelism. Then rewrite the sentences so they are parallel.

1.　　　Leslie has to rewrite her essay. She has errors in verb tenses, fragments, and there are run-together sentences also. She is not pleased about rewriting, but the professor says she has to do it.

2.　　　Quietly and with dignity, the young man put on his coat and left the room. The others had started imitating and laughing at people's accents. He disliked such behavior and would not take part in it.

3.　　　Tony decided not to join his friends that evening. His cold being worse, having homework to do, and he wanted to sleep early. He did not get his homework done, however, because of his cold, but he did get a good night's sleep.

4.   Lifting weights, aerobics, the golf course, and softball playing keep me very fit. Twice a week I lift weights and take an aerobics class at school. On weekends I play golf or softball with friends.

5.   Maria can work the point-of-sale cash register, sells clothing, and tagging new merchandise. She has worked in clothing stores before and feels comfortable in them. She should have no trouble finding another job in one.

6.   We asked the professor if he counted quizzes and that he drop the lowest grade. He agreed not to count the quizzes, but he did not agree to drop the lowest grade. He said, however, that he would allow essays to be rewritten for a possible better grade.

7.   Tony studies computers and knows a lot about them, but he thinks he lacks knowledge in the arts, especially painting. He wants a course that teaches about modern art, showing a lot of paintings, and to explain their meanings. Art 105: The History of Modern Art probably will suit him just fine.

Exercise 21   Finding and fixing parallel structure

Underline the two or three sentences in each paragraph that have errors of parallelism. Then rewrite those sentences using parallelism.

1.   I like watching quiz shows on television. They teach me interesting information and providing entertainment at the same time. I wish more quiz shows were shown in the evening when I am at home and they should be on the weekend also. The contestants seem really smart; they know all the answers. I can't begin to answer some of the unusual questions they are asked. I hope I never have to go on a quiz show and make a real fool of myself.

2.   Maria reads the newspapers every day to find out what is happening in the world and looking at the local events. She follows U.S.

politics fairly closely. Also she reads local news, especially about social programs and also about cultural events. She likes keeping current on what is going on and to have knowledge about world events. She considers reading the papers every day as part of her education. She really has the right idea about education.

3.   Being thrifty is a way of life for Joe and Tony. They do not make long-distance phone calls if they can write letters. They reuse plastic and paper bags. They like to invite friends over for a meal and that is cheaper than going out. They shop often in thrift stores, looking for good used clothes and to find household utensils. They get books and magazines from the local library instead of buying them. They walk or take a bus everywhere and that saves a lot of transportation cost.

4.   The best burritos come from the Mexican restaurant near me. The guacamole is freshly made, the beans have been cooked a long

time, the tomatoes are juicy and ripe, and the salsa is hot. All these ingredients come with a choice of shredded beef or having slices of chicken. The vegetarian burrito has all the vegetables and with rice also. The burrito is never rolled in advance but is made to order. It is never soggy or with dried edges.

Chapter 7

Getting Down to Details

WRITING AND READING

Before Reading "Cooking en Papillote"

WORDS AND PHRASES TO LOOK FOR

en papillote: French for "in parchment," wrapped in paper
parchment: a type of paper
retains the aromas: keeps in the good smells
generates: produces
considerable strain: a lot of pressure
materializes: appears
overlapping: one part over another part
ovenproof: can stand oven temperatures without breaking

QUESTIONS TO ANSWER AS YOU READ

1. What are some advantages of cooking *en papillote?*
2. What does a dish cooked *en papillote* look like after cooking?
3. How do you seal the edges of the parchment?
4. Try folding a piece of paper according to Rombauer's instructions. Is it easy or difficult? Why?
5. What foods do you think can be made *en papillote?*

Cooking en Papillote

This is a delightful way to prepare delicate, quick-cooking, partially cooked or sauced foods. The dish, served in the parchment paper in which it was heated, retains the aromas until ready to be eaten. As the food cooks, some of the unwanted steam it generates evaporates through the paper. Just the same, the paper rises and puffs as heating progresses, putting considerable strain on the folded seam. So, note the following directions carefully.

To make a *papillote:* fold a parchment of appropriate size in half, crosswise. Cut from the folded edge to the open edge, a half heart shape, so that when the paper is opened the full heart shape materializes.

Be generous in cutting—allowing almost twice again as much paper as the size of the object to be enclosed. Place the food near the fold—not too close to the seam. Turn the filled paper with the folded edge toward you. Holding the edges of the paper together, make a fold in a small section of the rim. Crease it with your fingers and fold it over again. Hold down this double fold with the fingers of one hand and with the other start a slightly overlapping and again another double overlapping fold. Each double fold overlaps the previous one. Repeat this folding, creasing and folding around the entire rim, finishing off at the pointed end of the heart with a tight twist of the parchment—locking the whole in place. Now butter the paper well. Place it in a buttered ovenproof dish in a 400° preheated oven for 5 to 6 minutes or until the paper puffs. In serving, snip about $\frac{3}{4}$ of the paper on the curved edge just next to the fold to reveal the lovely food and release the aroma.

Irma S. Rombauer and Marion
Rombauer Becker, *The Joy of Cooking*

Using Specific Words

Using specific words instead of general ones will help make your points clear, interesting, and exciting. Specific words also help to add variety to your sentences, because you don't use the same words over and over.

Although introductions, topic sentences, and conclusions probably use general words, the body paragraphs with examples and details should be more specific. Thus, instead of a general word, such as *dog, soup,* or *car,* use an appropriate specific word: *cocker spaniel, vichyssoise,* or *Corvette.* Instead of a common verb, such as *walked,* use *ambled, careened, marched, minced, rambled, sauntered, strolled, strutted,* or *wandered.* Choose the words that seem appropriate and feel natural to you.

Rather than calling something good or bad, wonderful or terrible, different or the same, choose a descriptive word that tells more than just what you think of it. Consider words that involve the five senses: sight, sound, smell, taste, and touch. How does that cocker spaniel look, sound, smell, or feel? How does that vichyssoise look, smell, or taste?

If you are writing about times, places, and numbers, try also to be specific. If something happened at a certain time, use *two o'clock, early afternoon, after an hour and a half,* or *in October.* Don't just leave it at *later, during the day,* or *a while ago.* Don't just say that a test was long; say that it took two and a half hours. If someone went to the beach or to a restaurant, say she went to Jones Beach or to Gino's Pizza. Don't say something cost *a lot,* say *$10.50.* Don't say there were *lots* of people in the room, say there were over one hundred people.

Take the time to choose specific words and appropriate descriptive words. Use a dictionary and a thesaurus for suggestions. But don't use words that you have never heard before or that you are unclear about. They might make your writing inaccurate, or your writing might sound unnatural. If you spend some time finding the right words, your writing will become lively and interesting. You will find that you enjoy writing more also.

EXERCISES IN USING SPECIFIC WORDS

Exercise 1   Choosing specific nouns

Underline the noun that is the most specific in the group. Use a dictionary.

1. novel   story   *The Great Gatsby*   book   Fitzgerald work

2. cottage   place   abode   one-story house   habitation

3. ball game   softball   sport   summer game   athletics

4. person   female   athlete   runner   sprinter

5. kale   food   salad   leaves   greens

6. colleague   person   friend   fellow   man

7. animal   dachshund   dog   puppy   lap dog

8. Granny Smith   Washington State apple   apple   red apple

9. three-year-old   girl   juvenile   toddler   child

10. drink   orange juice   Tang   fruit drink   ade

11. over half an hour   a time   a while   an hour   50 minutes

12. exercise   training   aerobics   calisthenics   workout

13. flower   blackeyed Susan   daisy   spring blossoms   blooms

14. picture   painting   a Renoir   an Impressionist

15. shellfish   clams   little necks   mollusks   bivalves

16. car   automobile   Lotus   sports car   two-seater

17. Macintosh   Apple   IBM   laptop   personal computer

18. blanket   cover   quilt   throw   coverlet

19. sunfish   boat   craft   sailboat   small boat

20. South America   São Paolo   urban area   big city   Brazil

Exercise 2   Finding specific nouns

Practice finding specific words to describe the following subjects. Use a dictionary and thesaurus after you have tried to find words on your own or with the class.

1. *dog*
   type:
   physical characteristics:
   color:
   personality:

2. *shirt*
   type:
   style:
   size:
   color:
   characteristics:

3. *room*

   type:

   size:

   color:

   characteristics:

   condition:

4. *shoes*

   type:

   color:

   style:

   characteristics:

5. *jacket*

   type:

   style:

   color:

   characteristics:

6. *tree*

   type:

   size:

   color:

   characteristics:

7. *a watch*

   type:

   color:

   size:

   style:

   characteristics:

8. *radio*

   type:

   style:

   color:

   size:

   characteristics:

Exercise 3   Finding specific nouns

Write down as many specific nouns as you can think of that mean the same or almost the same. For example, for *dog* you might write *cur, mutt, puppy, purebred, terrier, corgi, German shepherd,* and many other breeds.

1. bag
2. blue
3. India
4. jacket
5. bed
6. shoes
7. red
8. black
9. white
10. car
11. fish
12. horse
13. bear
14. cat
15. table
16. chair
17. glass
18. cup
19. airplane
20. box
21. soup
22. dessert
23. tree
24. bicycle
25. skates
26. book

27. plate

28. boat

29. hat

30. pen

31. tooth

32. pants

33. skirt

34. spoon

35. fence

36. paper

37. ball

38. card

39. jewelry

40. necklace

For which did you find the most words?

Which words were difficult?

Exercise 4 Finding specific verbs

After each verb write in as many other verbs as you can think of that mean the same or almost the same. For example, for *walk* you might write *amble, careen, march, mince, ramble, saunter, stroll, strut,* and *wander.*

1. eat

2. sing

3. run

4. speak

5. climb

6. look

7. turn

8. dance

9. swim

10. cut

11. clean

12. work

13. sleep

14. read

15. throw

16. sit

17. drink

18. steal

19. write

20. break

21. watch

22. fall

23. close

24. pull

25. hold

26. hit

27. push

28. sew

29. jump

30. act

31. trick

32. criticize

33. fly

34. spin

35. complain

36. want

37. enter

38. scare

39. take

40. get up

For which did you find the most words?

Which words were the most difficult?

Writing Specific Paragraphs

In most essays, the thesis statement and the following topic sentences in each paragraph probably need to be more general than the body paragraphs. But these body paragraphs must have more specific details in them to make the points clear.

For example, if you are writing an essay about a poor restaurant, you probably want to cover in separate paragraphs the appearance of the place, the service, and the food. Your first topic sentence might be that the restaurant looked really run down and dirty; that is a general statement about the appearance. You should *not* simply repeat this topic sentence in different words. Don't, for example, say that the façade looked old, that the walls and floors looked dirty, and that the tables did not seem very clean. You have mentioned parts of the restaurant, but you have not given a clear picture of the run-down, dirty appearance. Instead, tell about the broken glass in the front window, the faded and limp curtains, the ketchup on the walls, the bread crumbs and paper napkins scattered on the floor, and the sauce-stained tablecloth. Each of these points needs detailed descriptions. That is, pull together specific nouns and verbs along with adjectives and adverbs to paint a vivid picture.

Using specific words in paragraphs, however, is not limited to descriptions. If you are giving reasons for your particular point of view, you need also to write specific paragraphs. For example, if you want to give reasons why you thought the service was so poor in that restaurant, you will tell in detail that the hostess put you next to smokers even though you asked for the nonsmoking section, that the waiter forgot menus and water, that the busboy took away your dish before you finished eating.

If you are explaining step by step how to do something, also use specific language. If you want to tell how to make a dish better than that restaurant did, tell each step with specific words.

Using specific words in paragraphs takes some practice and requires a great deal of thought. Your essays will be much better, however, if you pay attention to the details.

EXERCISES IN WRITING SPECIFIC PARAGRAPHS

Exercise 5   Specifics in paragraphs

In the following essay, underline the thesis statement and the topic sentences, and then circle the specific parts of the body paragraphs.

I Quit

I have been working at the same job as a stock boy in a supermarket for two years now, and I think it is time to quit and find a new job. I am quite dissatisfied with the location, the working conditions, and particularly the boss.

Waiting for the bus and then riding it for half an hour and then walking another twenty minutes take too much time. I must spend at least an hour going to work and then coming home. There are other supermarkets much nearer to me where I might find work. But I would not mind the commuting time if I liked the other parts of the job.

Being a stock boy really requires a lot of hard, physical labor. I have to help unload large cartons of supplies from trucks that deliver at any time. The boxes of sponges and paper towels can be light, but the huge crates of liquid detergent, fruits, vegetables, and cans of almost anything are really heavy. I get sore arms after an hour of such work. Then I also stock the shelves, which means a lot of bending and squatting.

My boss also seems unfair to me. He often makes me help unload for almost two hours and calls on me often to clean up a broken glass jar or other food spilled in the aisles. I also locate items for customers, read labels for elderly people, and comfort lost kids while looking for their parents. But my boss never compliments me for taking the time to help customers even though he profits from it. On the contrary, he criticizes me for not having finished stocking the shelves. I don't think he appreciates me.

Next week I will apply at the supermarket just three blocks from my home. But in the meantime I have to do well at my present job so that the boss will give me a good recommendation.

Exercise 6   Writing specific paragraphs

Change the underlined nouns, verbs, adjectives, and adverbs to more specific words to have specific paragraphs. Change any other words you need to.

1.   The person wore a nice outfit to the party. He had on a black shirt, pants, and boots. He also wore some jewelry and carried a jacket. His friends said he looked nice.

2.   The car drove very fast down the street. It drove around the corner so fast that it drove on two wheels. A police car was following the car and wanted to catch it.

3.   The person did her homework. She read some chapters on one subject and then read a part of another book on another subject. After a while she did not do any more homework.

4.   The kitchen was very dirty. The stove had dirty spots on it, and the oven was also very dirty. The sink was full and the counter around it also had things on it. The refrigerator also looked dirty. The floor was especially dirty.

5.   Our evening <u>was</u> <u>fine</u>. We <u>went</u> to <u>a movie</u> that we both <u>liked</u>. Then we <u>ate</u> <u>something</u> at <u>a restaurant</u>. The <u>food</u> <u>was</u> good. We <u>were</u> both <u>happy</u> with it. Also both the <u>movie</u> and <u>restaurant</u> did not cost <u>very much</u> because we <u>had a discount</u>.

Exercise 7   Specifics

Rewrite the following essay by replacing general words with specific words to make specific paragraphs. Also give the essay a more interesting title. Make this story sound true.

The Story of a Life

He came from his country at a young age with his parents. They settled in this part of America where his parents went to work. They struggled hard, but now they are all right.

First, they had to find which part of the country to live in. They knew someone in this town so they decided to settle here. They found a place to live that is all right but not perfect for all of them.

His parents looked for work for a long time. Now they both work hard and do not get very much money. But their children helped out with things. They are doing all right, and they have managed to buy some things that they need.

He had to work for a while, but now he doesn't have to work so much and can go to college. He hopes to have a bright future in his profession. Things are turning out all right for them.

Exercise 8   Specific paragraphs

Rewrite this essay by replacing general words with specific words to make specific paragraphs. Also add a thesis statement to the introduction and a conclusion if you want. Give the essay a more interesting title.

Exercising

Exercising has been around for a long time. We can see many people of different ages exercising.

Some people belong to a gym or health club and exercise there often after other things. These places cost a lot of money but they seem popular. People go to health clubs for different reasons. There are many advantages to belonging to a health club.

People also can buy equipment to use at home, or they can watch a video of exercises if they don't want to buy equipment. This method is not as good as going to a health club. But this method is better than not exercising.

Most people like to go outdoors for exercise. They can do lots of different things there. There are many benefits to exercising outdoors although there are also some disadvantages. I prefer going outdoors for exercise. I feel better when I do. Everybody should do some exercise.

Suggestions for Essay Topics

Use freewriting, brainstorming, or clustering to get started, and then write on one of these topics.

1. Write an essay discussing whether Rombauer's directions are easy or difficult. Give reasons for your opinions.
2. Write an essay explaining Rombauer's step-by-step approach to cooking.
3. Write an essay telling how to make a particular dish that you know how to make. It can be very simple or quite complicated.
4. Write an essay telling how to do something that you know how to do well. It does not have to be something for which you have a special technique; it can be something you do every day but understand well.
5. Write an essay telling step by step something you have learned in another class or have read about in a book or magazine.

Once you have written a rough draft of your essay, look it over to make sure you have **topic sentences** and **body paragraphs,** an **introduction** with a **thesis statement, specific words** and **specific paragraphs,** and a **conclusion.** Also check that you have **descriptive detail** and **consistent voice** and **point of view.** See also that you have **sentence variety.**

GRAMMAR

Sentence Problems I: Subject-Verb Agreement

In addition to fragments, sentences need further attention in various areas. One such area is making sure of subject-verb agreement, which means that the verb must "agree" with the subject in number (singular or plural) and person (first, second, or third). For example, in "The cat drinks water, "cat" is the singular subject and "drinks" is the singular form of the verb. The same applies for plural subjects, as in "The cats drink water," "cats" is plural and "drink" is the plural form of the verb. Usually, this is easy, but a few problems need attention.

If the subject has more than one part (called a compound subject) and the parts are joined by *and,* use a plural verb: "The cat and dog drink water." If the compound subject is joined by *or,* use a verb that matches the nearest subject: "The cats or the dog drinks water." If you don't like how it sounds, turn the subjects around ("The dog or the cats drink water.") or recast the sentence ("The water is for the dog and cats to drink.").

If other information comes between the subject and verb, ignore the other information and match the verb to the subject. For example, in "The cats in my house drink water" the plural subject "cats" needs the plural verb "drink." Or in this example, "The cats, as well as the dog, drink water," notice that "dog" is not part of the subject, so the verb must match "cats."

Even when the subject comes after the verb, the subject and verb must agree. Notice that in this example, "In my house are two cats," "cats" is the subject, not "house." Also when using "there" and "here," match the verb to the subject: "There *are* two *cats* in my house," "There *is* a *cat* in my house," "Here *is* the *cat*," "Here *are* the *cats*." With questions beginning with "Where," "who," "what," and "how," also match subject and verb: "Where *are* the *cats?*" "Where *is* the *cat?*"

With pronouns ending in -one (one, every-, any-, some-), -body (body, every-, any-, some-, no-), and -thing (thing, every-, any-, some-, no-), always use a singular verb: "Someone likes my cats," "Somebody likes cats," "Something is wrong." "Each," "either," and "neither" also take singular verbs when they are used as the subject: "Each is right," "Either is right," and "Neither is right."

Finally, collective nouns, such as audience, class, committee, crowd, family, group, can take either a singular or plural verb depending on the intention, but actually most American writers think the plural form sounds wrong. Most people prefer, for example, "The committee *is* divided" to "The committee *are* divided." So use the singular form or recast the sentence.

EXERCISES IN SUBJECT-VERB AGREEMENT

Exercise 9   Finding subject-verb agreement

Underline the subject and the verb that goes with it. Notice whether they are singular or plural.

1.   My friend Kim reads the comics every day. She turns to them before looking at the news or anything else in the papers. She keeps up with so many comic strips that she takes a very long time to get through the papers. I think she should cut down on the number of comic strips she reads.

2.   Most people have a favorite chair for sitting, but I prefer to sit on my bed. I can arrange my cushions and pillows just right for my back. Then I stretch out my legs. I feel really comfortable this way. I do my homework, watch television, and read this way. I like to eat this way too, but I have to be careful not to get crumbs in my bed.

3.   Many people in this country do not vote. They do not think that voting is important, not even the big elections. They do not take an interest in local or national politics, so they do not know the issues. People need to understand what different politicians stand for, and then they need to vote for the ones they agree with. Voting is important.

4.   There is a Gay Rights demonstration on campus today. Everybody I know is marching in it. Leslie is carrying a big banner with "Gays Have Rights" written on it. Anybody can march, not just gays, so many people who believe that gays have rights are also marching. Neither Leslie nor I am gay, but we support their cause.

5.   All his books sit on one shelf next to his desk. There are only about ten of them. This semester's textbooks make up six of them. Two others are last semester's textbooks that he could not sell back. One other is a dictionary that he got as a high-school graduation present, and the other is a diary. He says the diary is blank because he has not written a word in it except his name.

6.   I find it hard to believe that someone has only ten books. He says that nobody in his family ever reads anything except a few ads in the mail. If somebody forgets and leaves a magazine in their home, some-one might read it although no one has done that. Now he leaves a book in the living room so anyone can pick it up, but nobody has yet.

7.   Our club wants to have a party, so a committee is planning it. The majority of the club wants a band to play. Luckily, a band called WOW! is willing to come. This group is just starting out and needs exposure, so even if the audience is small, it will do. A crowd still makes them very nervous.

Exercise 10   Making subjects and verbs agree

Fill in the appropriate form of the verb, choosing from the ones listed under the blank.

To Eat or Not to Eat Meat

Everybody _____ food preferences, but my family
                    has, have

_____ the worst or the best, depending on how you
        is, are

_____ at it. We all _____ different ideas about
    looks, look   has, have

food. We get along fairly well, but our family reunions _____
                                                              is, are

really complicated.

My sister and her family _____ meat of every kind.
<u>eats, eat</u>

They _____ steak and chops, roasts, ribs, and chicken, and
<u>likes, like</u>

also _____ lots of vegetables and not much dessert. My
<u>eats, eat</u>

brother, along with his wife and one child, _____ not eat
<u>does, do</u>

red meat, but they eat chicken and fish. Eggs and milk also

_____ up part of their diet. Their other child _____
<u>makes, make</u>   <u>eats, eat</u>

hamburgers and hot dogs whenever she _____ the chance,
<u>gets, get</u>

but she _____ strange about not having red meat often.
<u>feels, feel</u>

My stepmother never _____ meat with milk or cream
<u>eats, eat</u>

although she _____ everything else, except pork. She
<u>eats, eat</u>

_____ never tasted a cheeseburger or a ham and cheese
<u>has, have</u>

sandwich or any meat dish with cream sauce. She _____
<u>does, do</u>

not miss them, however, and _____ lots of things to eat.
<u>finds, find</u>

Also she _____ the best rugelach in the world.
<u>makes, make</u>

My father and I _____ no meat at all. Also we
<u>eats, eat</u>

_____ not have fish, eggs, or dairy products. Vegetables
<u>does, do</u>

and beans _____ up most of our meals, and tofu
<u>makes, make</u>

_____ often on our plates. My father _____ with a

appears, appear   bakes, bake

variety of grains, so we _____ wonderful breads to eat.

                                    has, have

There _____ times, especially on vacation, when eating

                is, are

_____ difficult, but we, along with my stepmother,

becomes, become

_____ to eat well.

manages, manage

When the clan _____ together, we _____

                    gets, get   has, have

some very heated discussions about food, but basically each of us

_____ and _____ each other's right to choose.

respects, respect   tolerates, tolerate

Sentence Problems II: Pronoun-Antecedent Agreement

This rather fancy-sounding term, *pronoun-antecedent agreement,* simply means that a pronoun must clearly and correctly refer to the word that came earlier in the sentence (the *antecedent*), usually a noun. The pronoun should agree in person (first, second, or third person), in number (singular or plural), and in gender (male or female). Also a pronoun should not be ambiguous or too far from the noun.

To agree in person, if the antecedent is third person, the pronoun referring to it should also be third person: *Leonard* took *his* child home; the *attorney* won *her* case; the *bank* changed *its* image. The same applies to first person and third person.

To agree in number, if the antecedent is singular or plural, the pronoun should also be singular or plural: *Leonard* took *his* mother with *him; Leonard and Karl* took *their* mother with *them;* the *chairs* need *their* cushions repaired.

Agreement in gender has some complications. If the antecedent is clearly feminine or masculine, then there is no problem: *Mr. Smith* lost *his* glasses; the *ballerina* liked *her* costume. If you know that a person is male or female, then use the appropriate male or female pronoun: The firefighter ran to her station; the boss opened his door. If you do not know the gender, do not assume that the person is male. Rather, use both genders or rewrite the sentence: The student took his or her exam early, or the student took the exam early. If possible, change to plural: The students took their exams early.

Another problem is that some indefinite pronouns (anyone, anybody, anything, everyone, somebody, each, etc.) and relative pronouns (who, whoever) are singular but do not seem clearly singular or clearly masculine or feminine. Writing "Everybody wants *his or her* child to succeed" is awkward, yet writing "their" for "his or her" is incorrect although we usually speak this way. One solution is simply to recast the sentence: Parents want *their* children to succeed. If that is not possible, use "his or her." "None" is clearly singular, but many people treat it as a plural ("None want *their* money back") even though they should write it as singular ("None wants *his or her* money back."). In the same way, collective nouns (club, company, family, group, etc.) are singular but sound plural sometimes; however, they should be treated as singular: The company held *its* annual picnic. Collective nouns are not masculine or feminine, but neutral.

Although spoken English allows some variation and laxness in rules, written English still adheres to definite rules.

EXERCISES IN PRONOUN-ANTECEDENT AGREEMENT

Exercise 11 Finding pronoun-antecedent agreement

Circle the parts of the pronoun-antecedent agreements and draw a line from one to the other in the following essay.

His and Hers Become Theirs

When Rosina and Tommy got married, they had to combine their two households into one. Their new apartment was not as big as their two apartments combined, so each could only bring some of his or her household things. How to accommodate each other was one of the first lessons they had to learn.

For the furnishings, Rosina brought her couch, and Tommy brought his dining room set. They each brought their chairs and bookcases, but they did not have enough room for all their furniture.

She had to get rid of her bed while he got rid of his desk and some of his books.

The kitchen is made up mostly of his cooking supplies, but she brought her food processor and her set of dishes. He actually did not like her dishes and wanted his instead. But finally they had to compromise and buy a new set. She wanted her posters on the walls, but he preferred his. So they each got rid of their pictures and put up some new ones they got as gifts.

Each wanted to arrange the furniture in his or her way, but finally they had to make an agreement: Rosina would do the living room and Tommy the kitchen. As for painting the apartment, whoever would do the work could have it his or her way.

They seem to have come through this first big hurdle in their marriage. They have learned to consult each other even when they get their way. And they are both willing to compromise. The future bodes well for them.

Exercise 12   Using pronoun-antecedent agreement

Fill in the correct pronoun to match its antecedent in the following paragraphs. If you think "his or her" sounds awkward, try writing the sentence another way.

1. Everyone should bring _____ family to this gathering.

   The men will all try _____ hand at cooking the hot dogs

   and hamburgers. The women will organize the games for the chil-

   dren. Each child will win a prize of _____ choice.

2. Each person has _____ special talent. Some people find

   _____ immediately and act upon it. Others do not find

   so quickly and have to explore _____ options. Even if

they do not find _____ special talent right away, they

should continue to look around seriously.

3. Going to college helps many people find _____ future ca-

    reer. Required courses give them a general education while elec-

    tives allow them to explore different interests. Whoever wants to

    discover _____ potential should investigate the local

    college.

4. Paola wants to stop _____ coffee-drinking habit. She

    thinks _____ nerves have suffered from too much coffee.

    She also thinks _____ health might suffer. She doesn't

    want to give up _____ morning coffee, but she will stop

    having coffee during the rest of the day.

5. Our club held _____ annual rummage sale. Everybody

    had to contribute something from _____ home. Some-

    body donated _____ ski equipment. Another person do-

    nated a popular album from _____ record collection. We

    were pleased that _____ club made $600 for charity.

Sentence Problems III: Misplaced and Dangling Modifiers

Misplaced and dangling modifiers are high-class errors. They often
occur when you revise your sentences or when you want sentence variety.
These modifiers are usually phrases and words that do not modify the

nearest noun or pronoun. The modifier can be either misplaced (it belongs elsewhere in the sentence) or dangling (it has nothing to modify). Whether a faulty modifier is misplaced or dangling does not matter very much; you just need to fix it by rewriting the sentence.

If the phrase or word is misplaced, then simply putting it elsewhere in the sentence solves the problem. For example, writing "The woman got on the bus in the suit," is wrong; it seems as if the bus wore a suit. In this case, "in the suit" should modify only "woman" and must be placed next to that word: "The woman in the suit got on the bus." However, if you wrote "The woman got on the bus in the rain," the phrase "in the rain" does not modify "woman" only and is correct. You must look carefully at the different parts of sentences to make sure that the modifiers are in the right places.

A modifying word, such as "almost," "even," "not," "only," can also be misplaced and give the wrong meaning to a sentence. For example, "I almost won a hundred dollars" means I came close but won nothing. But compare it to "I won almost a hundred dollars," which means that I won $95. Although the context of the sentence usually clears up such misstatements, you should not rely on it. You should make every sentence correct.

A modifier that dangles simply means that it cannot be placed in another part of the sentence in order to make sense. The whole sentence usually needs rewriting. For example, in "Having worked all day, a movie would be relaxing," the modifier "Having worked all day" must modify the nearest noun, "movie," but it cannot because the movie did not work all day. You can write "Having worked all day, you should relax at the movies," or "After you have worked all day, a movie is relaxing," or "A movie is relaxing after you have worked all day." Notice that usually you can either give the dangling modifier a word to modify ("you") or turn it into a dependent clause ("After you have worked all day"). Notice also that dangling modifiers often come at the beginning of sentences, so be careful of those phrases you have used for sentence variety.

EXERCISES IN MISPLACED AND DANGLING MODIFIERS

Exercise 13   Finding modifiers

Underline the sentence with the misplaced or dangling modifier in each paragraph. Then rewrite the sentence so it makes sense.

1.   Don was upset that he had lost his wallet on the bus. He reported the loss to the police and then started to walk home because he had no money on him at all. Lying in the street, Don found his wallet. He grabbed it and pulled it open, but he was not surprised to find that all the money was missing.

2.   Not having any credit cards, he did not feel too bad. Don had ten dollars in the wallet only. He felt happy that he did not lose the photos of his family, but he was especially glad to have the wallet back. It was a graduation gift from his parents and meant a lot to him.

3.   Happy to have his wallet, the walk back home was not so long. Don decided to go through the park to enjoy the nice weather. He went along the river, over the bridge, and through the picnic grounds. He thought about how he could prevent losing his wallet again, but he could not think of anything.

4.   Near the river Don found a dollar lying in the path. At the picnic grounds he found some pennies, dimes, and quarters. Someone must have been doing cartwheels on the grass. When he got home, his cousin gave him the five dollars she owed him. He almost got ten dollars back.

5.   Don resolved to be more careful about his wallet with a sigh. He did not like to think about thieves trying to rob him. But he also

thought that maybe the wallet had fallen out of his pocket, like that cartwheeling person on the picnic grounds. He would no longer carry his wallet in his back pocket.

Exercise 14   Finding modifiers

Underline the sentence or sentences with misplaced or dangling modifiers in each paragraph. Then make the sentences correct.

1.   I read an exciting story called "The Monkey's Paw" in my English class. It deals with a family who gets a magic monkey's paw from an old friend that grants three wishes when it is rubbed. The mother, father, and son are all very excited about becoming rich and famous through these wishes.

2.   Making the first wish, a large sum of money comes to them the next day. A man knocks at the door and informs the parents that their son has been killed by machinery at the factory where he works. The factory is compensating them with $10,000. That is how their first wish came true.

3.   The parents do not want the money and want their son, feeling extremely sad that night. The father wants to throw away the monkey's paw only, but the mother grabs it and makes another wish. For this

second wish, she asks for her son back. Immediately after her wish, they hear a faint knock at the door.

4.   They are not sure whether they heard a person knocking or the wind blowing. But the mother rushes down the stairs to open the door, expecting her son. The father is horrified that a maimed, disfigured son will be there, so he grabs the monkey's paw from his wife's hand.

5.   Just as his wife reaches the door, he wishes that the son is not there. She opens the door and sees only a tree branch waving in the wind. The father does not see his son there to his great relief. So they learn that money cannot buy happiness and that greed can bring great sadness.

Sentence Problems IV: Is When, Is Where, Is Because

Many students fall into writing sentences using "is when," "is where," and "is because" incorrectly. The first two, along with "is why," "is how," and "is what," have their uses, and the last one is often used in speaking, but usually they should be avoided.

If you write "Dancing is why I live," "Dancing is how I exercise" or "Dancing is what I love," the use of "is why," "is how" and "is what" is correct although wordy, informal, and awkward. Write "I live for dancing," "I exercise by dancing" or "I love dancing" instead.

Only if you are speaking of time may you use "is when," as in "Monday is when class meets." This sentence could be turned around to read "When the class meets is Monday." Do not use it, for example, like this: "Happiness is when you eat ice cream." Since even the correct use is rather awkward, avoiding "is when" all the time is safest. The same applies to "is where." You may use it when location is concerned, as in "The beach is where we meet." This can be turned around to read "Where we meet is the beach." But avoiding this structure altogether is better.

Only when the sentence begins with "it," "here," "that" or "this" can you use "is why," "is how," "is what," "is when," and "is where": "It is why I live," "Here is what I want," "That is how it works," "This is when he helps," "This is where I sit." Try to have "it," "that," and "this" refer to something specific, and use this construction sparingly.

"Is because" is heard so often in sentences such as "The reason why I'm late is because . . . " that we think it is correct. Although we may speak as we wish, writing "is because" is incorrect. Avoid using it altogether. Write the sentence "I'm late because . . . " Notice that you will be omitting several useless words as well.

Although writing correctly is the major reason for not using these constructions, avoiding them also avoids wordiness. You may think that extra words help expand your essay to the required length, but you want quality words, not just empty fillers.

EXERCISES IN "IS WHEN," "IS WHERE," AND THE LIKE

Exercise 15   Finding "Is when . . ."

Underline any "is when," "is where," "is how," "is what," and "is because" sentence in the following paragraphs. Decide which ones need rewriting and rewrite them.

1.   Surfing is when Tony is happiest. The reason why he likes surfing is because he just loves the water and the waves. Surfing is how he gets his exercise too. That is what he really loves.

2.   Spring break is when Tony goes surfing. That time is when the weather is just warm enough. A wetsuit is what Tony does not like

about surfing. Still, if wearing a wetsuit is what he has to do to surf, he is willing.

3.   Watching Tony surf is why I go to the beach. The reason why I love to watch Tony is because he is so graceful and beautiful when he surfs. Surfing is how he can use his whole body in harmony with nature.

4.   Surfing well is where Tony and I differ. Balancing is what I just can't do. The reason for that is because I have no confidence. Also the big waves are what I'm scared of. Losing that fear is how I'll be a better surfer.

5.   Meanwhile, watching Tony is what I'll do until I learn how to do it. Practicing sometimes on his board is how I develop some skill. Also buying my own board is what I need to do. Then surfing on my own is where I'll improve.

Exercise 16   Correcting "Is when. . . "

Underline the sentences using "is why," "is when," "is where," "is how," "is what," and "is because." Then rewrite them if they are incorrect.

Mini-Vacations

I work and go to school full time, so I hardly ever have time to myself. During school vacations is when I sign up for extra hours at work. And short school holidays are where I catch up on school assignments. So taking an overnight mini-vacation is what I do to relax.

Since I can't really have a good vacation at home, I pack an overnight bag and go to the bus station and choose a town that is about two hours away. The reason why I go by bus is because the bus is cheaper than the train and I arrive in the middle of town. Then I find a motel room and settle in.

I get brochures at the motel and go out to see the sights. Maybe seeing the zoo or a museum is what I do. Sometimes a restored part of town makes a nice walk. I usually have lunch and also browse in the stores. In the evening I buy some snacks and watch television in the motel.

The next morning I lounge in bed as long as I like. Then I have a leisurely breakfast somewhere and come home. Taking these mini-vacations is why I don't miss the big vacations.

EXERCISES IN SENTENCE PROBLEMS

Exercise 17   Correcting sentence problems

Read this essay and do the following:

1. Underline and correct subject-verb agreement errors.
2. Underline and correct misplaced and dangling modifiers.
3. Underline and correct "is why," "is when," "is because" errors.

Do each type of error separately so you don't miss any.

Finding Biological Parents

Cass was adopted at birth, so he only knows his present parents. They have been wonderful for him, sending him to school, giving him a comfortable home, and loving him. But now that Cass is grown up, he wants to find his biological parents. Who they are is what he wants to know.

At first, Cass did not tell his parents that he was looking since they might be hurt. Not knowing what else to do, asking for help in the public library is where he started. The library suggested that he contact the Salvation Army, which have extensive records of this kind. But Cass almost had no clues to go by, so finally he discussed the matter with his parents.

His parents supported his wish and tried to help. Finding out their surname and city is what made the difference. Then Cass got the telephone book and wrote a letter to everyone by that name in that city. Everybody did not reply; he got five negative letters back only out of twenty. But after waiting another two months, a reply came from his biological parents.

Cass is going to visit them next month. He is taking along a large photo album his parents prepared for him. It shows how he looked at every age. He hopes this meeting will go well.

Exercise 18   Correcting sentence problems

Read this essay and do the following:

1. Underline and correct subject-verb agreement errors.
2. Underline and correct misplaced and dangling modifiers.
3. Underline and correct "is why," "is when," "is because" errors.

Do each type of error separately so you don't miss any.

A Red Party

For my daughter's tenth birthday, we are having an all-red party. The reason for this is because red is her favorite color. We made invitations on red paper and asked everyone only to wear red.

We are decorating the living room with red balloons and red crepe paper. A red tablecloth, along with red paper plates and cups, are what the table is covered with. We even found red plastic forks and spoons. We have big red pencils, bags of red jelly beans, and little red boxes to give as prizes.

Deciding to have lunch for everyone, red food has to be served. We are making red Jell-O with cherries in it. For a main course we are making spaghetti with tomato sauce and a radish salad on the side. For dessert we are making cake with red frosting and strawberry ice cream with red candles on it.

A new red dress, as well as red socks and a red hair ribbon, are what my daughter is wearing. That is what I gave her as a present. I'm only wearing a red sweater and nothing else red.

Chapter **8**

Teaching and Explaining

WRITING AND READING

Before Reading "Left and Right: The Bias of Language and Custom"

WORDS AND PHRASES TO LOOK FOR

bias: leaning or favoring one side as opposed to the other
permeate: spread throughout
left and right hemispheres of the brain: the two sides of the human brain
anarchy, anarchist: absence of government; a believer in it
connotations: meanings suggested by a word in addition to its dictionary meaning
ominous: threatening, being a bad sign of something
sinister: evil, wicked
dexterity: skill with mind and especially hands
adroitness: skill and cleverness, especially with the mind
gauche: socially awkward and incapable
derogatory: belittling, negative
cognate: similar or same as another word
derive: come from, trace from
rectitude: correctness in morals and honesty
conversely: on the contrary, in opposition
autonomy: self-government, independence
fascist: governed by dictatorship

nonverbal message: body language, communication without words

synonyms: words with same or similar meanings in same language

malicious: spiteful, mean, evil

indispensable: absolutely necessary

buttonholed: keeping someone in order to talk

QUESTIONS TO ANSWER AS YOU READ

1. What are some words connected with the right hand? With the left hand?
2. In French and English, how have the words *right* and *left* been defined?
3. What are some examples given by Edwards of how *right* and *left* have affected our political and social thinking?
4. Why do some parents force their children to use their right hands? What are the advantages?
5. In what ways have left-handers been accommodated in your world? Should they be?

Left and Right: The Bias of Language and Custom

Words and phrases concerning concepts of left and right permeate our language and thinking. The right hand (meaning also the left hemisphere of the brain) is strongly connected with what is good, just, moral, proper. The left hand (therefore the right hemisphere) is strongly linked with concepts of anarchy and feelings that are out of conscious control—somehow bad, immoral, dangerous.

Until very recently, the ancient bias against the left hand/right hemisphere sometimes even led parents and teachers of left-handed children to try to force the children to use their right hands for writing, eating, and so on—a practice that often caused problems lasting into adulthood.

Throughout human history, terms with connotations of *good* for the right-hand/left hemisphere and connotations of *bad* for the left-hand/right hemisphere appear in most languages around the world. The Latin word for left is *sinister*, meaning "bad," "ominous," "sinister." The Latin word for right is *dexter* from which comes our word "dexterity," meaning "skill" or "adroitness."

The French word for "left"—remember that the left hand is connected to the right hemisphere—is *gauche,* meaning "awkward" from which comes our word "gawky." The French word for right is *droit,* meaning "good," "just," or "proper."

In English, "left" comes from the Anglo-Saxon *lyft,* meaning "weak" or "worthless." The left hand of most right-handed people is in fact weaker than the right, but the original word also implied lack of moral strength. The derogatory meaning of "left" may reflect a prejudice of the right-handed majority against a minority of people who were different, that is, left-handed. Reinforcing this bias, the Anglo-Saxon word for "right," *reht* (or *riht*) meant "straight" or "just." From *reht* and its Latin cognate *rectus* we derived our words "correct" and "rectitude."

These ideas also affect our political thinking. The political right, for instance, admires national power, is conservative, resists change. The political left, conversely, admires individual autonomy and promotes change, even radical change. At their extremes, the political right is fascist, the political left is anarchist.

In the context of cultural customs, the place of honor at a formal dinner is on the host's right-hand side. The groom stands on the right in the marriage ceremony, the bride on the left—a nonverbal message of the relative status of the two participants. We shake hands with our right hands; it seems somehow wrong to shake hands with our left hands.

Under "left handed," the dictionary lists as synonyms "clumsy," "awkward," "insincere," "malicious." Synonyms for "right handed," however, are "correct," "indispensable," and "reliable." Now, it's important to remember that these terms were all made up, when languages began, by some persons' left hemispheres—the left brain calling the right bad names! And the right brain—labeled, pinpointed, and buttonholed—was without a language of its own to defend itself.

Betty Edwards,
Drawing on the Right Side of the Brain

Writing to Teach Clearly

Most people think teaching should be left to teachers, who earn their living at it. But all of us have to teach others a variety of skills and lessons. Knowing how to do it effectively will save time and energy and also will result in great satisfaction for both the teacher and the student.

First, you should consider the *purpose* of the lesson. Will you tell everything the student needs to know and expect mastery of the skill? Or will you teach some basics and expand on the information later as the student improves? For example, if you teach someone how to use an air conditioner or a heater, you had better be thorough. But if you are teaching someone to paint with oils, you do not need to point out all the techniques immediately. Of course, sometimes the skill is just too complicated to teach all at once, so you need to decide the purpose. Also, why teach this skill: for the fun of it, for basic knowledge, for safety?

Next, you need to understand your *audience*. Are you writing for your peers? They already know a lot, so you can assume some knowledge on their part. Are you writing for children? You do not want to condescend to them, but you need to realize they do not know very much about your lesson. Are you writing for your boss or your professor? They may know as much or more than you, so you must assume knowledge on their part. Then also consider whether or not your audience wants to learn what you are teaching. If you think they do, you can assume they want to share and collaborate with you. If you think they do not want to learn but have to, you should make your lesson sound important, necessary, or fun to learn.

Finally, related to audience, you need to decide on your *diction*—that is, the words you choose to express yourself. You want simple words and short sentences for children; you probably will not use many pronouns and no or few technical terms. For your peers you want to sound intelligent and knowledgeable and give them confidence in your ability to teach them something. You should use the correct technical terms, but you should define most of them. For your boss or professor, you want especially to sound knowledgeable and well educated. Do not start using thesaurus words you never heard of, but do try to find the exact words you need. Use whichever technical terms are necessary and only define the really unusual ones.

Giving some thought and planning to your purpose, audience, and diction will make your lesson clear and effective.

EXERCISES IN TEACHING CLEARLY

Exercise 1   Purpose, audience, and terms

Read the following paragraphs and then write the **purpose,** the **audience,** and the **technical terms.**

1.   Students learn to analyze and discuss stylistic elements, such as tone, or to replicate organizational strategies found in, for example, a research report. While exercises in style related to the annotated bibliography help students to emulate other writers, exercises drawn from models in a common reader lead them to experiment with their emerging textual authority to transform text and to create it. (Felicia Mitchell, "Balancing Individual Projects and Collaborative Learning in an Advanced Writing Class")

Purpose:

Audience:

Technical terms (if any):

2.   As I stretched my legs on my shelf bed, I felt a cold, rough object against my toes. I threw back the blanket and saw a red snake coiled up. It was as surprised as I was and slithered off outside. After that, we always pounded our beds with a long stick before jumping in. Then I woke up one night feeling a sharp pain on my nose and found myself staring at two black, beady eyes. I screamed. Father came running to see what was wrong. A big rat about the size of a baby kitten had tried to eat my nose. (Mary Paik Lee, *Quiet Odyssey: A Pioneer Korean Woman in America*)

Purpose:

Audience:

Technical Terms (if any):

3.   Thurgood Marshall had as great an impact on the history and deliberations of the United States Supreme Court as anyone who has ever lived. That is a statement that could be made with almost equal confidence even if he had never joined the Court. Tall (six feet two), charming (he was a riotously funny story-teller), and physically courageous (his life was often in danger as he travelled thousands of miles a year throughout the hostile South), the young Marshall was, as a legal strategist, farseeing to the point of genius. (Hendrik Hertzberg, *The New Yorker*)

Purpose:

Audience:

Technical terms (if any):

4.   The report also makes other recommendations, two of which are embodied in the president's new national service plan. In addition to allowing students loan forgiveness in exchange for service and an income-contingent repayment plan, the report recommends preserving and fully funding the Pell grant program and providing tax-related incentives to encourage Americans to save for college. (*On Campus*)

Purpose:

Audience:

Technical terms (if any):

5.   Afar off upon a large level land, a summer sun was shining
bright. Here and there over the rolling green were tall bunches of
coarse gray weeds. Iktomi in his fringed buckskins walked alone
across the prairie with a black bare head glossy in the sunlight. He
walked through the grass without following any well-worn footpath.
(Zitkala-Sa, *Old Indian Legends*)

Purpose:

Audience:

Technical terms (if any):

Exercise 2   Purpose, audience, and language

Read the following short essay and answer questions at the end
about the **purpose, audience,** and **language.**

Counting with Your Fingers

If you like counting with your fingers, be cautious as you travel
abroad because you might just add up to total confusion. In Germany,

for example, to signal "one" a person uses the upright thumb instead of the forefinger. Therefore, in a German *gasthaus* beer garden, to order "one beer" you would flash the "Thumbs-Up" gesture. Many Westerners use the forefinger to signal "one," more or less ignoring the thumb. But, do that in Germany—casually hold up the forefinger and forget the thumb—and it could be seen as meaning "two," with the result that you'd be drinking two beers instead of one.

In Japan, they use the fingers to count visually just as most cultures do. However, in Japan counting begins with the index finger (not the thumb) to designate "one"; then the index and middle fingers combined equal "two"; the combination of index, middle and ring fingers is "three," and adding the little finger equals "four." Then the Japanese show the upright thumb alone to mean "five." So if you order "One beer" with your thumb in Japan you may well receive five beers. (Roger E. Axtell, *Gestures: The Do's and Taboos of Body Language Around the World*)

Purpose:

Audience:

Are there any unclear words?

What made this clear or not clear to you?

Exercise 3   Purpose, audience, and language

Read the following short essay and respond below.

Noradrenergic System

The *locus ceruleus* [Latin, blue place], which lies in the caudal midbrain and upper pons at the lateral margin of the periaqueductal gray matter, is made up of noradrenergic neurons that have extensive axonal connections with the entire forebrain. At least five noradrenergic tracts, including the central tegmental tract, run rostrally from the locus ceruleus to the diencephalon and telencephalon; among their terminations are the hippocampus and cerebral cortex. Fibers from this nucleus also run through the superior cerebellar peduncle to reach the cerebellar cortex. Recent physiological studies by Roger Nicoll and his colleagues at the University of California in San Francisco have demonstrated that the axons of these neurons mediate an excitatory modulation in the regions where they terminate. This excitatory modulation is due to the closure of a K+ channel by means of cyclic AMP-dependent protein phosphorylation. (James P. Kelly, "Cranial Nerve Nuclei, the Reticular Formation, and Biogenic Amine-Containing Neurons.")

Purpose:

Audience:

Technical terms (some of them):

Was this short essay clear? If so, why? If not, why not?

Exercise 4   Writing for an audience

You have been hired to write responses to people inquiring about visiting your town, which wants to encourage tourism for families. The town has rolling hills for walking, a fine arts museum, a natural history museum, shops and eating places in a restored old section, and a theater doing melodramas. Weather, accommodations, safety, and traffic may also be mentioned. Consider purpose, audience, and diction as you write.

1. Write a paragraph aimed at parents with small children.

2. Write a paragraph aimed at ten- to twelve-year-olds.

3. Write a paragraph aimed at a young couple.

Giving Logical Explanations

Teaching and explaining need especially clear, logical, and well-planned writing. There are several ways to do this.

If your topic requires a step-by-step process, chronological order makes logical sense. Simply explain each step as it comes. Do not backtrack; do not have any step out of time order. Explanations or theories should come before the step-by-step process begins. If you need to explain theory about one part, do it at that step; don't go back to it after completing other steps. For example, if you are giving instructions about baking a cake, you should start with gathering the equipment, then proceed step by step through mixing the different parts, putting the parts together, preparing and pouring the batter, and baking it.

If your topic has different aspects that may be done in any order or all at the same time, you still need to have a logical sequence. You could begin with the least important part and go to the most important part. If the parts all seem equally important, then go from the one that needs the shortest explanation to the one that needs the longest. If that doesn't seem right, consider going from the least frequent aspect to the most frequent one or from the easiest to the hardest. In any case, have some logical organization to the different parts. For example, if you are giving instructions about dog care, you should mention walking, bathing, and feeding the dog. The order might be bathing, feeding, and walking to go from the least frequent to the most frequent. You could also go from the easiest to the hardest task, probably feeding, walking, then bathing; or from the hardest to the easiest, probably bathing, walking, then feeding. You must decide which organization makes the most sense for your topic.

For all the methods, use transitional expressions from one paragraph to the next and also within paragraphs. You want to be sure that each step is followed clearly by the next step. You don't have to use the mechanical first, second, third, fourth sequence; try first, next, then, after that. Also you don't have to start each paragraph with one of the transitional words. Writing "after you have . . ., then . . ." will break up the mechanical beginnings.

Giving logical explanations needs some advance planning, but once the organization is established, writing the essay should not take much time.

EXERCISES IN GIVING LOGICAL EXPLANATIONS

Exercise 5   Steps in order

Decide the order of these steps by numbering these sentences from the first to the last.

1. Studying for an exam
   __ Pay particular attention to the important parts underlined in your notes.
   __ Read the textbook chapter.
   __ Gather together your textbook, notes, and handouts.
   __ Make sure you know what material is covered in the exam.
   __ Read over your notes and underline important parts.

2. Getting ready to hit a baseball
   __ Turn your head toward the pitcher.
   __ Stand with your feet about shoulder-width apart.
   __ Grip the bat with both hands and hold it over your shoulder.
   __ Bend at the waist and knees to a comfortable position.
   __ Stand between one and two feet from the plate.

3. Cooking pasta
   __ Measure out the amount of dried pasta you need.
   __ Add the pasta all at once to the boiling water.
   __ Add a little salt and a teaspoon of oil to the water.
   __ Bring a large pot of water to a boil.
   __ Carefully remove and taste one strand to test for doneness.
   __ Cook for about ten minutes.

4. Eating a mango

___ Starting at the stem end, peel the mango with your fingers as you would a banana.

___ Pick your teeth carefully afterwards.

___ Stand over a sink so you can drip without fear.

___ As you take bites, be careful of the large, flat, hairy seed in the middle.

___ Eat the mango from the top to the bottom.

___ Also wash your hands.

5. Becoming familiar with a textbook

___ Open to a random chapter.

___ Look at the cover, spine, and back; read them.

___ Read the table of contents.

___ Look for an index, a glossary, an answer key, and other helpful sections of the textbook.

___ Read the title page.

___ See the number and average length of chapters.

___ See if there are graphs, pictures, and charts to help you.

___ Look at the subheadings in the chapter.

Exercise 6   Step-by-step process

Read the following short essay. Then make a list of the step-by-step process of bathing a cat. If anything in the essay seems out of place, correct it on your list. If anything seems left out, add it to your list. Use fewer or more than five steps if you want.

Bathing a Cat

Bathing a cat can be traumatic unless it has been accustomed to this from an early age. If possible get a helper to hold and calm the cat while you wash it. Place a rubber mat in the bottom of the basin or bowl to give the cat a good footing, and fill it to a depth of about 10 cm (4 in.) with warm water. (Test with an elbow, as for a baby.)

Holding the cat gently but firmly, wet the head first, then the rest of the body. Then using a safe cat or baby shampoo, work up a lather, being extremely careful not to get soap in the eyes or ears. (Some experts suggest plugging the ears with absorbent cotton but this may alarm the cat.) Thoroughly rinse the cat, using a spray if possible, then wrap it in a towel. Dry it very carefully with this, or with a hair-dryer set to 'warm' and held at a safe distance. Avoid drafts until the cat is dry. (Michael Wright and Sally Walters, *The Book of the Cat*)

1.

2.

3.

4.

5.

Exercise 7   Writing directions

Here are Rosina and Tommy's directions to get from their college to their home. Cross out the unnecessary parts. Add parts you think are necessary. You may make up the information.

Leave by the south exit and turn on to Apple Road. Be careful of traffic coming both ways and obey the stop lights. Notice the fruit store on the right and then the large supermarket on the left after you go a few blocks. Then turn left on to the beautiful and scenic (ha ha) Peach Blossom Road. Go about fifteen minutes until you reach Orange Tree Lane. A little farther up Peach Blossom Road is Rosina's former elementary school, definitely worth a detour. Orange Tree Lane has no orange trees, but it will have a little blue house, number 27. You can't miss it. The whole trip should take about half an hour. Don't get lost! But call if you do.

Now write directions for getting from your college to your home. Write for walking, car, or public transportation.

Exercise 8   Directions in order

Write step-by-step directions for the following activities. Use easy to hard, least frequent to most frequent, or another order that makes sense, but do not use chronological order.

1. Joining a school club or civic organization.

2. Staying in college.

3. Cleaning a house or a room.

Suggestions for Essay Topics

Using one of the prewriting techniques—freewriting, brainstorming, or clustering—write on one of these topics.

1. Write an essay explaining Edwards's purpose and how she supports her purpose through her major points and her organization.
2. Write an essay that further supports Edwards's essay by discussing more areas and examples of discrimination against left-handers.
3. Write an essay about how you have been discriminated against. Consider race, religion, nationality, sex, weight, height, age, poverty, handicap, job, or another area that has affected you.
4. Write an essay justifying the bias against left-handers; that is, give the right-hand majority's point of view. Explain your reasoning carefully and clearly.
5. Write an essay explaining how we discriminate against another "difference" and give some possible solutions for change.

Once you have written a rough draft of your essay, see if it has **body paragraphs** with **topic sentences;** an **introduction** and a **conclusion; descriptions, examples and details;** a **consistent voice** and **point of view; sentence variety;** and **clear explanations.**

GRAMMAR

Using Commas I: Independent and Dependent Clauses

Commas are needed in independent clauses and dependent clauses. A comma and a coordinating conjunction (for, and, nor, but, or, yet, so) join two independent clauses. A comma comes after a dependent clause at the beginning of a sentence. Also dependent clauses in the middle of a sentence have commas before and after the dependent clause.

As discussed in Chapter 5, **compound sentences** that have a coordinating conjunction (for, and, nor, but, or, yet, so) should have a comma before the coordinating conjunction: Kim studied English, **and** Larry studied math. Unless the sentence is very short, a comma is always necessary.

For dependent clauses at the beginning of the sentence, a comma is usually necessary: "While Kim studied English, Larry studied math." If the sentence were reversed, however, with the dependent clause at the end of the sentence, no comma is needed: "Larry studied math while Kim studied English." This order is considered the normal sequence and has no pause between the clauses.

However, if the dependent clause at the beginning of a sentence is the subject of the sentence, then no comma is needed: "**That Larry needs to study** goes without saying;" "**What he needs** is discipline." The same follows for dependent clauses that are the objects of sentences: "She wants **what everyone wants.**" "Kim knows **that she will pass English.**" Knowing which is which can be tricky, but if the sentence makes sense without the dependent clause, then commas are needed; if they don't make sense, then commas are not needed.

Finally, a dependent clause in the middle of a sentence takes commas before and after it if the dependent clause contains added, but not crucial, information. For example, in the sentence, "My brother, who lives in Bombay, is coming to visit," "who lives in Bombay" could be omitted and the sentence, "My brother is coming to visit," would have basically the same meaning. If the information in the dependent clause is crucial to the meaning, no commas are needed: "People who vote are doing their duty." If "who vote" (the dependent clause) is omitted, the sentence would have entirely the wrong meaning. It is important to remember that the dependent clause in the middle of a sentence must have either both commas or no commas, not just one of them.

EXERCISES IN COMMAS I: INDEPENDENT AND DEPENDENT CLAUSES

Exercise 9   Identifying commas

Identify the commas in the following sentences by numbering them.

1. After a dependent clause.
2. Around a dependent clause.
3. Before a coordinating conjunction in a compound sentence.

a. __ Children learn from the outside world, so they need to be exposed to different experiences.

b. __ If they experience varied situations, they learn from each of them.

c. __ Parents should talk often to their children, so the children will get used to the sounds of voices.

d. __ Although babies cannot understand words, they learn early to recognize certain voices.

e. __ Every night parents should read bedtime stories, which prepare a child for reading, and tuck the child in bed.

f. __ Daily rituals give the child a sense of security, but they do not need to be followed slavishly.

g. __ Children need some freedom of choice in their activities, for they learn through trial and error.

h. __ They need to get dirty sometimes, and they should be allowed to make a mess once in a while.

i. __ Children should be kept away from danger, but they should be allowed to explore their world.

j. __ They should have simple toys, which do not have to be expensive.

k. __ Playing with objects around the house rather than toys develops imagination, which will enhance learning.

l. __ Children love a "choo-choo" made of chairs or cardboard boxes, and they will spend hours playing with it.

m.__ Even though they might make a mess, children also love to play with plastic cups and water at the kitchen sink.

n. __ Children need to develop a sense of security, so they need to have limits set for them.

o. __ They need to feel independent, yet they want to feel loved.

Exercise 10   Identifying commas

Read the following paragraphs and circle commas that are examples of

1. A comma after a dependent clause.

2. Commas around a dependent clause.

3. A comma before a coordinating conjunction in a compound sentence.

Blessed are the multicultural societies, for they shall inherit the holidays. Malaysia, with its rich blend of races and religions, is by that definition probably the most blessed country in the world. It has 40 official days off, including state holidays. So says the latest *World Holiday and Time Guide.* Malaysians are truly eclectic. They observe Hari Raya Puasa, Lunar New Year, Deepavali, and Christmas. Colonial Hongkong is blessed too since it celebrates both Chinese holidays and those grafted on by the British. The Chinese may not care much about the royal family, but they don't mind having a barbecue on the Queen's birthday. (*Asiaweek*)

If dandelions were rare and fragile, people would knock themselves out to pay $14.95 a plant, raise them by hand in greenhouses, and form dandelion societies and all that. But they are everywhere and don't need us and kind of do what they please. So we call them "weeds," and murder them at every opportunity. Well, I say they are *flowers,* by God, and pretty damn fine flowers at that. And I am *honored* to have them in my yard, where I want them. Besides, in addition to every other good thing about them, they are magic. When the flower turns to seed, you can blow them off the stem, and if you blow just right and all those little helicopters fly away, you get your wish. Magic. Or if you are a lover, they twine nicely into a wreath for your friend's hair. (Robert Fulghum, *All I Really Need to Know I Learned in Kindergarten*)

A school diploma is virtually useless on the job market, and so is a college degree. But school prepares for college, which prepares for postgraduate school, which prepares for entry into well-paid professions. In 1981 the average high-school graduate made $18,138, whereas the average for those with five or more years of college was $32,887. Lifetime earnings for the high-school graduates averaged $845,000, compared with $1,503,000 for five-year collegians. Yet an underlying flaw vitiates the comparison, for college draws people of higher intelligence and those from richer families. Their lifelong earnings largely reflect these particular factors. (Tertius Chandler, "Education—Less of It!")

Exercise 11   Using clauses and commas

Fill in an appropriate clause as indicated and make sure you have put commas in the right places.

Reading

Although Mario _____ he doesn't

have much time for reading. He works all day as a receptionist.

When he _____ he reads a little,

but he _____. In the evening, he

_____ and he _____.

Maybe when he _____ he will

_____.

His boss, Ms. Singh, says he _____.

She says in the past he _____ but

now he _____. Although he

_____ maybe this _____.

In the future, Mario _____ yet he

_____.

Using Commas II: Phrases and Words

Some phrases and words at the beginning, middle, and end of sentences, need commas, but vary. Although a comma is not always used in short sentences, usually it is needed in one of the following categories:

1. Dependent phrases that add information that is not crucial to the meaning (after, although, because of, since, when, while, including, such as, etc.)
2. Transitional phrases and words (however, of course, on the other hand, first, finally, etc.)
3. Phrases that show a reversal (not he, excluding her, only me, unlike them, etc.)
4. Phrases and words that are out of their normal order (Very tired, Kim went to sleep.)
5. Exclamations (well, oh, no, yes, oh no, no way, etc.)
6. Speaking to someone (Kim, everyone, students, etc.)

At the beginning of sentences, many short phrases and words need commas after them:

1. **Because of Larry,** Kim studied math. (Dependent phrase)
2. **Of course,** Larry already knew English. (Transitional phrase)
3. **Unlike Kim,** Larry had not studied for the exam. (Reversal)

4. **Anxious,** Larry gathered his notes. (Out of normal order)
5. **Uh oh,** I didn't study enough. (Exclamation)
6. **Students,** listen to me. (Speaking to someone)

In the middle of sentences, these same types of phrases and words need to be set off by commas:

1. Kim, **because of Larry,** studied English. (Dependent phrase)
2. Kim liked, **on the other hand,** studying math. (Transitional phrase)
3. Everyone, **except for Larry,** knew about the exam. (Reversal)
4. Larry, **very anxious,** gathered his notes. (Out of normal order)
5. Not Larry, **no,** he didn't like math at all. (Exclamation)
6. Study hard, **everyone,** and pass the exam. (Speaking to someone)

Also, at the end of a sentence, these same types of phrases and words need a comma before them:

1. Kim studied English, **though tired.** (Dependent phrase)
2. Kim already knew math, **however.** (Transitional word)
3. Larry is not studying English, **only math.** (Reversal)
4. Larry gathered his notes, **anxious to start.** (Out of normal order)
5. Larry did not like math at all, **no way.** (Exclamation)
6. Listen to me, **Kim.** (Speaking to someone)

EXERCISES IN COMMAS II: PHRASES AND WORDS

Exercise 12   Identifying commas

Circle the commas and number them as follows:

1. Phrase or word that adds noncrucial information.

2. Transition phrase or word.

3. Reversal phrase or word.

4. Phrase or word out of normal order.

5. Exclamation.

6. Word spoken to a person or people.

You will notice that some commas fall into two or more areas. Pick one or put in both of them.

a. __ Larry, will you please clean your room?

b. __ I would like it done today, not next week.

c. __ If not today, then when will you do it?

d. __ Well, please clean it as soon as possible because it is a mess.

e. __ Doing it today, however, will gain you my undying gratitude.

f. __ If, on the other hand, you do it immediately, I'll help you do it.

g. __ You know me, Larry, I love cleaning house.

h. __ Maybe I can get a housekeeping job, including doing windows.

i. __ But coming home, tired from cleaning three houses, I may regret my career choice.

j. __ It will be for the experience, not the money.

k. __ Meanwhile, let's clean up your room right now.

l. __ For two months, you have not even made your bed.

m. __ Change the sheets, including the pillowcases, along with sweeping under the bed.

n. __ Nobody else should do this job, only you.

o. __ Good luck, I'll check on the room in a couple of hours.

Exercise 13 Identifying commas

Circle the commas and number above them as follows:

1. Phrase or word giving added information.
2. Transition phrase or word.
3. Reversal phrase or word.
4. Phrase or word out of normal order.
5. Exclamation.
6. Word spoken to a person or people.

Some of them fall into two or more areas; choose one or write both numbers.

What is painful varies from person to person. Most people, for example, find it easy to recall positive memories, harder to bring back painful ones. For depressed people, though, positive memories come to mind less easily than negative ones. The self-system is, in part, a topographical chart of these painful areas. Where self-esteem is low, where the self-system feels vulnerable, such points of pain are strong. Where these pain nodes lie, I propose, lacunas perform their protective duty, guarding the self-system from anxiety. (Daniel Goleman, *Vital Lies, Simple Truths: The Psychology of Self-Deception*)

I went into his room five mornings ago, same as always. I tried to feed him a little rice porridge, same as always. He was not eating very much at the end. Every day I had to fight to open his mouth and pour something down his throat. Really, he was more trouble than a baby, wouldn't eat, always soiling his bed. That morning I was so exasperated I shouted, "Goddess of Mercy, open his mouth!" Suddenly, he was staring at me with clear eyes. I thought, Huh? Can he hear me? I said to him, "Eat a little, eat, eat." And he looked at me and said, "Then give me something proper to eat." (Amy Tan, *The Kitchen God's Wife*)

We like to talk to each other so we keep finding new substitutes for real conversation. These days sports have driven out the weather as the number-1 topic when we don't want to think much about what we're saying. "Hey, how about those Dodgers!" has temporarily replaced "Is it cold enough for you?"

A real conversation takes too long for most of us. We greet each other on the street, in an elevator or pushing a shopping cart. This is no time to talk politics, the economy or whether we're spending too much on arms.

There are several other reasons why conversation may be a dying art. First, good talk takes time and we aren't willing to spend it on something that seems like doing nothing. Second, the best conversations are between two people, not among three, four or ten. The best conversations are those in which the participants can't wait to say what they have to say and, if there are more than two conversationalists, they don't get a turn often enough. (Andy Rooney, "Talk, Talk, Talk")

Exercise 14   Using commas

Use the following words in a short paragraph. Be sure also to put in the correct commas.

1. Dependent phrases and words: *because of, including, since*
    Transitions: *however, nevertheless, on the other hand*
    Reversals: *excluding, except for, not counting*

2. Speaking to someone: (*any name*)
    Exclamations: *no, well, (make up your own)*
    Out of normal order: *repeatedly, exhausted*

3. Dependent phrase or word: *after, such as, though*
    Transition words: *in addition to, first, second, of course*

Using Commas III: Series, Titles, Addresses, Dates, Misunderstandings

The comma is certainly our most common piece of punctuation. In addition to being used in compound sentences and dependent clauses, and with phrases and words, commas also have other uses.

Clauses, phrases, and words in a **series** (that is, with three or more items in a row) should always be separated by commas in sentences. For example, the three independent clauses in a series in this sentence have commas between each part: Kim studied her notes, Larry reread the chapters, and Ming wrote down questions. The same follows for dependent clauses: Before she sat down, after she had eaten a snack, and when she felt comfortable, Kim started studying. The three phrases in a series in this sentence also have commas between each part: Kim studied her notes by writing down major topics, underlining main points, and memorizing important definitions. The three words in a series in this sentence also have commas between each part: Larry reread his notes, chapters, and questions; Larry gathered together his disorganized, scribbled, incomplete notes.

A series of only two adjectives also needs a comma: the big, bad wolf; the long, difficult exam. Both the adjectives describe the noun. However, in "the long math exam," no comma belongs between "long" and "math" even though both adjectives describe the noun. To decide on the comma, add "and" between the two adjectives. If the "and" makes sense, then a comma may replace the "and." If an "and" does not work, no comma is necessary. So "the long and difficult exam" works, but "the long and math exam" does not work. In a different way, "the light green car" does not need commas because "light" describes "green," not "car," but the same "and" test may be applied.

Commas are also used around **titles** at the ends of names, in **addresses,** and in **dates** written the American way: Sally Lopez, M.D., lives at 12 Main Street, New Town, Any State 34567; she was born on April 18, 1960, in West Town, North State. Juan Smith, Jr., lived at 1234 K Street, SE, Washington, D.C. He was born on 11 May 1965 in Jamaica. Notice the two methods of writing dates. No commas are needed if just the month and year are mentioned: She graduated in June 1987 with a B.A.

Finally, sometimes the reason for a comma is simply to avoid **misunderstandings.** For example, a comma makes these sentences clear: "Kim, look at the math text;" "Students, should studying come first?" "After washing, Larry went to bed." If the commas were omitted, these sentences would seem ungrammatical or need rereading to understand.

**EXERCISES IN COMMAS III: SERIES, TITLES,
ADDRESSES, DATES, MISUNDERSTANDINGS**

Exercise 15   Identifying commas

In the following short paragraphs, underline the series of words,
the titles at the ends of names, the addresses with commas, and the dates
with commas.

1.   My readers can also check the legitimacy of fund-raising groups
        by writing to the Philanthropic Advisory Service, Council of Better
        Business Bureaus, 4200 Wilson Blvd., Suite 800, Arlington, Va. 22203-
        1804 or the National Charities Information Bureau, 19 Union Sq. W.,
        Department 250, New York, N.Y. 10003-3335. Be sure to enclose a
        self-addressed, stamped envelope. (Ann Landers)

2.   Dr. Martin Luther King, Jr., spent the evening of April 3, 1968, in
        Memphis, Tennessee, where he gave a speech that reflected his dis-
        couragement with the slow progress of his pacifist movement. He
        seemed somewhat disheartened, but not defeated. The very next day,
        April 4, 1968, as he stepped from his hotel room, he was killed by a
        single bullet.

3.   The shortest interval that has elapsed between the death of a
        saint and his canonization was in the case of St. Anthony of Padua,
        Italy, who died on June 13, 1231, and was canonized 352 days later on
        May 30, 1232. The other extreme is represented by Pope St. Leo III,
        who died on June 12, 816, and was made a saint in 1673—857 years
        later. (Norris McWhirter, ed., *Guinness Book of World Records*)

Exercise 16   Identifying commas

In the following paragraphs, underline the series of words, the titles
at the ends of names, the addresses with commas, and the dates with
commas.

1.   The National Museum of African Art, 950 Independence Ave. SW (357-4600, TTY 357-4814), collects, catalogs, polishes, and shows off artifacts from Sub–Saharan Africa. Thoughtful exhibitions stress the insufficiency of names for an art whose artists, countries, and time periods most often cannot be known. Art objects include masks, textiles, ceremonial figures, and fascinating musical instruments, like a harp partly made of pangolin scales. A permanent display touts sophisticated bronze works from the Kingdom of Benin, in modern-day Nigeria. Temporary shows fluctuate between art-for-art's-sake ("Icons") and cultural-theoretical displays ("Africa Illustrated," Westerners' sketches of Africa). (Stephen Burt, ed., *Let's Go: The Budget Guide to Washington, D.C.*)

2.   People bring a variety of problems to psychotherapy. Some suffer from disabling anxiety attacks or headaches, some from compulsive habits such as excessive drinking, overeating, or refusing food altogether, some from feelings of worthlessness or depression, some from inability to have intimate relationships. Others do not feel particularly troubled but feel that life is empty and unsatisfying. Psychotherapy's immediate concern is helping people overcome these problems and the unhappiness they cause, but psychotherapy is also aware that these problems have a common base. In each condition the person does not feel free to be him- or herself and to live productively because of constriction from within. While this lack of freedom manifests itself differently in different people, it is always a fundamental issue for psychotherapy. (Otto Ehrenberg, Ph.D., and Miriam Ehrenberg, Ph.D., *The Psychotherapy Maze*)

3.   *A Year Off*, published by CRAC Publications, Hobsons Press (Cambridge) Ltd., Bateman Street, Cambridge CB2 1LZ (tel: (0223) 354551) provides information about voluntary service, work camps and summer projects, paid work, *au pair* work, study courses, scholarships and travel, adventure, and expeditions. Aimed at people with time to spare between school and higher education, it discusses the pros and cons of using that year in this special way, giving the view of

both students and career experts. (Melissa Shales, ed., *The Traveler's Handbook*)

Exercise 17   Using commas

Fill in the appropriate information with commas wherever necessary.

My Life

I was born on _____ in

_____. My _____

and _____ were born on

_____ and _____.

We lived at _____ in

_____. We moved to

_____ on _____.

Now I live at _____ in

_____ and have lived here since

_____. Living with me are my

_____ my _____

and my _____. We like living here, but

we would like to move to _____. Maybe

someday we will make the move.

Chapter 9

Argumentation

WRITING AND READING

Before Reading "The Case Against Bilingualism"

WORDS AND PHRASES TO LOOK FOR

bilingualism: knowing two languages
diversity: variety, difference
our common language: the language we all speak, English
social glue: what keeps the society together
multicultural: several cultural, or national, groups
designate: appoint, specify, indicate
xenophobic: hating or fearing foreigners
contend: argue, assert, compete
color blind: not judging people by color, not seeing color
linguistically: having to do with language
cacophony: harsh, clashing sound
nurture: raise and promote
confining: keeping within limits, imprisoning
self-perpetuating: making itself continue
linguistic ghettos: groups restricted by language
proficiency: great competence or skill
to assimilate: to absorb or incorporate into
multilingual: knowing three or more languages

1. According to Sundberg, what holds our country together? Who agrees with her?
2. According to Sundberg, what is wrong with bilingualism?
3. What are some reasons for a common language?
4. What are some reasons for bilingual education?
5. Which side do you agree with? Why?

The Case Against Bilingualism

The United States is a country of great diversity, and English, our common language, is the social glue that holds this multicultural country together, making all of us, regardless of national origin, Americans.

For that reason laws proposed in Congress and in some of the states that would designate English as the official language of the United States should not be regarded as xenophobic or anti-immigrant, or even racist as some critics recklessly contend. Governor Richard Lamm of Colorado has a good answer to these charges. He says, "We should be color-blind but not linguistically deaf. We should be a rainbow but not a cacophony. We should welcome different people but not adopt different languages" (quoted in "English Spoken Here," *Time* 25 Aug. 1986:27).

John Hughes, Pulitzer Prize-winning journalist, writing in the *Christian Science Monitor*, makes a related point:

> English is the common tongue of the majority of Americans. It might have been Dutch or Italian or some other European language. But it is English, and it is important that, whatever other languages they nurture, Americans command the primary language that binds them together ("For US, It's English," 28 June 1985:27).

Bilingualism, which became official US policy with the passage of the Bilingual Education Act in 1968, has made it harder for immigrants to enter the mainstream of American life by allowing them to avoid learning English, thus confining many of them to self-perpetuating linguistic ghettos. Since that act was passed, I have seen no statistics that show that either proficiency in English or the quality of education in the United States has improved. On the contrary, the National

Advisory and Coordinating Council on Bilingual Education, the body that oversees administration of this act, wrote in its recent annual report: "There is simply no evidence that bilingual education should be the preferred approach to instruction in all language-minority students" ("New Directions in Late 80's Pursued," Tenth Annual Report of NACCBE, US Department of Education, March 1986). This attempt to change an educational system which has worked so well to assimilate immigrants into the mainstream of American life for over two hundred years has been a grave error.

There is no reason to fear that repeal of the Bilingual Education Act, or passage of an act declaring English the official language of the United States, would discourage the study of foreign languages. By eliminating bilingual and multilingual courses, the government would have millions of dollars to spend on foreign language courses for all students, as well as on the basic education courses that are suffering severely from lack of funds.

Trudy J. Sundberg,
English Journal

Using Argumentation

Possibly the most important writing you do deals with arguing in order to persuade. Most research papers in school or work, proposals, editorials, and sermons, along with many letters and essays, argue a point of view. These writings try to persuade the reader to agree with the writer. The writer must, therefore, use clear and logical arguments.

First, start by writing down the argument you wish to make; this is the same as a **thesis statement.** It should express your point of view on a topic that has more than one side to it. Make this thesis statement specific.

Next you need **evidence** that supports your argument. You may use your own or someone else's experience, your observations, statements from authorities in the area, statistics, and facts that are well known or from reliable sources. Make sure you stick to your point; use only the part of the evidence that supports your point, not the whole event.

Using your own or someone else's **experience** gives a personal touch that adds interest. If you have derived pleasure from owning goldfish, for example, you can list the benefits: their beauty, ease of care, low cost, and the like. Or if someone you know has goldfish, she or he might have even more reasons. Use these as evidence. In addition to experience, use your own **observation.** Maybe you have seen someone enjoying goldfish; you can tell about that by watching the person.

Citing an **authority** in the area also is good evidence. The person does not have to be famous but must be an expert in that field. This expert could be the owner of a pet store (but be careful if he or she sells only goldfish), a writer about goldfish, an ichthyologist (a specialist on fish), the manager of an aquarium, or someone of that sort.

Statistics and **facts** both make excellent evidence if you can find them. Perhaps the number of people in the country who buy or own goldfish will make a good point. Also citing recent studies about the calming effects of watching goldfish would be excellent. You can find this type of information in the library.

If you know about evidence that goes against your argument, you should mention it and then **refute** it—that is, tell why it is wrong. Perhaps you have heard that goldfish die rather easily. You should then argue that care and attention will solve such problems. Or you could be ingenious and argue that the fast turnover rate will allow you to acquire even more goldfish!

Organize your arguments from the least important topic to the most important. Usually refuting the opposing evidence comes first because you want to build your case from weakest to strongest. However, sometimes opposing evidence comes within one of your points and has to be dealt with there.

Finally, restate your original argument. With solid evidence and good planning, your argument will be persuasive.

EXERCISES IN ARGUMENTATION

Exercise 1   Analyzing arguments

Decide if the following paragraphs present an **experience,** an **observation,** an **authority,** a **statistic,** or a **fact.**

1.   A typewriter or computer keyboard supposedly has the letters placed according to frequency of use. This placement provides the maximum efficiency for finger movement. But the most frequently used letter in English is e, followed by t, a, o, i, n, s, h, d, l, and u. Thus the keyboard has no logical placement at all.

Type of evidence: _____

2.   About 44 million people in the United States receive Social Security. The average payment in 1992 was $653, but the maximum was $1,128. Although raises in Social Security benefits are geared to the cost of living, they are not geared to increases in the cost of health care.

Type of evidence: _____

3.   AIDS is no longer a disease of gay males and drug addicts. Even in high school, we were warned constantly about contracting AIDS. The school nurse distributed pamphlets about how anyone can get AIDS. In health class, we studied the ways to prevent AIDS. Our student council decided on free distribution of condoms. Some parents and students objected, but either way, AIDS has certainly become part of our lives.

Type of evidence: _____

4.   Everyone should try to drink at least eight glasses of water a day. Dr. Lopez, our basketball coach, says that becoming dehydrated, especially while exercising, is very dangerous.

Type of evidence: _____

5.   War has rarely solved any problems. We need peaceful negotiations between countries and between people. Or, failing that, we need "passive resistance," the method advocated by Gandhi and also by Martin Luther King, Jr.

Type of evidence: _____

Exercise 2   Arguments, evidence, and conclusions

Underline the **argument** (the thesis) and the **conclusion** in this essay. Then write what kinds of evidence the essay used.

The Coffee Drinker

Paola brews coffee automatically, so it's ready when she wakes up in the morning. She drinks two cups and then puts the rest, four or five cups' worth, in a thermos for work. Then in the evening after dinner she drinks another cup or two. She drinks too much coffee and should stop this addiction.

I have seen her nervous and jittery when I meet her after work. She usually says she had too much coffee, but then she drinks a cup or two to "calm her nerves." Sometimes she complains that she does not sleep well either. I am sure that coffee is causing it.

The average coffee drinker has two or three cups of coffee a day, about 227 milligrams of caffeine. Paola has much more than that, usually about eight cups a day. That's about three times more than the average! She could well be in danger of getting heart disease and cancer, problems that have been associated, although not definitively, with excessive coffee drinking.

Coffee drinking is an addiction. It does not have the bad health or societal problems of cocaine or heroin, but it is still an addiction. People going "cold turkey" have withdrawal symptoms in the same way that other addicts do. They get headaches, tiredness, influenza symptoms, and cravings for coffee. If they get the chance, they drink coffee as soon as they can. It is just lucky for them that coffee is not expensive or illegal!

For these reasons I think Paola and other heavy coffee drinkers should cut down their consumption of this addictive and dangerous beverage. They should switch to juice or water. They would be calmer and would cut down their chances of heart disease and cancer.

Type of evidence: _____

Type of evidence: _____

Type of evidence: _____

Exercise 3   Finding arguments and evidence

Underline the **argument** (thesis) and the **evidence** in the following essay. Then write whether the evidence is **personal experience,** an **observation,** an **authority's statement,** a **statistic,** or a **fact.**

The Homeless Issue

The number of homeless people has increased greatly in this town. Male and female, young and old, educated and uneducated can be seen in many parts of town, even in the good neighborhoods. They continue to increase and have become a danger to us all. We need a program that counsels and rehabilitates these people.

About ten years ago we saw very few such people, just a small group of "bums," older male down-and-outs who had succumbed to alcoholism and frequented a rather seedy part of town. As a twenty-year-old, I only saw them if we happened to drive by that part of town. Looking at the bums fascinated us. They seemed exotic members of a different culture.

These days many of the bums are female, and often younger than I am. Maybe a few are alcoholics, but most seem high on drugs. And they have spread to all neighborhoods, even Ashton Park. The panhandlers may genuinely need money for food, but many of them frighten me. I don't walk at night anymore for fear of muggings. Recently our neighbor told about her uncle who was robbed in the street last year, and my sister's purse disappeared in a fast-food restaurant. Our homes are always in danger. We have had two break-ins in recent times. Cars seem constantly vandalized and stolen. Everybody uses special locks and alarms and carries the car radio with them.

This kind of persecution has to stop. Decent, law-abiding citizens have become victims of these drugged harassers. Maybe they could not help becoming drug addicts, so they need help. We must put them in detoxification programs. Both sides will benefit.

Type of evidence: _____

Type of evidence: _____

Type of evidence: _____

Exercise 4   Using evidence

Write a paragraph using evidence to support an argument:

1. Personal experience about why you like your favorite fast-food restaurant.

2. Authority for why we should all exercise. (Remember that the authority does not have to be a famous person.)

3. Observation showing that winter (or spring) is coming.

4. A statistic about your college's student population, proving that it is increasing (or parts are increasing). (Consult your college catalog for information.)

5. A fact about your college that makes it a good choice for students.

6. Personal experience to persuade someone to apply (or not to apply) for a job where you work.

7. A fact about your family's history to show why you live where you
   live.

8. Personal experience, observation, and authority to persuade someone to read (or not to read) one of your textbooks.

Avoiding False Arguments

   A number of illogical and false methods of argumentation exist and
should be avoided. Although some politicians and salespeople use such
tactics, they know what they are doing and hope to fool people with such
arguments. Everyone has been fooled at one time or another, but astute
people will notice false arguments, such as overgeneralizations, distraction, name-calling, references to character, false authorities, and climbing on the bandwagon, to name some of the most common ones.

   Overgeneralization means using one event or observation to make a
general statement for everyone. Just because Joe likes goldfish is not a
reason why others will like them. He may have some valid reasons, but
further evidence that goldfish make good pets will be necessary.

   Distraction (also called a *red herring*) means mentioning irrelevant
points to distract from relevant points. For example, Candidate X will
tell voters to remember her work for the rain forest when asked about

taxes. Or Candidate Y will emphasize his military service when asked about overcrowding in schools.

Calling names, such as nut, criminal, or murderer, weakens an argument. Opposers of abortion should not call abortionists "baby killers," no matter what they think. They should use more logical arguments to persuade against abortion. Using name-calling adjectives, such as crazy, silly, ridiculous, or stupid, also serves only to make an argument seem desperate and emotional, not clear and logical.

References to character apply traits from one part of a person's life to another part. Because a politician is divorced does not mean he or she cannot serve well in office. Or just because Joe dislikes dogs does not mean he would also be a mean parent or a poor president or even a bad person.

Celebrities make *false authorities* except in their area of expertise. Many advertisers use such celebrity endorsements to convince people that somehow they will be more like their favorite celebrity if only they use the same product as that person. A basketball player can be an expert on sneakers and many other things, but probably not on cars or frozen foods. Einstein was an authority on a great deal, but not on VCRs.

Climbing on the bandwagon means doing what others are doing simply because others are doing it. This false argument is commonly used by advertisers; one commercial even shows a bandwagon with people climbing on. Because many people will vote for a particular candidate is not reason enough to vote for that candidate. Even if a product is bought by more people than any other of its kind, that is not in itself a good reason for buying it.

False arguments seduce by their appeal to the emotions but will not stand up under logical analysis. Although there are many others, recognizing some of the most common false arguments will help a writer avoid their use.

EXERCISES IN FALSE ARGUMENTS

Exercise 5:   Overgeneralization and distraction

Read each paragraph and write at the bottom whether the argument is an overgeneralization or distraction.

1.   My sister gets As in English but only Cs, and sometimes Ds, in math. I guess girls are just good at language and terrible with numbers. Why should girls even bother with fields like physics or

engineering when they know they are so poor at math? They should become teachers, nurses, and secretaries; that's what they do well.

False argument: _____

2.   Getting rid of that old classroom building will provide a beautiful grassy area for picnicking, lounging, playing frisbee, or napping. Students will really enjoy life on campus.

False argument: _____

3.   All the social sciences must be awfully boring. Why would anyone take history, political science, and psychology courses if they didn't have to? When I took Introduction to Sociology, it was a really dull course.

False argument: _____

4.   Never mind the past. I'm promising no new taxes from now on.

False argument: _____

Exercise 6   Name-calling and references to character

Read each paragraph and write at the bottom whether the argument is name-calling or a reference to character.

1.   The senile Senator Jones opposes universal health care because he has never been unemployed or uninsured. He does not know what being poor feels like. He has never wondered about his next meal. And now he's so old he can't think straight.

False argument: _____

2.   The mayor is in favor of raising the school tax again. She really believes in soaking people for everything they've got. What a Nazi!

False argument: _____

3.   Don't vote for Sam Smith-Jones for City Council. He hates fast cars and roaring motorcycles. He doesn't like rock music and prefers listening to chamber music! He never goes fishing or hunting.

False argument: _____

4.　　Vote for Sam Smith-Jones for City Council. He has a loving wife, three wonderful children, and two friendly dogs. He likes watching football and playing baseball, just like you and me. He putters in his back yard and really enjoys a good barbecue.

False argument: _____

Exercise 7　False authority and the bandwagon

Read each paragraph and write at the bottom whether the argument is using false authorities or climbing on the bandwagon.

1.　　Be just like Supermodel Tanita. Use Glorious Shampoo and you too will have soft, manageable, shiny hair. The guys will fight over you. The photographers will love you. You'll be the center of attention wherever you go.

False argument: _____

2.　　Drink Juicy Cola. Everybody does.

False argument: _____

3.　　Aristotle would love this new complete-in-one-volume encyclopedia. He could look up all the facts about microwaves, black holes, and computers that he didn't know, to say nothing of catching up on the latest in poetics and ethics.

False argument: _____

4.　　Virtually everyone has tried smoking. Why? It is adult, sophisticated, cool. You too should join the crowd and light up. You'll be glad you did. You'll look elegant and sexy with that cigarette dangling from your lips or your fingers.

False argument: _____

Exercise 8　Identifying false arguments

Read each paragraph and write at the bottom whether the argument is an **overgeneralization**, a **distraction**, **name-calling**, a **reference to character**, using **false authorities**, or **climbing on the bandwagon**.

1.   We were thinking of renting an apartment in Ashton Hill because the schools, shopping, and neighborhood seemed really good. We liked the closeness to Mulberry Park also. But last week a hit-and-run accident occurred just three blocks from the new apartment. I think it will be too dangerous to live there.

False argument: _____

2.   My friends don't listen to chamber music, so why should I?

False argument: _____

3.   All my friends get wasted on the weekends. That's the thing to do. It's cool. We have a great time. I enjoy hanging out with them, and they like me because I'm just one of the guys.

False argument: _____

4.   Buy Brand Y jeans. Be part of the in-crowd and buy a pair today. You'll fit right in with the hottest folks around since everybody wears Brand Y jeans.

False argument: _____

5.   Forget taxes. Look at the wonderful new program for fighting crime: more police on the street, bigger prisons, tougher judges, longer prison terms, no parole, and no plea bargaining.

False argument: _____

6.   Loggers of the Northwest are crazy. Don't they realize that cutting down the trees will cause erosion and will so deplete the supply that soon we'll have no more wood? They are really stupid and short-sighted.

False argument: _____

7.   The author is a known alcoholic. He has been married twice and had many love affairs. He wastes large sums of money on luxurious vacations. He hates children and small animals. He detests television, movies, popular music, and any kind of sport, game, or exercise. Any book by him has to be bad.

False argument: _____

8.   I heard that a terrorist shot a person coming out of a restaurant in Paris. That must be a really dangerous city, and eating out

must be pretty hazardous too. I'm glad I'm here, safe in New York City.

False argument: _____

Suggestions for Essay Topics

Using one of the prewriting techniques—freewriting, brainstorming, or clustering—write on one of these topics.

1. Write a letter to Trudy J. Sundberg telling her how you agree or disagree with her argument. Use evidence from your personal experiences and observations to support your position.
2. Write an essay explaining which kinds of evidence Sundberg has used. Give examples from her essay.
3. Write an essay in your own words that explains Sundberg's major points. Do not quote her or use her quotations.
4. Write an essay arguing in favor of bilingual education. Use evidence from personal experience, observation, and authorities. Use statistics and facts if you want to.
5. Write an essay arguing your view on the duties of public schools. You might consider the topics of religious education, sex education, moral education, driver education, physical education, or any others.

Once you have written a rough draft of your essay, see if it has **body paragraphs;** an **introduction** and a **conclusion; descriptions, examples and details; consistent voice** and **point of view; sentence variety; specific words** and **transitions; logical explanations;** and **effective arguments** with evidence.

GRAMMAR

Using Apostrophes

The apostrophe, which looks like an above-the-line comma, has three basic uses: (1) to show possession in nouns, (2) to replace missing letters in contractions, and (3) to show the plural form of numbers, letters, and abbreviations.

1. **Possession** in a grammatical sense means that one thing belongs to another thing. Thus, "Kim's hat" means the hat that belongs to Kim,

as "Kim's hats" means the hats that belong to Kim. In the same way, "today's weather" means the weather of today, and "the cities' problems" means the problems of the cities. You can test whether or not you are showing possession by turning the words around to " . . . that belongs to . . . " or " . . . of . . . ."

To put the apostrophe in the right place, follow these steps: first, write down the singular or plural form of the noun you want; second, add an apostrophe to the end; third, add an *s* if there is no *s* before the apostrophe; otherwise, add nothing. Sometimes singular possessives add another *s* when an additional syllable is pronounced. Study these examples:

Singular	*Singular possessive*	*Plural*	*Plural possessive*
boy	boy's toys	boys	boys' toys
woman	woman's work	women	women's work
child	child's hands	children	children's hands
society	society's morals	societies	societies' morals
boss	boss' (boss's) ideas	bosses	bosses' ideas
James	James's feet	Jameses	Jameses' feet
weekend	weekend's weather	weekends	weekends' weather

2. Apostrophes also indicate missing letters in **contractions.** The apostrophe is placed where the missing letter or letters would be: could've, isn't, it's, that's, you're. We need contractions in speech, but in essays the words should be written out. However, some contractions do not have any other form: jack o'lantern, o'clock, O'Leary, rock 'n' roll.

3. Apostrophes indicate some plurals of numbers (10's), letters (a's), and abbreviations (M.D.'s) although just adding *s* is enough (3s, ts, M.D.s), but notice that a's and i's need the apostrophe to avoid confusion. Many abbreviations have plural forms but should be written out instead (avenues, not aves.; hours, not hrs.; numbers, not nos.).

On public signs and in some people's writing the apostrophe sometimes appears in plural nouns and even verbs for no reason. This misuse of apostrophes has caused much confusion, but remembering the above uses for apostrophes will make them clear.

EXERCISES IN APOSTROPHES

Exercise 9   Uses of apostrophes

Circle the apostrophes in the following essay. Then number them in the margin as follows:

1. Possession in a noun.

2. Contraction.

3. Plural: *a.* number, *b. letter,* or *c.* abbreviation.

Marian Anderson

Marian Anderson's life was one of serenity and acceptance despite the controversy that often swirled around her. Born in Philadelphia in 1897, Anderson started early on her life's career: She began singing at age three and joined the church choir at age six. Because her father died young and her mother took in laundry to support her three children, Anderson didn't start lessons until her teens, after her church choir gave benefits to raise money for her to study music.

Although she won competitions and had highly successful concerts in the early 1920's in the United States, prejudice against the black singer forced her to pursue her career in Europe from the late 1920's through the early 1930's. So many had called her the greatest singer of our times that she was convinced to return to the United States under the impresario Sol Hurok's management. In 1935 she triumphed in a New York concert and gave dozens of concerts a year through the 1930's.

Marian Anderson became famous throughout the United States, however, through an act of prejudice. When Hurok tried to schedule a concert in Washington, D.C.'s Constitution Hall, the headquarters of the Daughters of the American Revolution, he was told that all dates were booked. The D.A.R.'s prejudice led First Lady Eleanor Roosevelt and numerous other women to resign their membership. Finally in 1939, Anderson sang in the Lincoln Memorial. This Easter Sunday concert was broadcast to the entire nation, and Anderson's picture in front of Lincoln's statue became a symbol for the young civil rights movement.

After that, she sang at Constitution Hall at the D.A.R.'s invitation, at the Metropolitan Opera's presentation of Verdi's "Ballo in Maschera," and at Dwight D. Eisenhower's and John F. Kennedy's inaugurations. She gave her last concert in 1965 but continued in the

1970's and 1980's to promote humanitarian causes and to encourage young singers' talents through scholarships. When she died in 1993, she had never expressed bitterness against bigotry or glee at overcoming prejudice. Her rich, deep contralto communicated more universal emotions.

Exercise 10   Uses of apostrophes

Underline the apostrophes in the following paragraphs. Then number them in the margin as follows:

1. Possession in a noun.
2. Contraction.
3. Plural: *a.* number, *b.* letter, or *c.* abbreviation.

a.   Any good investigator will tell you that one of the best ways to find out what's going on in someone's house is to bag the household's trash. The debris of our lives goes in the garbage can and becomes fair game for the astute "garbageologist" who sifts through the envelopes, liquor bottles, handwritten notes, and doodles that we consign to the dump. (Edmund J. Pankau, *Check It Out!*)

b.   I admit it. I talk to my cat. And I don't mean just talk. I mean TALK. Real meaningful conversation. In fact, more satisfying conversation than I have with most people. Naturally, I want to do everything I can to keep Cleo her healthy best. So, I asked my veterinarian what food he recommends. Without skipping a beat, he said, "Hill's Science Diet." He said just as I have to eat a proper balance of foods to keep healthy, Cleo has to have a balance that's right for her. That's exactly what she gets with Hill's Science Diet. He called it Nutrient Precision. I like that. I'm so glad I asked because Cleo is very important to me. After all, she's the only one I know who can actually keep a secret. (Magazine ad for Hill's Science Diet)

c.   Every school day, 6,250 teachers are threatened with injury and 260 are actually assaulted. Just before Christmas a fifth-grade boy arrived at his school in Chicago one morning toting a concoction of household cleaners, including bleach, and poured it into his teacher's coffee. The teacher did not drink the brew, and the boy's classmates turned him in. Last week an eighth-grader in Washington shot a school guard in the stomach after he broke up a fight between rival gangs. (Jon D. Hull, "The Knife in the Book Bag," *Time*)

d.   When the world had to be glimpsed through a tobacco haze, matchbooks were plentiful. In today's increasingly smoke-free atmosphere, those little cardboard covers are becoming rare birds. But it's a safe bet that somebody started collecting them soon after a Philadelphia patent lawyer named Joshua Pusey invented book matches in 1892. It took a while for Pusey's invention to catch on because the striking surface was on the inside cover, dangerously near the matches. (Bill McTernan, "Matchbooks Make a Striking Collection," *Newsday*)

Exercise 11   Using apostrophes

In the following essay, fill in the blank with appropriate words and apostrophes.

Penmanship

_____ always been proud of my nice
                    I have

handwriting even though penmanship _____
                                                had not

been taught since grade school. I dot my _____
                                                          plural i

and cross my _____ carefully. I write
                        plural t

numbers particularly clearly because _____
                                                              I am

majoring in accounting. My _____ very
                                    handwriting is

legible, and I pride myself on nice penmanship. Still

_____ careful never to criticize
             I am

_____ because _____
   handwriting of people   I have

learned a lesson.

   I spent a summer in France and got nothing but criticism for

my handwriting. I had written to _____
                                          friends of my cousin

telling them I was coming. When I got there, they

_____ know when _____
             did not   I would

arrive. They read English all right, but _____
                                                      could not

understand my numbers and words. They said my

_____ looked like _____,
          plural 7   plural 1

and that my _____, _____,
                     plural p   plural r

and _____ _____
            plural 4   did not

look like any letters or numbers _____ ever
                                              they had

seen. Since then _____ noticed that
                          I have

_____ varies but not because
    handwriting of other people

_____ sloppy. _____
                    they are   That is

just how they were taught.

Now _____ more sensitive to these
                        I am

differences and realize that good handwriting is all relative. I

_____ criticize _____
                    will not   handwriting of people

anymore. They just learned to write in a different way.

Exercise 12   Using apostrophes

Write paragraphs using the following words with apostrophes. You don't have to use all of them in each group, but try to use as many as possible.

1. grandmother's birthplace, grandfather's town, grandparents' home, can't, shouldn't, isn't, haven't

2. college's quality, Ph.D.'s, M.A.'s. B.S.'s, professor's duty

3. o'clock, 9's, 6's, clock's hands, doesn't, I'm

4. it's, today's weather, spring's (contraction), tree's leaves, hasn't, can't, won't

Using Semicolons and Colons

The semicolon, which looks like a comma with a dot above it (;), seems like an advanced form of punctuation, but it really is not. We all need it in our everyday writing. The same follows for the colon, two dots one above the other (:).

In compound sentences when no coordinating conjunction (for, and, nor, but, or, yet, so) is used, a *semicolon* and not a comma separates the two parts. These two parts should be related to each other: I like swimming; it is fun. You could also put a period between them or reword them in some way, but using a semicolon is simple and clear. Just be sure that the two parts could each stand alone.

The semicolon sometimes replaces a comma to avoid confusion in a sentence with many commas. For example, in this sentence, "I went swimming with Pedro, my nephew, Maria, the lifeguard, and Rover, my dog," is Pedro the nephew? Is Maria the lifeguard? Better add semicolons: I went swimming with Pedro, my nephew; Maria, the lifeguard; and Rover, my dog. The sentence could be reworded to avoid the problem, but using semicolons makes the sentence clear without rewording.

The *colon* indicates that more precise information will follow a complete sentence. This information may be one word, a phrase, a series of items, or a whole sentence:

He loves just one thing: money.
She had a dream: to go to college.
I ate three vegetables: sweet corn, peas, and green beans.
One idea dominated his mind: he had lost his freedom.

Notice that the first part must be a complete sentence. Do not put a colon in such sentences as "The students are Kim, Larry, and Maria" and "Another person going was Mario." Although some exceptions exist, following this rule for colons will always make them correct.

Colons have several other uses: to indicate hours, minutes, and seconds (3:45:05); to indicate a subtitle after a title (*Let's Go: The Budget Guide to the USA*); to cite verses from the Bible (Joshua 6:20–21); to separate some parts of a business letter (Dear Madam:, To: Managers, KD:jm); to start a list (Rule 1: Walk; Rule 2: Don't run); and to separate some parts in a footnote (New York: Macmillan, 1995). None of these occurs frequently in essays, but added altogether they make colons common in writing.

EXERCISES IN SEMICOLONS AND COLONS

Exercise 13   Identifying semicolons and colons

In the following paragraphs,

1. Underline the two independent clauses separated by a semicolon.

2. Double underline any other uses of the semicolon.

3. Circle the independent clause before a colon.

When designing your daily menu, keep in mind this dialectical harmony. When serving food that comes from the sea, combine it with the appropriate food that grows on land; a serving of animal food (yang) should be balanced with vegetables or fruit (yin); foods rich in potassium (yin) go best with those rich in sodium (yang). Don't worry, you need not be a scientist. The macrobiotic principle is common sense and once your intuition is revitalized you will realize that you have known and used it all along, albeit only haltingly. With a little practice macrobiotic cooking will become second nature; with a bit more it may well become your primary nature. (Lima Ohsawa, *The Art of JUST Cooking*)

In high school I had always been on the outside looking in. When my classmates stayed after school to rehearse plays, take part in sports, or play musical instruments, I went home to do housework and milk cows. I was determined to help my children expand their horizons by taking advantage of all the things the city offered. On weekends we rented bicycles and rode through Golden Gate Park; we picnicked on the ocean beaches; we visited the zoo; we saw the exhibits at the museums. At home, when our studies were done, we played chess. When I was a child, if I was not studying, I had to be working, or if I was not working, I had to be studying. So now I played with my children—chess, tennis, swimming. I believed that life was meant to be enjoyed, not suffered. (Kartar Dhillon, *Making Waves*)

But even more wonderful than any human effort or revised interpretation are the organisms of the Burgess Shale themselves, particularly as newly and properly reconstructed in their transcendent strangeness: *Opabinia,* with its five eyes and frontal "nozzle"; *Anomalocaris,* the largest animal of its time, a fearsome predator with a circular jaw; *Hallucigenia,* with an anatomy to match its name. (Stephen Jay Gould, *Wonderful Life: The Burgess Shale and the Nature of History*)

At first I did not recognize him, nor he me. The boy I had known had been left behind long ago. In my eyes Huberto Naranjo was elegant: dark sideburns, oily pompadour, tight pants, cowboy boots, and metal-studded belt. His expression was vaguely arrogant, but in his eyes danced the spark of mischief that nothing in his stormy life could erase. He was barely fifteen, but he looked older because of the way he stood: legs apart, knees slightly bent, head thrown back, a cigarette dangling from his lower lip. I recognized him by his desperado-like bearing; he had walked exactly the same way as a kid in short pants. (Isabel Allende, *Eva Luna*)

I am having a minor infatuation with the Shepherd's Garden Seeds catalogue (no relation to Shep Ogden's catalogue), so I ended up ordering more than I meant to from them. But the description of the Kidma cucumbers was hard to resist: "Developed for eating out of hand, they are perfect when picked at 5 to 8 inches long. These cucumbers are not marketed commercially because they are too delicate to stand shipping." This is the luxury of the kitchen garden— growing things that you cannot buy at the store. And from Shepherd's Garden Seeds I also got Chioggia Striped beets (described as an Italian variety), which I tried late last summer at a friend's house; they revealed pink-in-white circles when sliced, and they were delicious plain, without a vinaigrette or butter. And I ordered Blue Lake string beans, which I have never grown; they are the most common string beans to grow, and, perversely, for just that reason I wanted to have them this year. But it was in the seeds for flowers that I lost myself: three packets each of Old Spice and Early Mammoth sweet peas. Where I will put them all, I don't know yet, but they'll all have to go in; there's no such thing as too many sweet peas. I also ordered packets of rose campion, cottage pinks, foxglove, stock, and double Canterbury bells. (Jamaica Kincaid, "Just Reading," *The New Yorker*)

Wisdom is better than possessions and an advantage to all who see the sun. Better have wisdom behind you than money; wisdom profits men by giving life to those who know her.

Consider God's handiwork; who can straighten what he has made crooked? When things go well, be glad; but when things go ill, consider this: God has set the one alongside the other in such a way that no one can find out what is to happen next. In my empty existence I have seen it all, from a righteous man perishing in his righteousness to a wicked man growing old in his wickedness. Do not be over-righteous and do not be over-wise. Why make yourself a laughing-stock? Do not be over-wicked and do not be a fool. Why should you die before your time? It is good to hold on to the one thing and not lose hold of the other; for a man who fears God will succeed both ways. (Ecclesiastes 7:11–19, *The New English Bible*)

Exercise 14   Using semicolons

Although these sentences are correct, change some of these commas to semicolons to clear up ambiguities.

1. We packed sandwiches, cookies, and oranges, rode two hours on the train, walked on the beach, and sang carols, hymns, and children's songs.

2. If you like sailing, biking, swimming, and hiking, if you want to sunbathe, sip drinks, and stroll in a garden, if you enjoy good company, leisurely meals, and soft music, then join us. We at Holiday Springs offer all these activities and nonactivities at low, low prices.

3. Strolling in the woods, picking daisies, daffodils, and irises, noticing the squirrels and birds, and listening to the rustle of leaves all make me very happy to live in the country rather than the city.

Replace some commas with semicolons to indicate that five people were there. Make the captain female and the nurse male.

4. Going on the boat trip were Tony, the captain, Maria, a nurse, Tommy, two students from the college, Kim and Bea.

Replace some commas with semicolons to indicate that eight people were there.

5. Going on the boat trip were Tony, the captain, Maria, a nurse, Tommy, two students from the college, Kim and Bea.

Replace some commas with semicolons to indicate that six people were there. Make the captain male.

6. Going on the boat trip were Tony, the captain, Maria, a nurse, Tommy, two students from the college, Kim and Bea.

Replace some commas with semicolons to indicate that Pei bought four books.

7. Pei bought a photography book, *Earth Watch*, a cookbook, *If It Doesn't Pan Out*, *The Awakening*, and *To the Lighthouse*.

Replace some commas with semicolons to indicate that six people celebrated.

8. Kim, a friend of mine, the manager, Leslie, the coach, the pitcher, the catcher, Maria, and Bea all went to celebrate the victory.

Exercise 15   Replacing with semicolons and colons

Read the following essay. Then replace some punctuation and words with semicolons and colons. You may change some other words too if you want, but concentrate on the semicolons and colons.

A Perfect Day

I enjoyed a perfect day last Saturday, and it went by so fast. The weather was perfect. The sky was clear. The sun was shining. The temperature was just right for a picnic.

At the grocery store I bought some picnic food. I bought tuna salad, three-bean salad, cornbread, and my favorite chocolate chip cookies. I packed these along with other supplies and headed for the beach. The bus came right away, and I did not have to wait. The beach had very few people, and I found the perfect spot near the water.

After a day of swimming, lounging in the sun, reading *The Awakening*, and eating my picnic, I headed home. Again the bus came right away, and I did not have to wait a minute.

When I got home, my friends Kim and Bea had just arrived. We told jokes, we listened to music, and we snacked. Then we went out to my favorite Mexican restaurant. It was great. I had all my favorite dishes. I had guacamole, refried beans, fajitas with salsa, and green salad.

I had a wonderful day. I wish it had lasted forever.

Exercise 16   Using semicolons and colons

Write paragraphs on the following topics using at least one semicolon and one colon in each one.

1. Using a vending machine to buy drinks and snacks.

2. The types of shoes you have.

3. The sports you enjoy playing or watching.

4. What you want for lunch or dinner.

5. What you have read this week or last week.

Using Hyphens

A hyphen (-) has many uses and has increased its number of uses in our complex world. Do not call a hyphen a dash.

The hyphen is most commonly used to divide a word at the end of a line and the beginning of the next line. A dictionary will indicate where the separation is possible, but do not separate a word with just one letter either at the beginning or the end. Divide only when necessary, not just to make lines even.

Hyphens connect a prefix and the main word (all-around, anti-gun control, pro-choice, self-esteem), especially those before a capital letter (mid-April), and some suffixes (president-elect, college-bound). Often-used words sometimes omit the hyphen (antifreeze, miniskirt, northbound).

Hyphens make combined phrases used as adjectives clear (behind-the-scenes action, high-school diploma, up-to-date information). Do not use hyphens with adverbs, *-ly* words (recently promoted manager), which are clear in themselves. Hyphenate these phrases only when they appear before nouns; otherwise write them without hyphens: "What happened behind the scenes?" "I went to high school"; "This dictionary is up to date."

We also use hyphens to make nouns and adjectives out of verbs that are made of verb plus preposition. For example, the verb "follow up" in "I will follow up on your progress" can be used as a noun by adding a hyphen, "I want a follow-up on your progress," or adjective, "I want a follow-up report on your progress."

Hyphens also indicate partial words (-ly words, pre- or post-war, Franco-, Anglo-, full- or part-time job). Compound names (ambassador-at-large, Asian-American, broker-analyst, Maria Smith-Jones, mother-in-law) and compound phrases (forget-me-not, so-so, touchy-feely, tractor-trailer) are often connected by hyphens. Some such words, however, often do not take hyphens (African American), while others sometimes do (vice-president) and sometimes do not (Vice President Gore).

Hyphens also connect two-word units of measure (kilowatt-hours, light-years), the parts of a telephone number or series of numbers (555-1234), and double-digit numbers and fractions (twenty-three and four-tenths), but not triple-digit numbers. All these uses can be extraordinarily complicated, but consult an up-to-date *American* dictionary (English usage differs). Then see how your word or phrase fits in the listed uses for hyphens.

EXERCISES IN HYPHENS

Exercise 17   Uses of hyphens

Circle the hyphens and number them in the margin as follows:

1. Divided word.

2. Hyphenated prefix.

3. Combined phrase used as adjective.

4. Verb plus preposition used as noun or adjective.

5. Partial word.

6. Compound name.

7. Unit of measure, number, or fraction.

Functional Illiteracy

The United States has a high literacy rate compared to many nations in the world, but not the highest. In the United States, children must attend school through most of high school or until they reach the age of sixteen. Thus almost everyone can write his or her name, some words, and some numbers. If they have achieved these skills by age fifteen, they are considered literate for purposes of literacy-rate calculations.

However, around twenty-seven million people are actually functionally illiterate. That is, they cannot find an address, fill out a simple job-application form, read a telephone book, or follow simple medicine-bottle instructions. Functionally illiterate people are not only limited in job opportunities but also may endanger themselves with their inability. They may mistake bleach for detergent or shampoo for medicine; they cannot read road-sign warnings while driving; they lack map-reading skill.

If they have jobs at all, they are limited to low-level blue-collar work, but in our technological-age workplace even low-level jobs require up-to-date technological skills, which mean reading how-to manuals, computer printouts, stick-on notes, and memos. And the out-of-work person certainly will have trouble finding a job that does not require any forms.

These jobless people must turn to welfare and often to crime. In fact, about one-half the people in jail are illiterate. This waste affects everyone in its costs to society.

Exercise 18   Uses of hyphens

Circle the hyphens and number them in the margin as follows:

1. Divided word.
2. Hyphenated prefix.
3. Combined phrase used as adjective.
4. Verb plus preposition used as noun or adjective.
5. Partial word.
6. Compound name.
7. Unit of measure, number, or fraction.

A Literacy Success Story

Maria Smith-Jones did not intend to, but she ended up a thirty-one-year-old semi-literate, or illiterate, as she finally admitted. After getting a high-school diploma, she worked at a dead-end job that paid poorly. Then she became a nurse's aide in a rest home and because of some on-the-job training was encouraged to become a nurse-practitioner. But she did not want to go back to school.

Maria knew she was functionally illiterate and had covered it up for many years. She always took the same bus to work, carrying a newspaper as if she had just read it, watched television to keep up, and commented on pictures in magazines as if she had read the article. She often said that she had forgotten her glasses or asked patients to read her memos for her "just for fun." To avoid reading a menu, she always asked for "the hamburger-and-coke special" at the fast-food restaurant. But one day her supervisor asked her to help sight-impaired patients read large-print books. She felt overwhelmed by her cover-up and had to admit her inability.

With better-late-than-never desperation, she inquired at the local library, found a just-retired tutor, and started lessons. After a year, she felt confident enough to help patients read. After more reading practice, she hopes to follow up on her long-delayed career as well.

Exercise 19   Using hyphens

Fill in the blanks with the indicated phrases listed in order. Decide whether or not to add the hyphens. Remember, add hyphens only for phrases used as adjectives.

1. back to school, high school, once a year, pen and pencil, loose leaf, out of stock

   In mid-August, clothing stores start _____

   sales for college and _____ students. The

   stores run big ads that claim _____ sav-

   ings. Supermarkets also feature _____ sets,

   _____ notebooks, and typing paper. Nobody

   sees an _____ sign on any of these items

   during this time of year.

2. community college, twice in a row, hungry for knowledge, senior citizen, hard to believe

   My brother's _____ record was none

   too sterling. _____ he failed algebra despite

   his _____ attitude that he hoped would in-

   fluence the _____ teacher. When he finally

   got a B, it was really _____.

3. out of date, up to the minute, out of the way, hard to find, off beat, run of the mill

   Being tired of _____ clothes, Kim de-

   cided to shop for an outfit that was _____ in

style. She searched in some _____

stores for some _____,

_____ clothes. She finally got an outfit that

is definitely not _____.

Exercise 20   Using hyphens

Use the following hyphenated words and phrases in paragraphs. You do not have to use all of them, but try to use as many as you can.

1. so-so, out-of-work, run-of-the-mill

2. run-in, stuck-up, up-to-date

3. ex-husband, husband-to-be, father-in-law, mother-to-be

4. Mexican-American, Chinese-American, inner-city

5. little-known, hard-won, hard-to-find, one-of-a-kind

Chapter **10**

Writing to Entertain

WRITING AND READING

Before Reading "The Discovery and Use of the Fake Ink Blot"

WORDS AND PHRASES TO LOOK FOR

regal: king- or queen-like, royal
dignitary: a high ranking person, ambassador
imperial: emperor-like
improvised jig: lively dance made up on the spot
Santa Anna: Mexican revolutionary and president, 1795–1876
Alamo: scene of massacre of Texans by Mexicans, 1836
substantially: significantly, importantly
cunning: sly, tricky, crafty
advent: arrival
disintegrating: breaking up, separating into parts
artifice: trickery, skill
robber barons: rich industrialists who cheated the poor
wherefrom: from where
tomfoolery: silliness, foolish acts
J. P. Morgan: American financier and robber baron, 1837–1913
staple: regularly stocked and used necessity
repertoire of diversions: array of entertainments
Empire (pronounced ahmPEER):   furniture style of Napoleon's era

QUESTIONS TO ANSWER AS YOU READ

1. List the different "diversions" Allen mentions.
2. List the historical events and people Allen mentions.
3. According to Allen, why didn't the first ink blot work and how did they make it work?
4. Is this a true story? If so, why? If not, why not?
5. What practical jokes do you know? Have you used them?

The Discovery and Use of the Fake Ink Blot

There is no evidence of a fake ink blot appearing anywhere in the West before the year 1921, although Napoleon was known to have had great fun with the joy buzzer, a device concealed in the palm of the hand causing an electric-like vibration upon contact. Napoleon would offer the regal hand in friendship to a foreign dignitary, buzz the unsuspecting victim's palm and roar with imperial laughter as the redfaced dupe did an improvised jig to the delight of the court.

The joy buzzer underwent many modifications, the most celebrated of which occurred after the introduction of chewing gum by Santa Anna (I believe chewing gum was originally a dish of his wife's that simply would not go down) and took the form of a spearmint-gum pack equipped with a subtle mousetrap mechanism. The sucker, offered a fresh stick, experienced a piercing sting as the iron bar came springing down on his naive fingertips. The first reaction was generally one of pain, then contagious laughter, and finally a kind of folk wisdom. It is no secret that the snappy-chewing-gum gag lightened matters at the Alamo considerably; and although there were no survivors, most observers feel things could have gone substantially worse without this cunning little gimmick.

With the advent of the Civil War, Americans turned more and more to escaping the horrors of a disintegrating nation; and while the Northern generals preferred amusing themselves with the dribble glass, Robert E. Lee passed many a crucial moment with his brilliant use of the squirt flower. In the early part of the War, no one ever came away from smelling the apparent "lovely carnation" in Lee's lapel without getting a generous eyeful of Suwanee River water. As things went badly for the South, however, Lee abandoned the once-fashionable artifice and relied simply on placing a carpet tack on the chair seats of people whom he did not like.

After the War and right up to the early 1900s and the so-called era of the robber barons, sneezing powder and a little tin can marked ALMONDS, wherefrom several huge spring serpents would leap into the victim's face, provided all that was worthy in the area of tomfoolery. It is said J. P. Morgan preferred the former, while the elder Rockefeller felt more at home with the latter.

Then, in 1921, a group of biologists meeting in Hong Kong to buy suits discovered the fake ink blot. It had long been a staple of the Oriental repertoire of diversions, and several of the later dynasties retained power by their brilliant manipulation of what appeared to be a spilled bottle and an ugly ink-stain, but was in reality a tin blot.

The first ink blots, it was learned, were crude, constructed to eleven feet in diameter and fooled nobody.

However, with the discovery of the concept of smaller sizes by a Swiss physicist, who proved that an object of a particular size could be reduced in size simply by "making it smaller," the fake ink blot came into its own.

It remained in its own until 1934, when Franklin Delano Roosevelt removed it from its own and placed it in someone else's. Roosevelt utilized it cleverly to settle a strike in Pennsylvania, the details of which are amusing. Embarrassed leaders of both labor and management were convinced that a bottle of ink had been spilled, ruining someone's priceless Empire sofa. Imagine how relieved they were to learn it was all in fun. Three days later the steel mills were reopened.

Woody Allen,
Getting Even

Writing to Entertain

Entertaining essays are probably the hardest essays to write. For this reason, good writing of this kind commands high sums of money, and the writers become famous. Still, we all do some amount of entertaining writing in letters to our friends and relatives, in essays to record our lives, and in memos at work when a light touch can make people pay attention.

We all have experiences worth writing about. An experience need not deal with traumatic life-changing events; the small occurrences usually make better essays.

Although you may think that making up funny events will be more entertaining, you should base your essay on facts and known events. Describing your family's Thanksgiving dinner can be very humorous if you describe the fuss and bother of preparations, the quirks and oddities of family members, the arguments among relatives, the little feuds. Or maybe nothing happens when you all get together. Then describe the monotony, the total boredom, the familiar stories, the predictable remarks and behavior. Anything can be humorous if it sounds real.

As with any piece of writing, have a **thesis** for your essay. Don't think you must start at the beginning and continue in chronological order: On May 6 we took the 8:45 train from Union Station and arrived at 11:03. Nobody will want to read more. Instead, decide on a thesis and keep it in mind as you describe just what fits your thesis. In the same way, decide what the Thanksgiving dinner is like: disastrous, deadly boring, or full of surprises. Then use that as the thesis.

For humorous effect, you can **exaggerate,** but don't overdo it. A little exaggeration makes the point; a lot makes the reader stop being involved with your story.

Use **details, careful descriptions,** and **precise words** to paint a picture of the person or scene. "My uncle is boring" and "we all ate too much" do not tell enough. Make clear what your uncle does or doesn't do. If you describe it precisely, you never have to add that he is boring; we get the picture from your words. Tell exactly what each person ate; then you won't need to say that it was too much.

If you do write fiction, base your characters and events on people and events you know. You may combine traits from various people, pull together different events into one event, exaggerate, and change the flow of the action. Then you can add some invented details if you want. If readers believe your story, then you have succeeded.

EXERCISES IN WRITING TO ENTERTAIN

Exercise 1   Analyzing entertaining writing

Read the following essay. Then in the margin find examples of these techniques and number them as follows:

1. Thesis.
2. Details and precise words.

3. Description.

4. Exaggeration (you think).

Cairo

It is the traveller's lot to dine at many table-d'hôtes in the course of many wanderings; but it seldom befalls him to make one of a more miscellaneous gathering than that which overfills the great dining-room at Shepheard's Hotel in Cairo during the beginning and height of the regular Egyptian season. Here assemble daily some two to three hundred persons of all ranks, nationalities, and pursuits; half of whom are Anglo-Indians homeward or outward bound, European residents, or visitors established in Cairo for the winter. The other half, it may be taken for granted, are going up the Nile. So composite and incongruous is this body of Nile-goers, young and old, well-dressed and ill-dressed, learned and unlearned, that the new-comer's first impulse is to inquire from what motives so many persons of dissimilar tastes and training can be led to embark upon an expedition which is, to say the least of it, very tedious, very costly, and of an altogether exceptional interest.

His curiosity, however, is soon gratified. Before two days are over, he knows everybody's name and everybody's business; distinguishes at first sight between a Cook's tourist and an independent traveller; and has discovered that nine-tenths of those whom he is likely to meet up the river are English or American. The rest will be mostly German, with a sprinkling of Belgian and French. So far *en bloc;* but the details are more heterogeneous still. Here are invalids in search of health; artists in search of subjects; sportsmen keen upon crocodiles, statesmen out for a holiday; special correspondents alert for gossip; collectors on the scent of papyri and mummies; men of science with only scientific ends in view; and the usual surplus of idlers who travel for the mere love of travel, or the satisfaction of a purposeless curiosity. (Amelia B. Edwards, *A Thousand Miles up the Nile*)

Exercise 2   Analyzing entertaining writing

Read the following paragraphs. Then underline examples of these techniques, and number them in the margin as follows:

1. Thesis or topic sentence.
2. Details and precise words.
3. Description.
4. Exaggeration (you think).

a.   Anyone who has sized up one of these burritos knows that the dirigible era did not end with the Hindenburg disaster. Rather than the slender tubes once common in Mexican restaurants, these are foot-long flour tortillas packed full with rice, beans, cheese, guacamole and anything else that once grew or moved. These entire meals in not-so-neat packages first took flight in Northern California, then traversed the country to New York. (Eric Asimov, *New York Times*)

b.   In the summer of 1942, I graduated from high school and started classes at Johns Hopkins University. Because of the war, colleges were running full tilt year round, so my transition from high-school senior to college freshman happened immediately. One day I took the commencement tuxedo back to the rental shop and next day I was listening to Professor Francis Murnaghan lecture on differential calculus. This was an alarming experience because, after my first ten minutes in the course, I knew I was going to fail calculus.

Dr. Murnaghan was a spirited, rosy-cheeked gentleman with silvery locks, who spoke with a pronounced Irish brogue. His energetic classroom manner was like a theatrical performance by an Irish character actor with a fondness for pixie roles. He never said "calculus," but always called it "the calculus" and urged us to think of it as a beautiful machine capable of doing magic things. (Russell Baker, *The Good Times*)

c.   For unwelcome house guests the Inspiration Shop has just about the cutest discouragers and annoyances I have ever seen.

These include inflammable ashtrays, a bathtub plug made of gelatin which looks exactly like the ordinary rubber plug, a charming assortment of cigarette boxes which you can't open —they are filled with cigarettes and are transparent—and a pair of bedroom slippers in which a mechanism has been cunningly concealed. The host or hostess should surreptitiously substitute these for the guest's own slippers. When he or she tries to put them on, they start moving across the floor. The guest is pretty sure to leave in the morning. If these devices do not work, the Inspirationers will show you the loveliest bathroom door you ever saw. It can't be locked or even closed, and is fine for the guest rooms of those who know the wrong kind of people. (James Thurber, *Thurber Country*)

Exercise 3   Adding a thesis, details, descriptions, and exaggerations

Edit this essay to make it more interesting. Give it a thesis, add some details and descriptions, and exaggerate a little.

My Father's First Ice Cream Cone

On July 4, 1958, our family was invited to a picnic at a neighbor's house. This sort of invitation did not happen often because we were (and are) Chinese and our all-American neighbors did not think we indulged in such all-American events as July Fourth picnics. They were right.

The fried chicken was all right, but the potato salad wasn't. The cole slaw was raw; we don't like raw cabbage. The dessert table had sweet apple pie, sweet chocolate cake, and various sweet cookies. We didn't care much for dessert.

The big eating event, however, was homemade ice cream in cones. My brother and I, little kids, had eaten them before. My mother chose not to sample one. My father, always ready for new adventure, took one of the ice cream cones. He had no experience with the proper licking technique, so he went at the ice cream directly with his mouth. How could he know that the ice cream just SAT on the cone and was not part of it? The ice cream fell out of the cone. He was sitting down, so reflex action caused him to try to catch it with his foot. But with a kick he sent it flying. Just at that moment the hostess, a nice woman with a flowery dress, was coming toward him (to offer napkins probably) and the ice cream landed on her skirt. Was he embarrassed!

My brother and I thought it was one of the funniest things we had ever seen. We could not stop laughing for days every time we were reminded of it.

Exercise 4   Writing to entertain

Write paragraphs on the following topics. Be sure to have a **thesis, details, and descriptions. Exaggerate** if you want. Use a nonchronological time sequence.

1. A new student's first day at college.

2. A typical family dinner.

3. A Saturday-night adventure.

4. The first meeting with a new boss, date, teacher, or someone else important.

Avoiding Stereotyping, Racism, and Sexism

All of us know we should avoid stereotyping (using one trait to define a whole group), racism (criticizing a whole race), and sexism (criticizing all women or all men), but many of these ideas have been deeply ingrained in our culture and are not easy to recognize even when we are aware of them.

Stereotyping is easy to fall into without thinking, yet in writing one must be careful not to do so. For example, do not assume that farmers are all backward, mothers are all cookie-baking types, football players are all illiterate, or politicians are all crooked. Yes, some of them are, but so are others. Stereotyping means forgetting the individual and concentrating on the false reputation of the group. We stereotype professions, women, nationalities, races—that is, everybody. We should always be careful not to make assumptions based on these stereotypes.

It is also so easy to define whole national groups—Arab terrorists, Irish drunkards, Korean grocers, Italian mafia—that we forget that such racial identities are not true for most people and can be very insulting. In writing, you should be careful not to assume such racist stereotypes; they replace individual characters with false generalizations.

Finally, do not base assumptions on sexist ideas. Women should not be stereotyped; they do not all have the same goals. They should be included in the world of people. For example, did you assume that farmers, politicians, Arab terrorists, and Korean grocers were all male? Maybe, in fact, most of them are, but do not automatically exclude women from these roles. Also consider that women can be criminals, drug dealers, firefighters, mail carriers, police officers, and supervisors. Although you may want to treat men and women differently in your writing, do so because they are individuals, not because they are men and women.

Do not think, however, that you must avoid issues about racism and sexism. These are fascinating topics to write about. Just be careful not to make assumptions about race and sex and then base your essay on these false assumptions.

EXERCISES IN AVOIDING STEREOTYPING, RACISM, AND SEXISM

Exercise 5 Analyzing paragraphs

Read the following paragraphs and then write what makes them **stereotypical, racist,** or **sexist.** Notice that some of the paragraphs are deliberately portraying such characters.

1. "D'you mean to tell me you've reached the age of twenty-four without reading Gibbon?" he demanded.

    "Yes, I have," she answered.

    "Mon Dieu!" he exclaimed, throwing out his hands. "You must begin to-morrow. I shall send you my copy. What I want to know is—" he looked at her critically. "You see, the problem is, can one really talk to you? Have you got a mind, or are you like the rest of your sex? You seem to me absurdly young compared with men of your age."

    Rachel looked at him but said nothing.

    "About Gibbon," he continued. "D'you think you'll be able to appreciate him? He's the test, of course. It's awfully difficult to tell about women," he continued, "how much, I mean, is due to lack of training, and how much is native incapacity. . . . " (Virginia Woolf, *The Voyage Out*)

How has this man been sexist?

2.   Whenever the moment comes to hail a cab, I'm ridden with anxiety. My stomach knots and my blood boils. During the last few months, I have recorded every incident when one of our fearless cabbies left me stranded on the street.

Reality check: More than 85 percent of those who passed me by were black or brown—whether African, African-American, Caribbean-American, Latino or Arab—people of color like me. This phenomenon is not simply black and white.

Yet I still consider this racist, as do many others. So where does that leave us? (Keith M. Brown, "The Shades of Racism," *Newsday*)

Why is this behavior racist?

Exercise 6   Analyzing paragraphs

Read the following paragraphs, and then write what makes them **stereotypical, racist,** or **sexist.**

1.   I didn't really socialize with people who are Hawaiian. One of my friends who is Japanese, married someone who is Hawaiian. That must have been a big shock to her family. It's a class thing. It's as if you're marrying someone who is a janitor, or something. I feel it's kind of marrying down when you marry Hawaiian. I mean to me, it's inconceivable. Why would I marry someone who is Hawaiian? They don't have my interests—they're not in my class. They're not in the top classes. I was the salutatorian in my high school class of seven hundred thirty students. I was in the top of all my classes in school. There weren't any Hawaiians in any of my classes. Maybe there were in my gym class but that wasn't based on ability. So the only Hawaiians I saw in high school were hanging around in their corners. (Andrea Kim, "Born and Raised in Hawaii, But Not Hawaiian," from Joann Faung Lee, *Asian American Experiences in the United*

States: Oral Histories of First to Fourth Generation Americans from China, the Philippines, Japan, India, the Pacific Islands, Vietnam and Cambodia)

How does this stereotype Hawaiians?

2.   Passengers had to be accommodated inside the coach, but as I was regarded as a "coolie" and looked a stranger, it would be proper, thought the "leader," as the white man in charge of the coach was called, not to seat me with the white passengers. There were seats on either side of the coachbox. The leader sat on one of these as a rule. Today he sat inside and gave me his seat. I knew it was sheer injustice and an insult, but I thought it better to pocket it. I could not have forced myself inside, and if I had raised a protest, the coach would have gone off without me. (Mahatma Gandhi, *An Autobiography*)

What would you have done in this situation?

Exercise 7   Finding stereotypes

Read the following essay and then answer the questions at the end.

Sexist Stereotypes

By excluding boys, the Ms. Foundation's Take Our Daughters to Work Day became another act of sex discrimination. By allowing only girls to discover careers and to see how men and women can work together, we make unfair assumptions: that boys would learn nothing from seeing women and men in nontraditional roles and that boys already know their career options.

To presume that a suburban white girl from a middle-class family has a greater need to expand her horizons and to raise her self-esteem than an inner-city black, Hispanic or Indian boy is not only sexist, it's racist. To assume that boys from fatherless homes have less need for role models is also sexist.

You fail to challenge several facts. One is that sexual stereotyping is a male-only problem. One of the best examples is that boys (and girls) who grow up in single-parent homes are raised by their mothers, as the courts and women will not accept men as primary caregivers. Men are also denied acceptance from society if they choose to stay home with their children; men are still expected to be the primary breadwinner by both men and women.

Let's make April 27, 1994, "Take a Child to Work Day" if you want to change stereotypes and encourage our sons to explore nontraditional male jobs. (Todd Walters, letter to the editor, *New York Times*)

Why do you think the Ms. Foundation made this event for girls only?

Do you think this event should be for both girls and boys? Why?

Exercise 8   Identifying stereotypes

Write a paragraph about stereotyping, racism, or sexism that you see around you, have experienced, have read about, or have heard about.

1. In your college or workplace.

2. Because you are male or female.

3. Among your friends.

4. Because of your work or lack of work.

5. In the national news.

Suggestions For Essay Topics

Using one of the prewriting techniques—freewriting, brainstorming, or clustering—write on one of these topics.

1. Write an essay explaining why Woody Allen connects the different practical joke devices with historical people and times.
2. Write an essay explaining what is funny about Allen's essay. Use some examples from his essay.
3. Write an essay that tells what is wrong with Allen's essay. Why is it hard to read and understand? What makes it not funny?
4. Write an essay telling about practical jokes you have used or heard about. You might consider if playing practical jokes is wise or not.
5. Write a humorous essay about the origins of a typical American holiday or ceremony. You might consider Thanksgiving, July Fourth, New Year's Eve, the high-school prom, a children's birthday party, or a wedding.

Once you have written a rough draft of your essay, see if it has **body paragraphs** with **topic sentences;** an **introduction** and a **conclusion; descriptions, examples** and **details;** a **consistent voice** and **point of view; sentence variety; clear explanations;** and **evidence.**

GRAMMAR

Using Quotation Marks and Direct and Indirect Discourse

Quotation marks (" ") have several uses: to indicate titles of short works; to indicate a word or phrase that is different in some way; and to indicate the exact word or words spoken or written by someone.

Put quotation marks at the beginning and the end of titles of works that are part of a book or magazine and not published separately. (Book and magazine titles are underlined or italicized.) Usually these include short stories, poems, and articles in a magazine or newspaper. But we also use quotation marks for other titles: songs, records and cassettes, television shows, paintings, usually films (sometimes underlined or italicized), and sometimes books (usually underlined or italicized). The quotation mark indicates that someone has given the work that title. You would not put quotation marks around your own essay title because you are not quoting someone else's title.

Put quotation marks around sarcastic and unusual ways of using a word (She is "exploring her options," not unemployed), words that are not appropriate for your essay but that express the mood (He acted like "mother's little helper"), words being referred to as words (How do you pronounce "exquisite"?), and translations of foreign words (*Mesa* means "table"). These uses do not occur often.

Quotation marks are most often used around the exact words that someone else has said either orally (He yelled, "My life with you is over." "So when are you getting out?" she yelled back) or in writing (The event captured the "collective imagination" of the nation). Direct quotation, or *direct discourse,* is necessary in research papers for quoting scholars and experts. Dialogue appears less often in essays and more in fiction.

If you need a period or comma at the end of the quotation, put it before the last quotation mark. Semicolons, colons, dashes, exclamations, and question marks go after the quotation mark unless the punctuation (usually exclamation points or question marks) is part of the quotation; then put it before the quotation mark.

With *indirect discourse,* you tell what someone said without the exact words but with the same sentiment. You should not use quotation marks, and you need to word the statement differently (He yelled that his life with her was over, so she asked him when he was getting out). Usually the person and the verb tense change. No question mark is used for an indirect question. In most essays, indirect discourse expresses enough; quoting people's exact words, if they are not particularly picturesque or memorable, is usually not necessary.

EXERCISES IN QUOTATION MARKS, DIRECT AND INDIRECT DISCOURSE

Exercise 9   Identifying quotation marks and indirect discourse

In the following paragraphs

a.   Underline the quotation marks for direct discourse.

b.   Circle quotation marks around special words.

c.   Double underline indirect discourse.

1.   As Kevin Padian of the University of California at Berkeley puts it: "Dinosaurs haven't gone extinct. You have a dinosaur bath in your

backyard, roast dinosaur at Thanksgiving, and eat dinosaur nuggets at McDonald's."

The name dinosaur was first used in print in 1842 by the English anatomist Sir Richard Owen, when it became clear that newfound fossils were from an unrecognized animal group. Owen combined two Greek words—*deinos,* or "terrible," and *sauros,* or "lizard," to describe the remarkable creatures. (Rick Gore, "Dinosaurs," *National Geographic*)

2.   In Selma, in 1965, King was the first black person to check into the Albert Hotel. And while he was checking in, a man came up to him and said, "Are you Martin Luther King?" And he said, "Yes." And the guy kicked him in the groin. It was a hard hit. And King had no emotion. His hands stayed at his side. He didn't flinch. If I hadn't seen it, I wouldn't have believed it. I was awfully impressed that he practiced what he preached, that he believed he was stronger than this man by not hitting him. (Julian Bond, "What Did We Lose?" *Life*)

3.   The mold that normally produces blue cheese produces traces of toxic substances, but not enough to hurt a human being in the quantities normally consumed, said Dr. Rodney S. Dietert, professor of immunogenetics and director of the Institute for Comparative and Environmental Toxicology at Cornell University.

Almost all blue cheeses are ripened by the mold Penicillium roqueforti, which does make about six alkaloid toxins, called mycotoxins, Dr. Dietert said. However, two of the six, the most potentially harmful, are not produced on cheese or break down immediately on cheese, he said.

"The four that are produced are detectable in parts-per-million levels," he continued. "There is no human data on their toxicity, but in rodents it takes an awful lot to do anything." By his calculations based on the most sensitive rodent studies, it would be necessary to eat more than 10 pounds of cheese a day for any harm to befall a person. (C. Claiborne Ray, "Q&A" item on blue cheese, *New York Times*)

Exercise 10   Identifying quotation marks and indirect discourse

Read this essay. Then find examples of the uses of quotation marks, and number them in the margin as follows:

1. Quotation marks around titles.
2. Quotation marks for direct discourse.
3. Quotation marks around words referred to as words.
4. Quotation marks around foreign words.

Underline examples of indirect discourse.

What's the Use of the Dictionary?

"You're always interrupting me," she complained, even as she continued to mutter about how much work she had to do and how little time she had to do it.

"But how can I look up a word that I don't know how to spell?" he shouted in total frustration. "Do I have to look through the whole dictionary to spell "pursuing?"

"No, you just have to look through the P section; at least you know the first letter." But she felt sorry for him and told him to look under "pu" rather than "pe."

A moment later, he wailed that he couldn't find it. "It only has "pursue"; I know how to spell that. I want "pursuing," and it's not here. This dictionary is no good; it doesn't have any words in it."

Since she didn't want him to have such a negative feeling about the dictionary, she stopped her work and showed him how to look under "pursue" to find other forms of the word. Sure enough, "pursuing" was there. He thanked her for her help, and then went on to his next task: finding out the languages of a long list of words meaning "goodbye." He thought it was a bit premature to say goodbye before he had said hello in any of these languages, but they had been discussing the word, and people in the class had mentioned "The Goodbye Girl," "A Farewell to Arms" (the movie), "Bye Bye Birdie," "Goodbye, Mr. Chips," and "Sayonara."

"Adieu" and "adios" were in the dictionary, along with "au revoir," but there was no sign of *arrivederci* or *sayonara*. He wondered what that meant. If the words were in an American dictionary, were they American words? Surely not. But how can we decide which ones get in the dictionary? Maybe the common ones get in, but *ciao* is very common and NOT in, and he didn't know anyone who ever said "adieu" or "au revoir."

He decided that dictionaries were a real mystery as he trotted off to the library to consult the foreign dictionaries.

Exercise 11   Using quotation marks

List some titles that need quotation marks.

Short stories:

Poems:

Newspaper articles:

Films:

Albums:

Songs:

Television shows:

Paintings:

Write a paragraph using some of these titles. Remember to use quotation marks.

Exercise 12   Using titles and quotations

Fill in the blanks with an appropriate title or quotation. Don't forget to use quotation marks in the right places.

My Media Life

We are bombarded by the media in our everyday lives. No one

can turn around without seeing newspapers, magazines, and televi-

sion shows. And then we listen to the radio, cassettes and CDs, watch videos, and go to the movies. I am no exception, of

course. I love all these media and take full advantage of them.

Every day on television I watch _____

and _____. Then once a week

my favorite shows are _____,

_____, and _____.

I don't even like _____, but I still watch it

sometimes.

I like films too. Recently I saw _____

and _____. I particularly recommend

_____.

But I like listening to music the most. Currently my favorite song

is _____, but two of my old favorites are

_____ and _____.

When I have nothing to do or even when I have lots to do, I

still enjoy having something to watch or listen to. Probably many

people feel the same way. Otherwise, why would the media be so

popular?

Other Punctuation: —, (), . . . , <u>underlining</u>, /, [], *, &, %, #, @

In addition to commas, semicolons, and colons, other important
pieces of punctuation are the dash (—) and parentheses (). The ellipsis

(. . .) and underlining are less important but necessary. The slash (/) and brackets ([]) are rarely used, while the asterisk (*), ampersand (&), percent (%), #, and @ should not be used at all in essays.

The *dash*—a long line or two hyphens on a keyboard—serves to emphasize **a piece of information, a short example, a short definition, a comment by the writer,** or **a contrasting thought.** The dash calls attention to itself and is rather informal. Put dashes (without spaces) at either end of the thought if it comes in the middle of a sentence, or replace the second dash with a period if it comes at the end of the sentence. Use dashes sparingly—two or three times at most in an essay; otherwise they become annoying and make the essay seem disorganized.

Use *parentheses* (parenthesis in the singular) to downplay (not emphasize) **a piece of information, a short example, a short definition, a comment by the writer, or a contrasting thought.** Parentheses may be used repeatedly if done in an organized way, such as giving a short example after each statement. Otherwise, use them sparingly since they can make sentences confusing. If other punctuation is needed, add it after the parenthetical item (never before).

Parentheses also (1) enclose numbers in lists, (2) enclose numbers after written-out numbers in business letters, (3) enclose area codes in telephone numbers, and (4) enclose footnote information. These uses occur rarely in essays.

An *ellipsis* (. . .) indicates words missing, usually in quoted statements at the beginning, middle, or end. It is important to indicate this to show that you have changed the quotation in this way. In writing dialogue, the ellipsis also shows words missing because the speaker trails off.

Underlining indicates three things: emphasis on a word or words (He loved it), the titles of whole books and newspapers (The Great Gatsby, The Los Angeles Times) and sometimes films (Citizen Kane), and foreign words (amor y pesetas). Published materials use *italics* (slanted type) instead of underlining.

The *slash* (/) has become more and more used but should be avoided except for three uses: to show a new line of poetry when you are quoting two or three lines (Roses are red;/ violets are blue), to show fractions (3/4) if many numbers and fractions will appear in your essay (if not, write out the fraction), and to show two or more words that apply (it is/was, his/her). However, avoid using the popular "and/or" in an essay, as well as such titles as writer/director; simply add "and" (writer and director) or commas (writer, director, and producer).

Brackets ([]) are like parentheses and sometimes replace them when more parentheses are needed within parentheses. Mostly, however, brackets indicate information inserted into a quotation. They tell us that the writer is making a change or adding a piece of information. Sometimes you will see "[*sic*]" after a quoted word that has an error in it; it means "thus" or "so" and indicates that the quoter knows of the error but is quoting it exactly.

An *asterisk* (*) at the end of a word tells the reader that a note comes at the end of the page. Advertisements use them for making disclaimers to offers; sometimes an essay might add a piece of information, but rarely. The *ampersand* (&) means "and"; it should not be used in an essay, nor should other symbols for "and"; write out the word instead. The *percent* (%) sign appears sometimes in business publications, but should not be used in essays; write out the word. Also do not use #; write "number" instead. Finally do not use @, which means "each." These symbols have their place in business forms but not in writing essays.

EXERCISES IN OTHER PUNCTUATION

Exercise 13   Dashes and parentheses

Underline the passages that have dashes and parentheses. In the margin, number the dashes and parentheses according to their use as follows:

1. Added information.
2. Example.
3. Definition.
4. Comment by writer.
5. Contrasting point.

a.   Jamaica, a thousand miles from St. Lucia and the Eastern Caribbean, is the largest (forty-five hundred square miles) and the oldest (it was captured by Oliver Cromwell's Navy in 1655) of the former British colonies in the West Indies. Because of its long-sustained ties with Britain, it was, by early in this century—in a number of its cultural and class dispositions—the most English of the Caribbean colonies. The black elite of its upper middle class came to be seen—and to see themselves—as "Afro-Saxons." (Jervis Anderson, *The New Yorker*)

b. Writing in the *Chronicle of Higher Education* (January 13, 1993), Christopher Shea says that fewer students scored 600 or above on the verbal SAT in 1992 than in 1972, even though more students took the exam. In absolute numbers, 116,630 scored above 600 in 1972 and only 75,243 in 1992—an enormous drop. Of course, with more students taking the SAT, you would expect to see a decline in the average score, but what could possibly explain the drop in the number of top scorers? (Albert Shanker, letter to the editor *New York Times*)

c. New World Monkeys range from Mexico through South America. Among them are the only primates with prehensile (grasping) tails. Old World Monkeys include the many tree- and ground-dwelling species of Africa and the Far East. The larger nonhuman primates—baboons, chimpanzees, and gorillas—are not native to North and South America. (Michael Dobrovolsky in William O'Grady, et al., *Contemporary Linguistics*)

d. A perfectly decent supper of fresh Portuguese sardines, olive toast, steak tartare and cappuccino *brulée* will set you back only $30 per person. And after the theater—when the Ivy is filled with people who look like winners in a genetic sweepstakes—you can have a decent hamburger and a terrific arugula salad (called rocket in Britain) with shaved Parmesan for less than half that price.

The Ivy's service is an interesting combination: Waiters go by the rules (for example, holding the champagne bottle properly by the punt, the indentation in the bottom) or are so casual they scrape off the plates right by your table. (George Lang, *Travel & Leisure*)

Exercise 14   Other punctuation

Circle the **ellipses, brackets, underlinings,** and **slashes.** Then in the margin write why they were used in that particular paragraph.

1.   St. Lucia seemed to [Derek Walcott] at times like an island of wrecked seafarers. He was to write in "Prelude," one of his early poems:

> . . . the steamers which divide horizons prove
> Us lost;
> Found only
> In tourist booklets, behind ardent binoculars.

And in "The Castaway," a later work, he referred to "the starved eye" of a Crusoe-like character who "devours the seascape for the morsel / Of a sail." (Jervis Anderson, "Derek Walcott's Odyssey," *The New Yorker*)

2.   At the celebration of Ekushey February in 1987, President Hussain Muhammad Ershad stated: "I had declared on January 24 in the Jatiya Sangsad that except in communication with foreign countries, in all other spheres in the government and private organisations, all letters and files will have to be maintained in Bangla." He added that the government is providing support for "a master-plan . . . for publication of a large number of books on modern scientific and technological subjects" and called upon "the intellectuals and others [to] come forward to establish Bangla in all institutions." To mark this step in the history of the nation, the president ordered that English-language street signs be replaced with ones in Bangla. (Richard W. Bailey, "English at Its Twilight")

3.   Does [Michael Caine] hope to keep on acting as well? "Yeah . . . [he sounds doubtful] reasonably so." What would stop him? "If I no longer got the parts. I wouldn't do second-rate movies." Of course, he could afford to give up work tomorrow. "But what would I do? Sit up in Chelsea Harbour watching television? Or sit around in the country, growing roses? I tried that. I stopped once, about five years ago, and it didn't work. . . . I kept turning down scripts, turning down scripts, and then finally a script came along and I thought, Oh, sod it, I'll go and do it, and I just started off again. . . . I really cannot vegetate. I haven't learnt that." (Lynn Barber, "The Caine Scrutiny," *Vanity Fair*)

4.　　　Zanshin is not easy to attain. Many years of mental and physical discipline are required before a martial artist can face an opponent without anxiety or tension. . . . The perfectly trained warrior faces his opponent, adopts a relaxed posture, and concentrates on his own energy center, the *hara* or *tanden* in the center of his body. The first opponent to break concentration is the one who loses. (Howard Rheingold, *They Have a Word for It*)

Exercise 15　　Other punctuation

Fill in the blanks with the appropriate punctuation and piece of information as indicated under the blank space.

　1.　Use **parentheses** and **dashes.**

Some dogs have long hair _____ while

examples

others have short hair _____. Maria's dog

examples

_____ has long hair.

name

　2.　Use **underlinings** and **quotation marks.**

We all know a number of words in foreign languages. For

example, in German I know _____, meaning

German word or phrase

_____ and _____,

meaning　　　　　　　　　German word or phrase

meaning _____. In Spanish I

meaning

can say _____, which means

Spanish word or phrase

_____. I also know some
            meaning

_____ words, such as
       name language

_____, meaning _____,
    foreign word or phrase   meaning

and _____, meaning
       foreign word or phrase

_____.
       meaning

3. Use **slashes** and **underlinings.**

I just read a book of poems called _____
                                    make up title

by _____. I particularly liked these two lines:
    make up author

_____
               make up two lines of poetry

_____.

I don't read much poetry, but I think these lines are great.

Exercise 16   Using punctuation

Write paragraphs using the indicated punctuation.

1. Use **underlining** and **ellipses, quotation marks,** and **brackets** (if you want) to quote a passage from your textbook.

2. Use **dashes** and **parentheses** to tell about your relatives.

3. Use **underlining** for emphasis and **dashes** to describe an exciting sports maneuver.

4. Use **underlining, parentheses,** and **slashes** to tell about a poem you read in a newspaper. You may make up the poem.

5. Add **brackets** and appropriate information in the following paragraph. You may make up the information.

She did not want to move to Springfield because Tootie was not allowed in the apartment complex. "I'll just console myself at Bill's Spot and stay right here," she sighed.

Ten Essays for Reading and Analyzing

Eggplant

Eggplant is a joy to grow. The plant is as beautiful as its fruit. Its culture is similar to that of tomatoes and green peppers. Plants require a long, warm growing season and should not be put outside until the weather is dependably warm. Eggplant seedlings are available in many garden supply houses at the same time of year (usually March or April) as tomato and green pepper plants. If you purchase seedlings, one or two (except for the midget variety) should be sufficient to produce all the fruit you are likely to use.

If you decide to raise plants from seed, do not be intimidated by reports of difficulty in germination or transplanting. Eggplants are just as easy to work with as tomatoes and are handled in the same manner. Plant seeds eight to nine weeks before it's time to put seedlings outside.

Depending upon the variety, the plants will grow from 2 to 3 feet in diameter and be bushy or flat as trained. They will begin to bear approximately 75 days after transplanting. Maturity dates for eggplant listed in catalogs usually indicate transplant time. Allow eight to nine weeks for seeds to germinate and reach transplant stage. As the blossoms appear (they are an attractive lavender), pinch off a few to keep the eggplant from setting too many fruits; about five or six per plant is best. Terminal growths on the stems can also be pinched back to maintain the shape of the plant—short and bushy or taller, as desired.

Don't wait too long to harvest. You can use the fruit any time after it is about half-grown. Don't wait until it overripens and loses its glossy shine. Not only will the fruit have a tough texture and a slightly bitter taste—the plant will stop producing.

Alice Skelsey, *Cucumbers in a Flowerpot.*

Recently Arrived

[The speaker, David Lee,] is twenty-eight years old and arrived in the United States from Taiwan in 1985. He speaks some English, but was more comfortable talking in Mandarin (a dialect of Chinese).

"I guess my goal is to go as high as I can, and keep aiming for the top and as much money as possible. I am doing it for my next generation. I want them to travel an easier path. But I haven't really found a way to do that yet. Right now, I'm taking fifteen hours of English classes a week.

"My first job in this country was to wash linen for a French restaurant. It was a tough job—seven days a week, twelve hours a day. I did it for three years and then was laid off. The restaurant wasn't doing very well. So I got some odd jobs, such as in a factory, hanging up clothes, and washing dishes in a restaurant. Then I saw an ad in the paper about a training program in setting jewelry. So that is what I am studying now. A friend of mine has a jewelry business in Taiwan, so I'm thinking maybe I can learn this and work out a profession for myself.

"My skills are in shipping—how to restore ships and the mechanical aspects of it. When I first came to this country, I tried to get a job in this area. But I couldn't find any. My life in this country has been very hard. Everyday, you work hard, and you want to do good, to earn a decent living. But after work there is nothing to do, unlike Taiwan, where there are lots of things to do for leisure. For instance, after work in Taiwan, you could call up friends, go have a late supper, take in a movie, or go for a stroll at night. Places are open twenty-four hours a day even. But in this country, things seem to close up by eight o'clock. And then, no one has time. If I have time, you don't have time. When you are free, I am working. So in terms of my existence, I feel it is pretty thin. At most I may call up my friends and chat on the phone. So it is not like the life I had in Taiwan at all, where whenever you were free you hung out or went out to eat. Here, we work long hours, but you can't say we do exceptionally well. We eat, go to sleep, then wake up and go to work. And everyday, it is the same thing. When you wake up, it's go to work. So mentally, the adjustment in lifestyle has been the hardest part for me. Nothing is fun anymore.

"My family is from Shantung, China. But I have never been there. I was born and raised in Taiwan, and that is where I feel my home and my country is right now."

Joann Faung Jean Lee, *Asian American Experiences in the United States: Oral Histories of First to Fourth Generation Americans from China, the Philippines, Japan, India, the Pacific Islands, Vietnam, and Cambodia.*

Young Women, Keep Your Own Names

To the Editor:

As Joan D., I graduated from high school, where I won honors and awards, including a scholarship.

I became Joan S. when I was 20 years old, readily relinquishing my identity, as that was the custom then. I changed my name on my college transcript and Social Security number, and as Joan S., I produced two children, obtained a teaching certificate, taught public school, divorced Mr. S., and entered graduate school.

Several years later I became Mrs. K., whereupon I changed my name on transcripts, credentials and Social Security number, a more complicated process this time. We moved to another community, and at the age of 30 I left behind an entire being, losing touch with students, friends, and professional acquaintances, who no longer knew who I was. As Joan K., I forged a new identity, raised two S's and two K's, taught part time at a university. and made a bit of a stir with my scribblings.

Many people, including my own children, have asked me why I became Joan D. again after so many years as Mrs. K. I reply: "It's my name. It's who I am." Statistically, my two marriages and two divorces are the norm. I had no intention when the story began of becoming three people. I didn't know I would have to go forth and attempt to forge a career for myself, not once, but thrice. My name changes have caused professional, as well as personal loss. It's a problem to be confused about one's own identity; but it's even more of a problem when years of professional training and experience and achievement are signed Anonymous. I advise my young women friends to retain their maiden name.

Joan Davis
Bellingham, Washington

New York Times, Letters, April 7, 1993

John F. Welch, Jr.

John F. Welch, Jr., may have inherited leadership of the company Thomas Edison created, but he's much more the J. P. Morgan type. Morgan, Edison's financial backer, was the one who built General Electric into one of the biggest corporations in the U.S. in no time, building both the equipment needed to generate and transmit electricity and the appliances that used that electricity. And CEOs like Welch have kept it there ever since. The $43 billion-in-revenues giant now runs 13 major businesses.

CEO since 1981, Welch has been called charming, voluble, energetic, brilliant, intimidating and a model for America's business managers. But perhaps the most lasting description is the nickname, "Neutron Jack," awarded to him after he fired thousands of employees but left their divisions standing.

However, there are signs that Welch, 57, may be mellowing. Recently, he has been stressing his program for democratizing GE through better worker-manager communication.

Mellowing or not, Welch has recast GE in his own image. Since taking over, he has made $10 billion worth of divestitures, announcing just last November that the company would sell its $6 billion-in-revenues aerospace operations to Martin Marietta. He has also made $19 billion worth of acquisitions. GE Capital, for example, has announced plans to buy Eastman Kodak Credit Corp. Over the past 10 years sales have climbed 10% a year, compounded, and earnings have grown 11% annually (excluding 1992's accounting change required by the Federal Accounting Standards Board; see page 74). Sales were up just 3% in 1992, and due to that accounting change, earnings dropped 52%. Without the charge, earnings would have been up 7%.

With the economy improving, GE's future looks, in a word, bright.

Nanette Byrnes, Financial World

Review of Matt Cartmill's View to a Death in the Morning

Matt Cartmill is a biological anthropologist, but don't let that stop you. His book on the history of our attitudes toward hunting is not only smart and thoughtful, it's fascinating. From the Renaissance, when only the nobility were allowed to hunt, he quotes a poem that describes in great detail the fewmets of a stag. (Fewmets are deer droppings, and a competent hunter had to be able to look at them and describe the animal, up to the number of points in the rack.) Felix Salten, the Hungarian who wrote the original *Bambi: A Forest Life* and encouraged millions of children to hate hunters, had his own private hunting preserve. In the eighteenth century it was the custom, after a stag had been run to the ground, to ask one of the ladies in the hunt to slit its throat.

The book is full of this kind of information, as well as a rich account of our centuries-old ambivalence toward hunting, especially deer hunting. Cartmill describes the many symbolic meanings that have been attached to deer: as a figure of cowardice in antiquity, when nobody objected to hunting; as a Christ figure in the Middle Ages; as the noble stag to Romantics; finally as Bambi (not to mention Donder and Blitzen) to us. The growing weight of this cultural baggage has burdened hunters. "Anybody who wants to kill an animal that stands for love, beauty, innocence, and Christmas," he notes dryly, "has a serious public-relations handicap to overcome."

Cartmill is most on target when he gets to the arguments about hunting, pro and con—he blows holes in both sides. You're hunting only to cull deer that would otherwise starve? Why not hunt ravens, then, or raccoons, which also starve in winter? You think it's wrong to kill innocent creatures? Then what are you doing with steak tartare in your mouth? Cartmill writes well, too; there's no trace of the usual impassable academic prose. Best of all, he's evenhanded. He doesn't despise hunting; he just wants to understand it. The result is endlessly informative and frequently entertaining. And your next slice of venison will taste much more interesting.

Anthony Brandt, *Men's Journal*

Alice's Snazzy Pajamas

Alice bought her pajamas in the lingerie department. They were a pale grey silk, with square-cut short sleeves and long pants. A little line of white piping edged the cuffs and ran the length of the shirt front, the buttons had the lustre of pearl. New they'd cost two-hundred and twenty dollars.

Alice got them at Goodwill for three bucks. She'd been desperate for a flannel nightgown, but when she'd gone through the ratty, worn pile of night clothes in the back corner of the store, she'd stopped short when she'd come across the pajamas. The seam under one arm was gaping open and they were wrinkled beyond belief, a dead giveaway of their authenticity. At first she couldn't believe it.

When she got them home, she took out Ivory Snow and washed them. She hung them on the back porch where she had her clothesline, putting pieces of Saran Wrap between the material and the pins. When they were dry she brought them inside and mended the arm, and then set up her ironing board. She had been waiting for this moment. Like magic the silk smoothed out and the garments became slinky and soft. She draped them carefully on a hanger in the doorway and stood looking at them for a long time. Then she spread them out on her bed and fingered the material: Never in her life had she owned anything like these. Never had she expected to. She was spellbound just looking at them.

Every night when she got off work, she'd start thinking about her pajamas. The winter streets were dark and slippery and the buses out of the city were packed, but Alice would fight her way to a seat, or stand patiently holding a strap, wrapped in a lot more than her thin cloth coat. She felt like someone special.

The pajamas got her through four and a half months. She would wear them for an hour or so every night after her shower and before going to bed. Sometimes she would arrange herself on the pillows on the sofa and read movie magazines. Other nights she'd prop herself up in bed and watch TV. It depended on her mood.

Then in March her sister came over. She'd left her husband, the bastard, and arrived on Alice's doorstep at nine o'clock one night with her two-year-old and the new baby. Alice had just been reading about the Academy Awards.

They put the baby to sleep in the laundry basket fixed up for a bed, and Alice gave her nephew something to drink and a paper and pencil to draw with while she tried to comfort her sister and get the whole story. The upshot of the evening was that the grape juice got knocked over and spread across the tablecloth. It also stained the pajamas. There was nothing to be done. Through her tears her sister decided to move in until she could get a place of her own.

It was crowded. There were only two rooms. But they worked it out for six weeks until her sister returned to the bastard to try again. They both knew she'd be back before long, but for now at least it seemed okay.

Alice never mentioned the pajamas. She tried washing them out, but nothing would remove the grape juice that wouldn't bleach out the color of the fabric as well. So after a couple of tries, she ironed them smooth, folded them in tissue paper, and put them away in the bottom drawer of her dresser with a lavender sachet. Every now and then she'd lay them out on her bed and admire them, folding the stained edge of the top back and covering the spots on the pant leg by turning them under. But she never put them on again. It wasn't the same.

Alice continued to visit Goodwill every week to look through the merchandise as usual. She always looked for nice things. She picked up a wool blazer for only seven dollars, and one time came across an almost new leather purse. Though she never found anything much in the lingerie corner, Alice kept looking. Knowing those snazzy pajamas were at home in her drawer was enough. She knew anything was possible.

S. G. Tyler, "Alice's Snazzy Pajamas,"
Four-Minute Fictions,
Robley Wilson, Jr., Ed.

Psychotherapy for Ethnic Minorities

Although we consider ours a pluralistic society, the different cultural groups that make up that society are, only too often, not allowed full privileges and are looked on askance because they refuse to lose their identities in the melting pot. Ethnic and racial minorities in our country are at a social disadvantage not only because of negative stereotyping but, generally speaking, in terms of education, job opportunities, and economic resources as well. This means that they have more problems to deal with and less ability to obtain needed services. It has been documented that minority people generally receive inferior mental health care, being unable to afford the relatively high fees of trained therapists or not having available trained personnel in the community. They are more likely to be assigned junior rather than senior staff members for therapy, to be diagnosed as having more severe pathology, to receive short-term rather than long-term treatment, and to be provided with medication instead of psychotherapy. Language creates another barrier, as there is a shortage of therapists who can work comfortably in languages other than English. This is especially true of non-Western languages, and the problem of finding a therapist is more acute for the growing Asian population in this country.

In addition to the difficulties involved in locating and paying for appropriate psychotherapy services, minority people must also find therapists who do not harbor racist sentiments. Racist attitudes are so deeply ingrained in our culture that it is very hard for anybody growing up in our society to be free of them, including people from minority groups themselves, who sometimes introject the negative attitudes to which they are subjected. Like others in the society, therapists tend to have ethnic and racial biases. Thus, if you are a member of a minority group, obtaining appropriate psychotherapy services will be more difficult for you than it is for others.

Otto Ehrenberg and Miriam Ehrenberg
The Psychotherapy Maze

A Conspiracy Against Silence

There's a conspiracy against silence in the world. We seem to prefer a shout to a whisper.

Everywhere you go, someone is making noise. They aren't making sounds, they're making noise. People who make noise for their own amusement intrude on the privacy of silence to which the rest of us are entitled.

Silence is the natural state. Any noise is a deviation from the norm. A lion doesn't roar for more than a few minutes out of twenty-four hours, and while I don't know any lions personally, I'll bet there are days lions choose not to roar at all. How often do you hear thunder, the eruption of a volcano or the rumble of an earthquake? These natural sounds are special and they only break the earth's silence on rare occasions.

I don't understand why some people insist on filling the air with noise. They can't stand to be in a car without having the radio on. They can't stand being anywhere with nothing but the natural sounds of earth in their ears.

The most loathsome telephone practice instituted since Alexander Graham Bell asked Watson if he was there is the hold button that automatically feeds music into the waiting caller's ear. In many offices, when you call and are put on hold, the company apparently feels the need to amuse, entertain or distract you, so it feeds music into the line. If I have to wait for someone on the phone, I don't want the thought of what I wish to say crowded out of my head by some inane bit of music.

Many airlines pipe music into the passenger section upon landing. I'm trying to gather my wits and remember which overhead bin I put my coat in and they're playing soothing music. Soothing music irritates me more than music that isn't soothing. Soothing music sets my nerves on edge.

I can stand the sound of a neighbor mowing his lawn because it is not a noise made merely for the sake of noise-making. The machine making the noise is performing a necessary function and I accept it.

It's the gratuitous noise that irritates me most. When a driver stops in front of a house in the neighborhood and blows the horn to attract the attention of someone inside, it's thoughtless and rude. We're all conditioned to the sound of a horn. Why should ten people have to bother to look out the windows of ten houses to find out the horn means nothing for them? As a matter of fact, I don't think there are more than ten times in a whole year of driving when it's necessary for someone behind the wheel to blow the horn.

I question the frequency of use of ambulance sirens. If the ambulance people use the siren, they ought to mean it. There ought to be a genuine medical emergency, not just a cowboy at the wheel.

In New York City there are 12,000 licensed taxis. Half the drivers are tuned to both a commercial radio station and the cab company's shortwave frequency, which advises them of pickups. The drivers play both radios simultaneously and keep turning up the volume on each to override the other until they can hear neither. The paying passenger, besieged in both ears, is helpless.

I realize now that when I was a kid, some of the boys I played with were constant screamers. They always made more noise by yelling louder than the rest of us. It's a trait some people carry with them through life. They do everything louder than everyone else.

Most people don't mind the normal and necessary sounds. If I'm writing, I can ignore a vacuum cleaner, a lawn mower or a conversation in another room, but when a kid goes past the house with his car windows open and rock music blaring from his radio, I forget what I'm doing. It's those unnecessary noises, deliberately made, that call themselves to our attention and get on our nerves.

We have a day to celebrate almost everything else. I propose A Day of Silence.

Andy Rooney, *Word for Word*

Improving Reading Efficiency

If you wish to become a better and faster reader, there are several things you can do to improve. First, read more than you are now reading. If you are a slow reader, you probably find reading tedious and unrewarding. But as you become more efficient, you will be rewarded more quickly and more often. Unless you develop the habit of reading for two hours or more at a stretch, two or three evenings a week, you will not get enough practice to become a skillful reader.

Second, read for main ideas, fitting the details into a larger framework. When you read a short story or novel, for example, look for the main elements—plot, character, and conflict—as you move quickly through descriptive details. Try to keep a steady rhythm, although you may slow down occasionally to savor some especially beautiful writing. When you read magazine articles or textbooks, skim over the chapter first to get a quick general impression, an overall framework upon which to hang the details as you read. This overview should take no more than a minute or two while you glance at the title, pictures, first paragraph, subheadings, and the first sentence of each paragraph. Then, as you read the entire chapter at your normal rate, you will perceive a meaningful pattern.

Third, force yourself to read faster, so that you break old habits of dawdling. If you read more slowly than your mind wants to move, your attention will wander just as a driver's attention may wander more at 15 miles an hour than at 55 miles an hour. Find out where your speed is now by timing yourself while you read for an hour. Set a goal of 500 words a minute on easy or familiar reading material, and at least 300 for harder material.

After you have practiced this way for a few weeks, you will feel discontented with your old slow reading habits. Once you have proven to yourself that you understand more as you read faster, you will never return to your old inefficient ways.

Helen Heightsman Gordon,
Interplay: Sentence Skills in Context

Guns

Last year's great North Pacific winter season has many surfers somewhat frothing at the mouth over the prospect of big surf this year in both Californian and Hawaiian waters. And many of their shapers will be taking advantage of Macho Surf Fever by experimenting with some of this year's short board innovations in the big gun arena.

Forward vees, concaves and more rocker are all certain to infiltrate quivers shaped by gun names like Pat Rawson, Eric Arakawa and Jeff Bushman. Rawson has been pulling his forward vees out to eight-six, full giant Sunset gun length, and plans on doing nine-sixes and up for Darrick Doerner and a few other select hellmen. "They (the forward vees) seem to surf the top of the wave brilliantly," Pat says. "They don't have the drive of the spiral vee bonzer bottom, but for what the kids wanna do, they've been great."

Bushman feels there'll be more room for experimentation in Pipeline boards. At Pipe, he says: "The goofy-foot surfers there are actually trying to slow their boards down so that they can ride deeper in the tube, so you can work on different tail rockers and forward vee at Pipe." He plans to pull the length of teamrider Ross Clarke-Jones' Waimea guns out to ten-five. "The common thought has always been that nine-six was the limit, and any longer wouldn't fit in the curve of the wave." Jeff will increase the rocker in certain areas to help that fit.

Arakawa is trying a different tack: he's pulling the tails in a lot narrower, especially for Sunset. His plan? Bring back the bottom turn. "Even good Sunset surfers have trouble with their bottom turns. I hope the narrower tails will help to set the turn a little more." But Eric sounds the note of caution in all the shapers' voices as they discuss taking hotdog ideas into big boards: "No matter what, we are going to see a lot of drifting and sliding in turns with all these rockers and tail concaves coming in." Perhaps once this winter's over, it'll be clearer than ever that a good gun is a simple thing.

Surfing Magazine, February 1993

Index

Abstract nouns, 45; exercises 46–48
Adjectives, 103–104; exercises 104–108
    in descriptions, 89; exercises, 89–94
Adverbs, 103–104; exercises, 104–108
    in descriptions, 89; exercises, 89–94
Agreement of pronoun and
        antecedent, 191–192; exercises,
        192–194
Agreement of subject and verb,
        187–188; exercises, 188–191
Allen, Woody, "The Discovery and
        Use of the Fake Ink Blot,"
        269–270
Ampersand, 288–290
And/or, 289
Anecdotes, 59
Antecedents, 191–192
Apostrophes, 247–248; exercises,
        248–254
Argumentation, 235–236; exercises,
        236–242
Asterisk, 288–290
Audience, 207; exercises, 207–214
Authorities in argumentation,
        235–236; exercises, 236–242

Body of the essay, 13–14; exercises,
        14–15
    writing, 34–35, 39–40; exercises,
        35–39, 40–44
Body paragraphs, 39–40; exercises,
        40–44

Book titles, 289
Brackets, 288–289; exercises, 291–292,
        294–295
Brainstorming, 4; exercises, 4–8

Chopin, Kate, "The Story of an
        Hour," 85–88
Chronological order, 214–215, 271;
        exercises, 215–218
Clauses, 129; exercises, 130–135
Clichés, 89
Climbing on the bandwagon,
        242–243; exercises, 245–247
Clustering, 4; exercises, 5, 7, 10
Collective nouns, 188
Colons, 254–255; exercises, 255–261
Commas
    in clauses, 220–221; exercises,
        221–224
    with phrases and words, 224–225;
        exercises, 225–228
    in series, titles, addresses, dates,
        misunderstandings, 229;
        exercises, 230–232
Common nouns, 45; exercises, 49–50
Comparisons, 89
Complex sentences, 135–136;
        exercises, 138–141
Compound sentences, 135–136;
        exercises 137–138
Compound–complex sentences,
        135–136; exercises, 138–141

Conclusions, 13–14, 63–64; exercises 64–70

Concrete nouns, 45; exercises, 46–48

Conjunctions, 108–109; exercises, 109–112, 114–115

  coordinating conjunctions, 220

Contractions, 248; exercises, 248–254

Controlling idea, 88–89; exercise, 94–95

Coordinating conjunctions, 220

Dangling modifiers, 194–195; exercises, 195–198

Dash, 288–289; exercise, 290–291

Demonstrative pronouns, 50

Dependent clauses, 129; exercises, 130–135

  using commas with, 220–224

Descriptions, 88–89; exercises, 90–94

  as purpose, 118; exercises, 121–122

  in entertaining essays, 271; exercises, 271–276

Descriptive verbs, 89

Descriptive words, 88–89; exercises, 90–94

Details

  in body paragraphs, 34–35

  in entertaining essays, 270–271; exercises, 271–276

  writing details, 39–40; exercises, 40–43

Diction, 207; exercises, 207–214

Direct discourse, 282–283; exercises, 283–287

Distraction as false argument, 242–243; exercises, 245–247

Each sign (@), 289; exercises, 290–291

Ellipsis, 289; exercises, 291–294

Entertaining essays, 270–271; exercises, 271–276

Exaggeration in essays, 270–271; exercises, 271–276

Examples, 34–35, 39; exercises, 41–44

False arguments, 242–243; exercises, 243–247

False authorities, 242–243; exercises, 245–247

Fanboys (coordinating conjunctions), 108

First person, 123–124; exercises, 124–125, 126–128

First person of verbs, 71

Focusing, 6

Foreign words, 283, 293

Fractions, 289

Fragments, 157–158; exercises, 158–161, 164–165

Freewriting, 3–4; exercises, 4–8

Future tense of verbs, 71–72, 78–79; exercises, 79–84

General words, 175

Hyphens, 261–262; exercises, 262–267

Implied topic sentence, 35

Indefinite pronouns, 50–51

Independent clauses, 129; exercises, 130–135

  using commas with, 220; exercises, 221–224

Indirect discourse, 282–283; exercises, 283–286

Introductions, 13–14; exercises, 14–18

  writing introductions, 58–59; exercises, 59–63

Irregular verbs, 71–72; exercises, 73–76

  list of types, 73–74

Is when/where/because/why/how/ what, 198–199; exercises, 199–203

Italics, 282, 289

It is/was, 151; exercises, 154–156

Length of sentences, 150
varying length, 150–151; exercises,
154, 155–156
Logical explanations, 214–215;
exercises 215–219

Malcolm X, 2, 146
Misplaced modifiers, 194–195;
exercises, 195–198

Name-calling, 242–243; exercises,
244–245, 245–247
Narrowing down, 8–9; exercises, 9–12
Newspaper titles, 289
Noun types, 45–46; exercises 46–50
Number sign (#), 288–290

Objective pronouns, 50; exercises,
51–56
Objects and subjects, 45–46
Observations in argumentation,
235–236; exercises, 236–242
Organizing an essay, 13–14; exercises,
14–17
Overgeneralization, 242–243;
exercises, 243–247

Paragraphs, 39–40; exercises, 40–44
Parallelism, 166; exercises, 167–173
Parentheses, 288–289; exercises,
290–291
Past participle of verbs, 71–72;
exercises, 72–76
Past tense of verbs, 71–72; exercises,
72–84
Percent sign (%), 288–290
Picturesque nouns, 89; exercises,
90–94
Plural verbs, 71–72
Plurals with apostrophes, 247–248;
exercises, 248–254
Poetry quoting, 289, 294

Point of view, 123–124; exercises,
124–128
Possession, 247–248; exercises,
248–254
Possessive pronouns, 51
Precise words, 271; exercises, 271–276
Prediction as conclusion, 63;
exercises, 64–68
Prefixes, 262
Prepositional phrases, 108–109;
exercises, 112–114
for sentence variety, 144–145;
exercises, 145–150
Prepositions, 108–109; exercises,
112–115
list of common prepositions,
112–113
Present participle of verbs, 72;
exercises, 72–75
Present tense of verbs, 71–72;
exercises, 72–84
Pronoun–antecedent agreement,
191–192; exercises, 192–194
Pronouns, 50–51; exercises, 51–56
Proper nouns, 45–46; exercises, 46–50
Purpose in essays, 118, 206–207;
exercises, 121, 207–213

Question as introduction, 59;
exercises, 59–63
as conclusion, 63; exercises, 64–68
Quotation as introduction, 59;
exercises, 59–63
as conclusion, 63; exercises, 64–68
Quotation marks, 282–283; exercises,
283–288

Racism, 276–277; exercises, 277–281
Recommendation as conclusion, 63;
exercises, 64–68
Red herring (distraction), 242;
exercises, 243–244
References to character, 242–243;
exercises, 244–247

Reflexive pronouns, 51; exercises,
    51–56
Regular verbs, 71–72; exercises, 72–73
Relative pronouns, 50–51
Run-together sentences, 161–162;
    exercises, 162–165

Second person, 123–124; exercises,
    126–128
Second person of verbs, 71–72
Semicolon, 254–255; exercises,
    255–261
  to correct run-together sentences,
    162; exercises, 162–165
Sentence as clause, 129
Sentence types, 135–136; exercises,
    136–141
Sentence variety, 144–145, 150–151;
    exercises, 145–150, 151–156
Series of phrases for sentence variety,
    151; exercises, 151–153, 155–156
Setting the scene as introduction, 59;
    exercises, 59–63
Sexism, 276–277; exercises, 277–281
Sic, 290
Simple sentences, 135–136; exercises,
    136–137, 139–141
Singular verbs, 71–72
Slash, 288–289; exercises, 291–292,
    294–295
Specific nouns, 175–176; exercises,
    176–180
Specific verbs, 175–176; exercises,
    180–182
Statistic as introduction, 59; exercises,
    59–63
Statistics and facts, 235–236;
    exercises, 236–242
Stereotyping, 276–277; exercises,
    277–281
Subjective pronouns, 50–51; exercises
    51–56
Subjects and objects, 45–46
Subject-verb agreement, 187–188;
    exercises, 188–191

Subject-verb-object (SVO), 144–145
Summary as conclusion, 64; exercises,
    64–68

Tense in verbs, 71–72, 78–79;
    exercises, 72–78, 79–84
Thesis statement, 13
  in introductions, 58; exercises,
    59–63
  in entertaining essays, 271;
    exercises, 272–276
Third person, 123–124; exercises,
    124–128
Third person of verbs, 71–72
Titles, 13–14, 289
Topic sentences, 13
  writing, 34–35; exercises, 35–39, 43,
    110–111
Transitional expressions, 97–98;
    exercises 98–102
  in logical explanations, 214

Underlining, 288–289; exercises
    291–295
Understood subject, 45

Verbals and verbal phrases, 144, 145
Verbs
  regular and irregular, 71–72,
    exercises, 72–78
  tenses, 78–79, exercises, 79–84
Voice, 118; exercises 118–120, 122–123

Who, whom, 50
Words Often Confused, 19; exercises,
    19–25
  list, 20–25

You understood, 45